The Harcourt Brace Casebook Series in Literature

"A Worn Path"

Eudora Welty

THE HARCOURT BRACE CASEBOOK SERIES IN LITERATURE
Series Editors: Laurie G. Kirszner and Stephen R. Mandell

DRAMA
Athol Fugard
"Master Harold"... and the boys

William Shakespeare
Hamlet

POETRY
Emily Dickinson
A Collection of Poems

Langston Hughes
A Collection of Poems

SHORT STORIES
Charlotte Perkins Gilman
"The Yellow Wallpaper"

John Updike
"A & P"

Eudora Welty
"A Worn Path"

The Harcourt Brace Casebook Series in Literature
Series Editors: Laurie G. Kirszner and Stephen R. Mandell

"A Worn Path"

Eudora Welty

Contributing Editor
Elizabeth Sarcone
Delta State University

Harcourt Brace College Publishers
Fort Worth   Philadelphia   San Diego   New York   Orlando   Austin   San Antonio
Toronto   Montreal   London   Sydney   Tokyo

Publisher   Earl McPeek
Project Editor   Matt Ball
Production Manager   Linda McMillan
Art Director   Vicki Whistler

ISBN: 0-15-505482-1
Library of Congress Catalog Card Number: 98-84577

Copyright © 1998 by Harcourt Brace & Company

All rights reserved. No part of this publication may be reproduced or transmitted in any form or by any means, electronic or mechanical, including photocopy, recording or any information storage and retrieval system, without permission in writing from the publisher.

Requests for permission to make copies of any part of the work should be mailed to: Permissions Department, Harcourt Brace & Company, 6277 Sea Harbor Drive, Orlando, Florida 32887-6777.

Address for Editorial Correspondence: Harcourt Brace College Publishers, 301 Commerce Street, Suite 3700, Fort Worth, TX 76102.

Address for Orders: Harcourt Brace & Company, 6277 Sea Harbor Drive, Orlando, FL 32887-6777. 1-800-782-4479.

(Copyright Acknowledgments begin on page 169, which constitutes a continuation of this copyright page.)

Web site address: www.hbcollege.com

Printed in the United States of America

8 9 0 1 2 3 4 5 6 7   066   10 9 8 7 6 5 4 3 2 1

About the Series

The Harcourt Brace Casebook Series in Literature has its origins in our anthology *Literature: Reading, Reacting, Writing* (Third Edition, 1997), which in turn arose out of our many years of teaching college writing and literature courses. The primary purpose of each Casebook in the series is to offer students a convenient, self-contained reference tool that they can use to complete a research project for an introductory literature course.

In choosing subjects for the Casebooks, we draw on our own experience in the classroom, selecting works of poetry, fiction, and drama that students like to read, discuss, and write about and that teachers like to teach. Unlike other collections of literary criticism aimed at student audiences, The Harcourt Brace Casebook Series in Literature features short stories, groups of poems, or plays (rather than longer works, such as novels) because these are the genres most often taught in college-level Introduction to Literature courses. In selecting particular authors and titles, we focus on those most popular with students and those most accessible to them.

To facilitate student research—and to facilitate instructor supervision of that research—each Casebook contains all the resources students need to produce a documented research paper on a particular work of literature. Every Casebook in the series includes the following elements:

- A comprehensive **introduction** to the work, providing social, historical, and political background. This introduction helps students to understand the work and the author in the context of a particular time and place. In particular, the introduction enables students to appreciate customs, situations, and events that may have contributed to the author's choice of subject matter, emphasis, or style.

- A **headnote,** including birth and death dates of the author; details of the work's first publication and its subsequent publication history, if relevant; details about the author's life; a summary of the author's career; and a list of key published works, with dates of publication.

- The most widely accepted version of the **literary work,** along with the explanatory footnotes students will need to understand unfamiliar terms and concepts or references to people, places, or events.
- **Discussion questions** focusing on themes developed in the work. These questions, designed to stimulate critical thinking and discussion, can also serve as springboards for research projects.
- Several extended **research assignments** related to the literary work. Students may use these assignments exactly as they appear in the Casebook, or students or instructors may modify the assignments to suit their own needs or research interests.
- A diverse collection of traditional and non-traditional **secondary sources,** which may include scholarly articles, reviews, interviews, memoirs, newspaper articles, historical documents, and so on. This resource offers students access to sources they might not turn to on their own—for example, a popular song that inspired a short story, a story that was the original version of a play, a legal document that sheds light on a work's theme, or two different biographies of an author—thus encouraging students to look beyond the obvious or the familiar as they search for ideas. Students may use only these sources, or they may supplement them with sources listed in the Casebook's bibliography (see below).
- An annotated model **student research paper** drawing on several of the Casebook's secondary sources. This paper uses MLA parenthetical documentation and includes a Works Cited list conforming to MLA style.
- A comprehensive **bibliography** of print and electronic sources related to the work. This bibliography offers students an opportunity to move beyond the sources in the Casebook to other sources related to a particular research topic.
- A concise **guide to MLA documentation,** including information on what kinds of information require documentation (and what kinds do not); a full explanation of how to construct parenthetical references and how to place them in a paper; sample parenthetical reference formats for various kinds of sources used in papers about literature; a complete explanation of how to assemble a List of Works Cited, accompanied by sample works cited entries (including formats for documenting electronic sources); and guidelines for using explanatory notes (with examples).

By collecting all this essential information in one convenient place, each volume in The Harcourt Brace Casebook Series in Literature responds to the needs of both students and teachers. For students, the Casebooks offer convenience, referentiality, and portability that make the process of doing research easier. Thus, the Casebooks recognize what students already know: that Introduction to Literature is not their only class and that the literature research paper is not their only assignment. For instructors, the Casebooks offer a rare combination of flexibility and control in the classroom. For example, teachers may choose to assign one Casebook or more than one; thus, they have the option of having all students in a class write about the same work or having different groups of students, or individual students, write about different works. In addition, instructors may ask students to use only the secondary sources collected in the Casebook, thereby controlling students' use of (and acknowledgment of) sources more closely, or they may encourage students to seek both print and electronic sources beyond those included in the Casebook. By building convenience, structure, and flexibility into each volume, we have designed The Harcourt Brace Casebook Series in Literature to suit a wide variety of teaching styles and research interests. The Casebooks have made the research paper an easier project for us and a less stressful one for our students; we hope they will do the same for you.

Laurie G. Kirszner
Stephen R. Mandell
Series Editors

Preface

"A Worn Path," one of the early short stories of Eudora Welty, is an American classic. Written in 1940, the story represents a period when Welty was experimenting with a new fictional mode and was in the process of discovering her own narrative path. In mid-October of that year she included a copy of "A Worn Path" with a letter to Diarmuid Russell, her literary agent, introducing it almost by way of a postscript: "I forgot to say, here is another story—I had to do something while waiting for you to read [*The Robber Bridegroom*]" (qtd. in Kreyling 47). The story's publication in the *Atlantic Monthly* the following February heralded Welty's entrance onto the national stage. After winning a second-place award, the story was reprinted in *O. Henry Memorial Prize Stories of 1941* and became a late-hour substitute for another story in Welty's first short story collection, *A Curtain of Green* (1941). Over the years "A Worn Path" has continued to earn Welty literary acclaim.

Two well-known women writers—who effectively bracket Welty's career—demonstrate the enduring appeal of "A Worn Path." In 1914, Katherine Anne Porter, already a successful short story writer, wrote the introduction to *A Curtain of Green,* Welty's collection of short stories in which "A Worn Path" appeared. She calls the story "beautiful" and singles it out as one of her personal favorites. In 1994, Beth Henley, a Pulitzer Prize–winning playwright, follows John Reid and Claudia Velasco's filmed version of "A Worn Path" with a videotaped interview (available from Harcourt Brace College Publishers). Seated in a room in Welty's Tudor-style house, the two authors—one young and one now old—discuss how the story was made.

Reading "A Worn Path" raises many questions: What happened to the grandson's parents? How did he happen to swallow lye? Is he dead? Is Phoenix Jackson a stereotype of a black woman, or does she reveal a humanity that transcends race? What does her journey represent? Why isn't the reader ever assured that Phoenix Jackson arrives home safely? As the sources selected for this volume indicate, critics have answered these and other questions in different ways.

The sources included in this Casebook are arranged in chronological order to make it easier for readers to see how literary scholars react to and answer each other. The two essays by Welty were selected because they have a direct bearing on the story and are often referred to in discussions of it. The nine scholarly articles were chosen because each focuses on "A Worn Path" and, either in its argument or in its review of scholarship or both, highlights the story's critical history. These articles present a wide spectrum of approaches covering three decades of Welty criticism.

- Welty, Eudora. "Must the Novelist Crusade?" 1965. Welty distinguishes between the purpose and methods of the novelist and the crusader. Although the novelist, inspired by imagination, seeks to bring alive lasting human truths through characters, the crusader is driven by the urgency of a particular crisis. Ultimately the novelist is the best crusader because the fictional work changes how readers think and feel. In this essay Welty speaks on behalf of all novelists as she subtly defends herself against charges of racism.
- Howell, Elmo. "Eudora Welty's Negroes: A Note on 'A Worn Path.'" 1970. Howell argues that the story is not a criticism of white society but a reflection of the actual social customs prevailing in Mississippi at the time. Phoenix feels no animosity toward the white people she meets because she is too noble to be tempted toward malice. Her strength and that of the story lie not in her race but in her triumphant humanity. Howell's interpretation is generally in line with Welty's stated views.
- Welty, Eudora. "Is Phoenix Jackson's Grandson Really Dead?" 1974. Welty discusses the origin of the story and answers the question that she says her correspondents ask her most frequently. Although she says she assumes the grandson is still alive, the question ultimately is irrelevant because the story is centered on Phoenix, her journey, and her hope. While reputedly written to answer students, Welty's essay actually addresses the growing number of critics who want her fiction to match their interpretations.
- Nostrandt, Jeanne R. "Welty's 'A Worn Path.'" 1976. Nostrandt suggests that the story may be based on the inversion of a Norse legend in which an old woman is transformed into a woodpecker because of her failure to respond to someone in need. Described in terms that are consistent

with a woodpecker, Phoenix Jackson attains her humanity because of her selflessness.

- Bartel, Roland. "Life and Death in Eudora Welty's 'A Worn Path.'" 1977. Bartel claims that Phoenix Jackson's grandson is dead and that Phoenix denies this fact so that her own life will still have meaning. This assumption explains much of her behavior and proves her name to be ironic. (Bartel ignores Welty's comments on this issue.)
- Walter, James. "Love's Habit of Vision in Eudora Welty's Phoenix Jackson." 1986. Walter argues that an epiphany occurs not in the protagonist but in the reader. The reader revises his or her initial estimate of Phoenix Jackson after seeing that she is guided by spiritual vision. This wide-ranging, moderate reading is in line with Welty's views.
- Robinson, David. "A Nickel and Dime Matter: Teaching Eudora Welty's 'A Worn Path.'" 1987. Robinson shows how the story's central incident—Phoenix's stealing the nickel dropped by the hunter—can be variously interpreted depending on what the hunter is assumed to know about the theft. This article is one of the first to grant the story a plurality of readings.
- Butterworth, Nancy K. "From Civil War to Civil Rights: Race Relations in Welty's 'A Worn Path.'" 1989. Butterworth sees Phoenix Jackson not as a stereotype but as a unique individual whose journey, nearly an allegory, represents the development of black-white relations from Reconstruction to the pre–civil rights era. The author reviews the articles representing the extreme positions on race and tries to mediate.
- Orr, Elaine. "'Unsettling Every Definition of Otherness': Another Reading of Welty's 'A Worn Path.'" 1992. Orr challenges previous readings of the story as failing to recognize Phoenix's intelligence and complexity. Phoenix—and metaphorically Welty as a writer—escapes each stereotyped interpretation with a unique response. Thus, linguistically, by the end of the story, Phoenix, like the mythic bird, re-creates herself. This reading opens up the story in new, surprising ways.
- Saunders, James Robert. "'A Worn Path': The Eternal Quest of Welty's Phoenix Jackson." 1992. Saunders sees Phoenix Jackson as representing those black women who, during a certain period in history, acted out of a deep moral center and became a mother to those around them. He cites as examples Faulkner's Dilsey, Margaret Walker's Virgy, and Angelou's Annie Henderson. The author is similar to Howell and Walter in his attention to character.

- Gardner, Joseph. "Errands of Love: A Study in Black and White." 1993. Gardner argues that the archetypal significance of Phoenix Jackson is based on a racial stereotype and that her universality derives from unexamined cultural assumptions. To make his point, Gardner contrasts her to Alice Walker's Rannie Toomer in "Strong Horse Tea." Gardner's position opposes that of Howell and Saunders.

As always, the invitation is for you to listen to the scholarly debate, find a place to enter, and then expand the discussion with your own well-reasoned view. To provide you with a model for writing about "A Worn Path," the Casebook includes a student paper that was selected because it illustrates both how to use MLA documentation style and format and how to incorporate sources found in the Casebook. The student writer, Daniel Collins, discusses what he finds most important about the story—the relationship between character (Phoenix Jackson) and act (her journey). Daniel begins by reviewing what other critics have found important in the story and then goes on to present his position. Notice that because Daniel uses the ideas of critics and references to the story to support and strengthen his own points, his voice controls and directs the discussion.

Acknowledgments

A number of people are directly responsible for the making of this Casebook. First, I want to thank Laurie G. Kirszner and Stephen R. Mandell, the Series Editors, for developing the casebook concept. I also want to thank Claire Brantley, the Harbrace representative who recommended me for the project; Michael Rosenberg, the Executive Editor who asked me to undertake it; and Dorothy Shawhan, my department chair, who encouraged me to accept. I also want to thank the librarians at Delta State University, especially Diane Coleman who provided me with a world of interlibrary loan materials. Finally, I want to thank the Harbrace editorial staff for all their help—especially Laura Newhouse, Katie Frushour, Linda McMillan, Matt Ball, and Vicki Whistler.

Elizabeth Sarcone
Delta State University

Contents

About the Series. v
Preface ix

Introduction 1

"A Worn Path": The Making of an American Classic 2
A discussion of the background of "A Worn Path" illustrating the
story's unique place in Eudora Welty's fiction
About the Author: Eudora Welty 12

Literature 15

"A Worn Path" 16
Discussion Questions 24
Research Topics 25

Secondary Sources 27

Welty, Eudora. "Must the Novelist Crusade?" *Atlantic* Oct. 1965:
104–108. Rpt. in *The Eye of the Story: Selected Essays and Reviews*. By
Welty. New York: Random, 1978. 146–58. An essay in which Welty
points out the differences between creative writing and crusading. 28

Howell, Elmo. "Eudora Welty's Negroes: A Note on 'A Worn Path.'"
Xavier University Studies 9.1 (Spring 1970): 28–32. An article that
finds no racial hatred in the story and sees Phoenix Jackson as a
universal figure who happens to be black. 37

Welty, Eudora. "Is Phoenix Jackson's Grandson Really Dead?"
Critical Inquiry 1 (Sept. 1974): 219–21. Rpt. in *The Eye of the Story:
Selected Essays and Reviews*. By Welty. New York: Random, 1978.

159–62. An essay in which Welty explains her views on this
frequently asked question. 41

Nostrandt, Jeanne R. "Welty's 'A Worn Path.'" *Explicator* 34
(Jan. 1976): item 33. An article that suggests the story draws upon
an Old Norse tale but inverts its bird imagery. 44

Bartel, Roland. "Life and Death in Eudora Welty's 'A Worn Path.'"
Studies in Short Fiction. 14 (Summer 1977): 288–90. An article that
argues Phoenix Jackson's grandson is dead. 45

Walter, James. "Love's Habit of Vision in Eudora Welty's Phoenix
Jackson" *Journal of the Short Story in English* 7 (Autumn 1986): 77–85.
A broad discussion that links Phoenix Jackson's patience and
persistence to her belief in the cyclic process of nature. 48

Robinson, David. "A Nickel and Dime Matter: Teaching Eudora
Welty's 'A Worn Path.'" *Notes on Mississippi Writers* 19.1 (1987):
23–27. An article suggesting that the scene in which Phoenix steals
the hunter's nickel is open to multiple interpretations. 56

Butterworth, Nancy K. "From Civil War to Civil Rights: Race
Relations in Welty's 'A Worn Path.'" In *The Eye of the Storyteller.* Ed.
Dawn Trouard. Kent: Kent State UP, 1989. 165–72; 212–13. An
article that interprets Phoenix's journey as a recapitulation of black–
white relations since slavery. 60

Orr, Elaine. "'Unsettling Every Definition of Otherness': Another
Reading of Welty's 'A Worn Path.'" *South Atlantic Review* 57.2
(May 1992): 57–72. A critical article that interprets the story as a
complex analogy of the writing process. 70

Saunders, James Robert. "'A Worn Path': The Eternal Quest of
Welty's Phoenix Jackson." *Southern Literary Journal* 25 (Fall 1992):
62–73. An article that argues that Phoenix Jackson epitomizes
participation in nature, preservation of innocence, and persistence. 86

Gardner, Joseph. "Errand of Love: A Study in Black and White."
Kentucky Review 12 (Autumn 1993): 69–78. An article that argues
Phoenix Jackson embodies Welty's unconscious stereotypical
assumptions about African-Americans. 97

Sample Student Research Paper 107

Bibliography............................115
Works by Eudora Welty 116
Autobiography, Biography, and Interviews 117
Criticism and Commentary................................ 117
Electronic and Other Media 151
Reference Guides and Bibliographies 153

Appendix: Documenting Sources..........155
A Guide to MLA Documentation Style....................... 156
Credits... 169

The Harcourt Brace Casebook Series in Literature

"A Worn Path"

Eudora Welty

Introduction

"A Worn Path": The Making of an American Classic

Most readers familiar with Eudora Welty would agree that "A Worn Path" occupies a special place in her work. Widely anthologized in short story collections and college literature anthologies, it has become one of Welty's best-known and most-admired stories.

PUBLISHING BACKGROUND

As the first story by Eudora Welty to be published in a national magazine, "A Worn Path" signaled the official launching of her career. But if the national publication in February 1941 marked the beginning of a new period, it came as the result of much hard work.

When Welty was unable to find a job in New York because of the Great Depression and returned home to Jackson, Mississippi, in 1931, she was confronted with two shocks: the sudden death of her father at age fifty-two and the newfound awareness of Mississippi's diversity and poverty, which she gained while working with the Works Progress Administration. The WPA had been set up in 1935 by President Franklin Roosevelt as part of his New Deal, his plan for providing recovery and relief from the Depression. Its purpose was to create jobs—by hiring workers to build roads, parks, and bridges—and to provide social services such as adult-education classes and free lunches for children. As a publicist in the state office, Welty traveled around Mississippi talking to people and reporting on WPA efforts. She documented what she saw by taking photographs, which she developed at night and studied in the mornings. In a 1977 interview, Welty said the experience was "the real germ of my wanting to become a writer, a real writer, a true writer. It caused me to seriously attempt it. It made me see for the first time, what life was really like in this state. . . . I didn't know what people were really like until then" (Conversations 178).

Almost from the moment Welty asked friend and fellow writer Herbert Creekmore if he knew where she could send her stories, Welty never lacked support or guidance. Following Creekmore's advice, Welty sent her first story, "Death of a Traveling Salesman," to John Rood, editor of the small but prestigious journal *Manuscript*. To her surprise, it was accepted and published in June 1936. Soon afterwards, Robert Penn Warren and Cleanth Brooks at the University of Louisiana began accepting her stories for the *Southern Review*. Through reading the journal and from her husband, Albert Erskine, who was also associated with the *Southern Review*, Katherine Anne Porter came to know Welty's work and befriended her. Acceptance by Porter, an older woman who was herself a short-story writer, helped crystallize Welty's growing sense of herself as an author.

The *Southern Review* was also instrumental in Welty's acquiring an agent. John Woodburn, an editor for the publisher Doubleday, Doran, heard about Welty during a scouting trip that took him to Louisiana. After stopping in Jackson to meet Welty and read some of her manuscripts, he passed on her name to Diarmuid Russell, the son of A. E. (George William Russell), the noted Irish poet. Russell, who had just opened an agency in New York, wrote Welty in May 1940 offering his services. (For the next thirty-three years, Russell represented Welty and gave her what she, in Jackson, could never have acquired for herself—an insider's knowledge of the publishing business.) In December 1940, after six months of rejections, Russell placed "A Worn Path" and "Powerhouse" with the *Atlantic Monthly*, one of the country's two oldest and most respected magazines. This remarkable achievement was quickly followed by another: In February 1941, *Harper's Bazaar*, a magazine rivaling the *Atlantic* in prestige, bought "The Key," one of Welty's more difficult stories. Acceptance by Mary Louise Aswell, *Bazaar*'s fiction editor, brought to Welty a woman who was to be of increasing importance to her artistic growth. For while Rood, Brooks, Warren, Erskine, and Porter helped Welty to see herself as a writer, and Russell and Woodburn won her national exposure, Aswell encouraged Welty to experiment—this at a time when Russell and others thought she should be more cautious.

Meanwhile, Russell had sold a collection of Welty's short stories to Woodburn at Doubleday, Doran. The final arrangements included a commitment by Porter to write an introduction to increase the chances for the book's success and replacing "Acrobats in the Park," a weaker story, with "A Worn Path." On November 7, 1941—exactly one month before the Japanese attacked Pearl Harbor and the United States entered World

War II—Doubleday, Doran came out with Welty's first book, *A Curtain of Green*. "A Worn Path" was the last story in the collection.

THE PLACE

On several occasions Welty has described her inspiration for "A Worn Path." According to Welty, she was with a friend along the Old Canton Road near Jackson, which was then still in the country. While her friend painted, Welty sat under a tree reading. Then, in the distance, Welty saw a woman come out of the woods, cross the field, and disappear back into the woods. The appearance of the woman caused Welty to remember a comment made by another woman she had met on a previous outing: "I was too old at the Surrender." Fusing the two experiences, Welty created Phoenix Jackson. When Welty changed the scene from the outskirts of Jackson to the Natchez Trace, she made imaginative use of the reading she had done for the WPA and the Mississippi Advertising Commission.

Often called the "Devil's Backbone," the Natchez Trace was originally little more than a loosely connected network of old buffalo trails and Indian footpaths. Once used as an important communication link, this narrow track stretching diagonally 450 miles from Natchez to Nashville took on its most colorful role when goods were routinely transported down the Mississippi River by flatboat. Because returning up the river meant poling against the current, the Trace became the overland road back. All sorts of travelers—politicians, soldiers, traders, preachers, and outlaws—were thrown together on the swampy, dangerous route. The Trace fell into disuse in about 1830 when the steamboat, invented in 1811, became popular. Over the next hundred years the legendary path was reclaimed by grass and forests. Then, in 1937, looking for WPA projects and needing the political influence of Mississippi Senator Pat Harrison, President Roosevelt used his emergency funds to conduct a survey for the construction of the Natchez Parkway, a road which would generally follow and so commemorate the old Natchez Trace.

Natchez, the "paved city" in "A Worn Path," is built on high bluffs overlooking the Mississippi River. Ever since the French built Fort Rosalie there in 1716, it has had an exceptional history. Successively governed by the French, British, and Spanish, Natchez served as the capital of the Mississippi Territory from 1798–1802. Its wealth and sophistication gave it a cultural and economic preeminence long after Mississippi's political headquarters moved to Jackson, a city newly created to be the state capital, in 1822. In the boom of the 1830s, rich planters made Natchez the center of the Cotton Kingdom. When it lost that position after the Civil War, Natchez made even greater financial gains through its railroads, river traffic, and venturesome merchants. During the Depression, while the rest of Mississippi suffered through the worst times since Reconstruction, Natchez experienced an economic renewal, triggered in 1931 when garden club women capitalized on the city's cultural heritage by organizing a tour of antebellum homes. The event was so successful, it was made an annual celebration. By the late 1930s and early 1940s the Natchez Spring Pilgrimage had become so profitable that historical restoration became an important local business.

The Natchez setting clearly locates "A Worn Path" in Mississippi and identifies Welty as a Southern author. But during the late 1930s when scholars were in the process of establishing the Southern literary tradition, the work of Southern writers was quickly labeled and pigeonholed. For Welty this often meant being unfavorably compared to William Faulkner, another Mississippian. More frequently it meant being dismissed as a regionalist— a term negatively associated with provincialism and local color. Few critics saw Welty's use of surface details, including habits of speech, for what it was—a disciplined means of portraying the complex inner landscape of her characters. As a response to this kind of categorization, in 1956 Welty wrote "Place in Fiction" (*Eye of the Story* 116–133), an essay that asserts that the world's great literature depends on its explicit fidelity to a particular location. When interviewers ask her who most influenced her work, Welty typically names Chekhov, Austen, and Woolf—clearly implying that her work is set in a particular place but not limited to it.

THE TIME

"A Worn Path" is set around 1940, the year it was actually written, and it is notable for being one of only a handful of Welty stories with an African-American protagonist. The story takes place during the Depression, shortly after President Roosevelt described the South as "the nation's number one" economic problem in 1938 and the phenomenal box office success of *Gone with the Wind* in 1939.

In the American South, only seventy-five years away from the end of the Civil War, 1940 was a time when segregation was institutionalized by both law and custom. Jim Crow laws kept races separated everywhere from water fountains to hospital waiting rooms, lynchings were not unheard of, and an elaborate social etiquette governed interaction between the races. That Welty was moved by the social and political injustice she found in Mississippi's rural black communities is documented in her publication of *One*

Time, One Place: Mississippi in the Depression; A Snapshot Album (1971), a collection of photographs she took during her work for the WPA.

Segregation policies were protected by the 1896 Supreme Court's "separate but equal" ruling and remained in effect until found unconstitutional in 1954 by the *Brown v. Board of Education* Supreme Court decision. Throughout the 1950s, Mississippi tried, in the words of Governor Hugh L. White, "every legal means" to save segregation. But the 1960s saw an eruption of violence. In 1962 James Meredith's admission to the University of Mississippi precipitated a bloody riot; in 1963 civil rights leader Medgar Evers was murdered in Jackson; in 1964 three young civil rights workers, Michael Schwerner, James Chaney, and Andrew Goodman, were murdered in Philadelphia, Mississippi; and in 1966, activist James Meredith was shot while marching from Memphis to Jackson. During this decade Welty published "Where Is the Voice Coming From?" (1963) and "The Demonstrators" (1966), two stories based on Mississippi's racial upheaval. The first of these stories shows remarkable daring—Welty wrote it the night Evers was murdered as a first-person narration by the murderer before Byron DeLa Beckwith had been named or charged.

Because these are the only two stories that acknowledge race as an issue, Welty has been routinely criticized for having no social conscience. But Welty is not without political and social vision. In an essay entitled "Must the Novelist Crusade?" (1965), she formally answers those who accused her of failing to address social problems by distinguishing the purpose of creative writers from that of crusaders and other social reformers. Though her methods are subtle and indirect, the characters Welty creates illustrate the effect of oppressive and racist political and social conditions. It is true, for example, that in "A Worn Path" there is no evidence of racial unrest, but despite her nobility, Phoenix Jackson's place in the Natchez community attests to Mississippi's deep social and economic divide.

THE WRITING STYLE

"A Worn Path" is among those early stories Welty says she wrote spontaneously without revising. But inasmuch as its nearly seamless movement between Phoenix Jackson's inner and outer world anticipates Welty's later style, its location as the final story in *A Curtain of Green* is particularly fitting. Beginning with Welty's second short story collection, *The Wide Net* (1943), critics have attacked all of Welty's books, with the exception of *The Ponder Heart* (1954), as being deliberately obscure. But from the outset Welty has not been without more perceptive readers. Referring specifically to "A Worn Path" in her "Introduction," Katherine Anne Porter was the first to call favorable attention to Welty's emerging technique. Mary Louise Aswell also saw the hidden current in her method and prompted Welty to continue to explore it. In "The Love and Separateness in Miss Welty" (1944), a now famous essay examining Welty's first two collections, Robert Penn Warren defended Welty against indictments by northern reviewer Diana Trilling. And Welty herself has provided subtle hints about how her own stories should be read. For instance, in an interview she describes the excitement she felt after first reading Virginia Woolf's *To the Lighthouse* (1927) and says that, for her, Woolf was "the one who opened the door" (*Prenshaw* 75). Clearly, Welty means that, for her, Woolf opened the door to recognizing the possibilities of using a feminine point of view and experimental methods. It is not hard to imagine how Welty, freed by Woolf's precedent, ignored her detractors and, following an inner authority, invented the oblique style she needed to get her stories told. *The Eye of the Story* (1978), a collection of selected essays, reviews, and reminiscences spanning thirty years, provides ample proof of Welty's fully realized aesthetic.

THE SOUTHERN LITERARY TRADITION

Frequently anthologized and studied by generations of students, "A Worn Path" is perhaps Welty's best-loved story. But, as a brief look at the history of Southern literature will show, the continuing popularity of it, along with several other isolated short stories, masks two important matters that have affected Welty's critical reception. First, Welty has been undervalued because of her assigned place in the Southern Renaissance. And second, her work has been only superficially understood by New Critics because of their narrow critical approach.

For most of the twentieth century, Southern literature has been defined by the work of a few men affiliated with Vanderbilt University and loosely identified as Fugitive-Agrarians. In the 1920s, these scholars belonged to a group called the Fugitives, which regularly met to read, discuss, and publish poetry. Later known as Agrarians, they became famous for the 1930 manifesto *I'll Take My Stand*, a collection of essays that defended the South and its traditions against what the Agrarians saw as the threat posed by progress and industrialization. Paralleling the attempts of historians to rid Southern history of its outmoded romanticism and defensive posture, these scholars, individually and collectively, began to rethink the nature and function of poetry. When they left Nashville, they took with them a common perspective and, using various literary vehicles, began to direct and dominate America's literary discourse.

The most famous of these men are John Crowe Ransom, Robert Penn Warren, and Allen Tate. Ransom is credited with originating the theory of literary criticism that took the name of his 1941 book, *The New Criticism*. Replacing older approaches to literature, New Criticism regarded the critic's task as the understanding and evaluation of a work through careful reading, with little reference to the author's biography or to the literary history or the cultural context of the work. It focused almost entirely on the images, symbols, and meanings to be discovered in the text. Editors of three influential journals—the *Sewanee Review*, the *Kenyon Review*, and the *Southern Review*, all associated with the Nashville group—promoted these new principles. What Ransom initiated and editors endorsed, Warren institutionalized. By co-editing a series of college textbooks (*Understanding Poetry*, 1938; *Understanding Fiction*, 1943; and *Understanding Drama*, 1945) Warren changed how teachers taught literature in classrooms across America.

But it was Tate who, in an often quoted passage, called the period he shared with his Vanderbilt colleagues the Southern Renaissance and defined its major theme: "With the war of 1914–1918, the South re-entered the world—but gave a backward glance as it stepped over the border; that backward glance gave us the Southern renascence, a literature conscious of the past in the present" (Tate 292). According to Tate, the sudden outburst of creativity in the South occurring between the two world wars happened because Southerners tried to move forward by forging a new understanding of their past. Tate's explanation soon became critical doctrine. Thus the Southern Renaissance was formally established.

In addition to the Fugitives, Agrarians, New Critics, and William Faulkner, other authors accepted as members of the Southern Renaissance include Caroline Gordon and Thomas Wolfe. Because Welty began publishing in 1940, after these novelists had already earned their reputations, she is generally regarded as part of the second generation of writers of the Southern Renaissance. But all too often, even while acknowledging Welty's achievements, the critical guardians of the Southern Renaissance tradition diminish or dismiss her. For instance, in *Renaissance in the South* (1963), John M. Bradbury finds Welty "indifferent to the larger social and political problems of her region" (108). And in *A Southern Renaissance* (1980), Richard H. King excludes Welty and other female writers because "they were not concerned primarily with the larger cultural, racial, and political themes" (9).

Such marginalization is currently being challenged by literary revisionists who see the Southern Renaissance as a male construct which, because its standards are limited to the experience of men, fails to accommodate women's ways of writing. When Brooks and Warren published two of Welty's short stories ("A Piece of News" and "Old Mr. Marblehall") in their first edition of *Understanding Fiction* (1943), Welty was officially accepted in the textbook canon and the new critical tradition, but, ironically, this inclusion—with its focus on isolated stories—delayed more accurate and more comprehensive assessments of her work. Referred to as "nutty mythosymbolist explications" by novelist Reynolds Price (Johnson 177), many interpretations of "A Worn Path" typify the kinds of misreadings Welty's fiction attracts. In "Is Phoenix Jackson's Grandson Really Dead?" (1974), Welty uses the question raised by so many students as an occasion to say that an interpretation should be consistent with a story's tone and intention. In interviews such as the one taped with Beth Henley, she counters "symbol hunters" by explaining that she chose *Phoenix* because it was a name actually given to slaves, not merely for its allusive value. Yet despite her commentaries on literary mishandling, Welty has generally remained more admired than understood.

GENDER, GENRE, AND THE ARTIST

"A Worn Path" is instructive because, while the point of view is that of a woman, little is known about Phoenix Jackson's personal history. Thus the story underscores two well-known facts about Welty: she is opposed to being labeled a feminist and she does not like being asked personal questions. In spite of rejecting the feminist tag, however, Welty shows her sensitivity to the position of women. For instance, a few weeks after finishing "A Worn Path," Welty responded to New York publishers' unrelenting demand for a novel by writing to her literary agent, Diarmuid Russell: "When I only think of a novel, it scares me. I never wanted to be contrary, but it is the natural thing for me to do what I can within a lesser space. I suspect that that comes from my being a female, and is permanent" (qtd. in Kreyling 49). Welty not only linked gender with genre but admitted that gender made a difference in content as well. When Mary Louise Aswell called attention to the "latent female psychology" in "The Winds," a short story Welty wrote in March 1941, Welty acknowledged that its slant was meant to be distinctively female (Kreyling 69). As for her desire for privacy, Welty has consistently resisted biographers, screened interviews, and kept any personal difficulties to herself. However, in 1984 she published *One Writer's Beginnings,* a series of three autobiographical essays, first delivered as lectures at Harvard, relating events in her early life that gave shape to her writing career. And it was she who gave Michael Kreyling the letters and the idea for *Author and Agent* (1991), a book recounting the partnership she had with Diarmuid Russell. Both efforts—her stand on the woman's movement and on biographical investigation—seem similarly directed. Welty has wanted her work to be read for itself—not reduced to propaganda or personal facts. As Will Brantley observes in response to *One Writer's Beginnings*, Welty presents herself as "an artist, not a woman who is also an artist" (117).

THE JOURNEY MOTIF

"A Worn Path" is noteworthy because it is based on a journey, a motif Welty often repeats. It occurs not only in her fiction, but also in pieces such as "The Little Store," an autobiographical account of growing up in Jackson, Mississippi; in fact, it is a central image in her work. In "Is Phoenix Jackson's Grandson Really Dead?," Welty takes time to suggest what the image means to her. By drawing a parallel between the course of Phoenix's errand and the process of writing, Welty says that like Phoenix, her aim has been to do her duty and follow her own path. Ruth Weston has said, "Whatever else Welty is writing about, she is always writing about writing" (76). Certainly Welty's remarks help explain the cryptic line Phoenix utters when she passes the boarded-up, weathered cabins sitting "like old women under a spell" (18). By "I walking in their sleep" Phoenix means she embodies earlier dreams of freedom. Similarly, like the former slave, the writer, emancipated from the demands of the publishing industry, the critics, the literary establishment, and the political activists, is free to "go [her] own way" (qtd. in Kreyling 136).

CURRENT RE-EVALUATION

"A Worn Path" has recently been made into a film accompanied by an interpretive discussion by the author. The 1994 videocassette, combining John Reid and Claudia Velasco's production and Beth Henley's interview, is part of what Jon Smith calls the effort "to bring Welty firmly into the American canon" (554). With the publication in 1980 of *The Collected Stories*—forty-one in all—and in 1984 of the autobiographical *One Writer's Beginnings*—a surprising best-seller—critics began taking notice. Now the full range of Welty's work—short stories, novels, essays, reviews, autobiography, and photographs—has made Welty's achievement as a woman of letters undeniable. As a result, Welty's work is currently undergoing an exciting reassessment of which this casebook is a part.

WORKS CONSULTED

Bradbury, John M. *Renaissance in the South: A Critical History of the Literature, 1920–1960.* Chapel Hill: U of North Carolina P, 1963.

Brantley, Will. *Feminine Sense in Southern Memoir: Smith, Glasgow, Welty, Hellman, Porter, and Hurston.* Jackson, UP of Mississippi, 1993.

Henley, Beth. *Interview with Eudora Welty.* Dir. John Reid and Claudia Velasco. Videocassette. Harcourt, 1994.

Johnston, Carol Ann. *Eudora Welty: A Study of the Short Fiction.* New York: Twayne, 1997.

King, Richard H. *A Southern Renaissance: The Cultural Awakening of the American South, 1930–1955.* New York: Oxford UP, 1980.

Kreyling, Michael. *Author and Agent: Eudora Welty and Diarmuid Russell.* New York: Farrar, 1991.

Loewen, James W., and Charles Sallis, eds. *Mississippi: Conflict and Change.* New York: Pantheon, 1974.

Manning, Carol S., ed. *The Female Tradition in Southern Literature.* Urbana: U of Illinois P, 1993.

Porter, Katherine Anne. "Introduction." *A Curtain of Green.* By Eudora Welty. Garden City: Doubleday, 1941. ix–xix. Rpt. in Johnston. 151–57

Prenshaw, Peggy Whitman, ed. *Conversations with Eudora Welty.* Jackson UP of Mississippi, 1984.

Price, Reynolds. "The Collected Stories of Eudora Welty." Review of *The Collected Stories of Eudora Welty.* By Eudora Welty. *New Republic* 183 (1980): 31–34 Rpt. in Johnston. 173–178.

Rubin, Louis D., Jr., et al. *The History of Southern Literature.* Baton Rouge: Louisiana State UP, 1985.

Sansing, David G., Sim C. Callon, and Carolyn Vance Smith. *Natchez: An Illustrated History.* Natchez: Plantation, 1992.

Smith, Jon. "The Welty Boom!" *Contemporary Literature* 36.3 (1993): 553–69.

Tate, Allen. "The New Provincialism." *Virginia Quarterly Review* 21 (Spring 1945): 262–72. Rpt. in *Collected Essays.* By Tate. Denver: Alan Swallow, 1959. 282–93.

Warren, Robert Penn. "The Love and Separateness in Miss Welty." *Kenyon Review* 6 (Spring 1944): 246–59. Rpt. in Johnston. 158–68.

Welty, Eudora. *The Eye of the Story: Selected Essays and Reviews.* New York: Random, 1978.

———. *One Time, One Place: Mississippi in the Depression; A Snapshot Album.* 1971. Rev. ed. Jackson: UP of Mississippi, 1996.

———. *One Writer's Beginnings.* Cambridge: Harvard UP, 1984.

———. Preface. *The Collected Stories of Eudora Welty.* By Welty. New York: Harcourt, 1980. ix–xi.

Weston, Ruth D. "The Feminine and Feminist Texts of Eudora Welty's *The Optimist's Daughter.*" 4 (Winter 1987): 74–91.

"*A Worn Path.*" By Eudora Welty. Dir. John Reid and Claudia Velasco. Perf. Cora Lee Day and Conchita Ferrell. Videocassette. Harcourt, 1994.

About the Author

EUDORA WELTY (1909–) is a Southern writer who is internationally recognized for her works of fiction. Originally labeled a regionalist, grouped with Southern writers whose subject was the Gothic and the grotesque, or—because of the coincidence of time and place—compared to William Faulkner, Welty is now celebrated for her singular achievement. Welty's recognition has steadily grown over the long span of her career, but since the publication of her last two novels, the *Collected Stories,* and the autobiographical *One Writer's Beginnings,* her popular and critical reputation has dramatically increased. Noted for her lyrical style and balanced, detached view, Welty approaches her subjects with a genuine respect and affection.

Born in Jackson, Mississippi, where she lives now and has lived most of her life, Eudora Alice Welty grew up with two younger brothers in a close-knit family two blocks from the state capitol. Both her father, a Republican from Ohio, and her mother, a Democrat from West Virginia, were once schoolteachers. After they married, they moved to Jackson where Christian Welty became a prominent Jacksonian and, eventually, president of the Lamar Life Insurance Company. Having gone to high school in Jackson, Welty spent two years at Mississippi State College for Women in Columbus and then transferred to the University of Wisconsin in Madison to complete her degree as an English major. On her father's recommendation, Welty then attended the school of business at Columbia University, where she studied advertising from 1930 to 1931. Unable to find a job in New

York, Welty returned to Mississippi in 1931, the same year her father died. During this period, Welty held a number of part-time jobs, including working for a Jackson radio station and serving as the Jackson social correspondent for the Memphis *Commercial Appeal*. Her first full-time employment, in 1935, was with the Works Progress Administration where she was the "junior publicity agent." In this capacity, Welty traveled the state interviewing people, writing newspaper copy, and taking photographs to publicize the various WPA projects. In 1936, following a Democratic defeat, the job ended abruptly. The same year saw the publication of her first short story, "Death of a Traveling Salesman." Welty's next job was with the Mississippi Advertising Commission where she wrote copy and took photographs to attract tourism and industry. She also continued to write fiction; during the next few years Robert Penn Warren and Cleanth Brooks, editors of the *Southern Review*, published six of her stories. After the publication of her first short story collection, *A Curtain of Green*, in 1941, Welty quit work to devote herself to her writing. Since the launching of her literary career, Welty has received many prestigious awards and honors, including her election to the American Academy of Arts (1971), the Pulitzer Prize for *The Optimist's Daughter* (1973), the Presidential Medal of Freedom (1980), and the Modern Language Association Commonwealth Award (1984).

Welty's major works include her first collection of stories, *A Curtain of Green* (1941); a novella, *The Robber Bridegroom* (1942); a second collection of stories, *The Wide Net* (1943); a full-length novel, *Delta Wedding* (1946); a collection of related stories, *The Golden Apples* (1949); a long story, *The Ponder Heart* (1954); another collection of stories, *The Bride of the Innisfallen* (1955); two stories published in *The New Yorker*, "Where Is the Voice Coming From?" (1963) and "The Demonstrators" (1966); a long novel, *Losing Battles* (1970); a collection of photographs, *One Time, One Place* (1971); and a loosely autobiographical novel, *The Optimist's Daughter* (1972). She has also published a collection of essays and reviews in *The Eye of the Story* (1978) and forty-one stories in *Collected Stories* (1980). The autobiographical *One Writer's Beginnings* (1984) made the best-seller list for months.

"A Worn Path" was sent along with "Powerhouse" to the *Atlantic Monthly* in October 1940. It was accepted in December and first published in February 1941. Later that year Welty's agent, Diarmuid Russell, and Doubleday editor John Woodburn encouraged her to use it to replace "Acrobats in the Park" for her first short story collection. "A Worn Path" won second prize in the O. Henry Memorial Award for 1941 and was collected in a 1942 volume with the other prize-winning stories. "A Worn Path" was included among the three short stories Welty recorded in 1952. In 1994, John Reid and Claudia Velasco directed a film version of the story, which appeared on Mississippi ETV and is now available on audiocassette from Harcourt Brace College Publishers.

Literature

EUDORA WELTY

A Worn Path
(1940)

It was December—a bright frozen day in the early morning. Far out in the country there was an old Negro woman with her head tied in a red rag, coming along a path through the pinewoods. Her name was Phoenix Jackson. She was very old and small and she walked slowly in the dark pine shadows, moving a little from side to side in her steps, with the balanced heaviness and lightness of a pendulum in a grandfather clock. She carried a thin, small cane made from an umbrella, and with this she kept tapping the frozen earth in front of her. This made a grave and persistent noise in the still air, that seemed meditative like the chirping of a solitary little bird.

She wore a dark striped dress reaching down to her shoe tops, and an equally long apron of bleached sugar sacks, with a full pocket: all neat and tidy, but every time she took a step she might have fallen over her shoelaces, which dragged from her unlaced shoes. She looked straight ahead. Her eyes were blue with age. Her skin had a pattern all its own of numberless branching wrinkles and as though a whole little tree stood in the middle of her forehead, but a golden color ran underneath, and the two knobs of her cheeks were illumined by a yellow burning under the dark. Under the red rag her hair came down on her neck in the frailest of ringlets, still black, and with an odor like copper.

Now and then there was a quivering in the thicket. Old Phoenix said, "Out of my way, all you foxes, owls, beetles, jack rabbits, coons and wild animals! . . . Keep out from under these feet, little bob-whites. . . . Keep the big wild hogs out of my path. Don't let none of those come running my direction. I got a long way." Under her small black-freckled hand her cane, limber as a buggy whip, would switch at the brush as if to rouse up any hiding things.

On she went. The woods were deep and still. The sun made the pine needles almost too bright to look at, up where the wind rocked. The cones dropped as light as feathers. Down in the hollow was the mourning dove—it was not too late for him.

The path ran up a hill. "Seem like there is chains about my feet, time I get this far," she said, in the voice of argument old people keep to use with themselves. "Something always take a hold of me on this hill—pleads I should stay."

After she got to the top she turned and gave a full, severe look behind her where she had come. "Up through pines," she said at length. "Now down through oaks."

Her eyes opened their widest, and she started down gently. But before she got to the bottom of the hill a bush caught her dress.

Her fingers were busy and intent, but her skirts were full and long, so that before she could pull them free in one place they were caught in another. It was not possible to allow the dress to tear. "I in the thorny bush," she said. "Thorns, you doing your appointed work. Never want to let folks pass, no sir. Old eyes thought you was a pretty little *green* bush."

Finally, trembling all over, she stood free, and after a moment dared to stoop for her cane.

"Sun so high!" she cried, leaning back and looking, while the thick tears went over her eyes. "The time getting all gone here."

At the foot of this hill was a place where a log was laid across the creek.

"Now comes the trial," said Phoenix.

Putting her right foot out, she mounted the log and shut her eyes. Lifting her skirt, leveling her cane fiercely before her, like a festival figure in some parade, she began to march across. Then she opened her eyes and she was safe on the other side.

"I wasn't as old as I thought," she said.

But she sat down to rest. She spread her skirts on the bank around her and folded her hands over her knees. Up above her was a tree in a pearly cloud of mistletoe. She did not dare to close her eyes, and when a little boy brought her a plate with a slice of marble-cake on it she spoke to him. "That would be acceptable," she said. But when she went to take it there was just her own hand in the air.

So she left that tree, and had to go through a barbed-wire fence. There she had to creep and crawl, spreading her knees and stretching her fingers like a baby trying to climb the steps. But she talked loudly to herself: she could not let her dress be torn now, so late in the day, and she could not pay for having her arm or her leg sawed off if she got caught fast where she was.

At last she was safe through the fence and risen up out in the clearing. Big dead trees, like black men with one arm, were standing in the purple stalks of the withered cotton field. There sat a buzzard.

"Who you watching?"

In the furrow she made her way along.

"Glad this not the season for bulls," she said, looking sideways, "and the good Lord made his snakes to curl up and sleep in the winter. A pleasure I don't see no two-headed snake coming around that tree, where it come once. It took a while to get by him, back in the summer."

She passed through the old cotton and went into a field of dead corn. It whispered and shook and was taller than her head. "Through the maze now," she said, for there was no path.

Then there was something tall, black, and skinny there, moving before her.

At first she took it for a man. It could have been a man dancing in the field. But she stood still and listened, and it did not make a sound. It was as silent as a ghost.

"Ghost," she said sharply, "who be you the ghost of? For I have heard of nary death close by."

But there was no answer — only the ragged dancing in the wind.

She shut her eyes, reached out her hand, and touched a sleeve. She found a coat and inside that an emptiness, cold as ice.

"You scarecrow," she said. Her face lighted. "I ought to be shut up for good," she said with laughter. "My senses is gone. I too old. I the oldest people I ever know. Dance, old scarecrow," she said, "while I dancing with you."

She kicked her foot over the furrow, and with mouth drawn down, shook her head once or twice in a little strutting way. Some husks blew down and whirled in streamers about her skirts.

Then she went on, parting her way from side to side with the cane, through the whispering field. At last she came to the end, to a wagon track where the silver grass blew between the red ruts. The quail were walking around like pullets, seeming all dainty and unseen.

"Walk pretty," she said. "This is the easy place. This the easy going."

She followed the track, swaying through the quiet bare fields, through the little strings of trees silver in their dead leaves, past cabins silver from weather, with the doors and windows boarded shut, all like old women under a spell sitting there. "I walking in their sleep," she said, nodding her head vigorously.

In a ravine she went where a spring was silently flowing through a hollow log. Old Phoenix bent and drank. "Sweet-gum makes the water sweet," she said, and drank more. "Nobody know who made this well, for it was here when I was born."

The track crossed a swampy part where the moss hung as white as lace from every limb. "Sleep on, alligators, and blow your bubbles." Then the track went into the road.

Deep, deep the road went down between the high green-colored banks. Overhead the live-oaks met, and it was as dark as a cave.

A black dog with a lolling tongue came up out of the weeds by the ditch. She was meditating, and not ready, and when he came at her she only hit him a little with her cane. Over she went in the ditch, like a little puff of milkweed.

Down there, her senses drifted away. A dream visited her, and she reached her hand up, but nothing reached down and gave her a pull. So she lay there and presently went to talking. "Old woman," she said to herself, "that black dog come up out of the weeds to stall you off, and now there he sitting on his fine tail, smiling at you."

A white man finally came along and found her—a hunter, a young man, with his dog on a chain.

"Well, Granny!" he laughed. "What are you doing there?"

"Lying on my back like a June-bug waiting to be turned over, mister," she said, reaching up her hand.

He lifted her up, gave her a swing in the air, and set her down. "Anything broken, Granny?"

"No sir, them old dead weeds is springy enough," said Phoenix, when she had got her breath. "I thank you for your trouble."

"Where do you live, Granny?" he asked, while the two dogs were growling at each other.

"Away back yonder, sir, behind the ridge. You can't even see it from here."

"On your way home?"

"No sir, I going to town."

"Why, that's too far! That's as far as I walk when I come out myself, and I get something for my trouble." He patted the stuffed bag he carried, and there hung down a little closed claw. It was one of the bob-whites, with its beak hooked bitterly to show it was dead. "Now you go on home, Granny!"

"I bound to go to town, mister," said Phoenix. "The time come around."

He gave another laugh, filling the whole landscape. "I know you old colored people! Wouldn't miss going to town to see Santa Claus!"

But something held old Phoenix very still. The deep lines in her face went into a fierce and different radiation. Without warning, she had seen with her own eyes a flashing nickel fall out of the man's pocket onto the ground.

"How old are you, Granny?" he was saying.

"There is no telling, mister," she said, "no telling."

Then she gave a little cry and clapped her hands and said, "Git on away from here, dog! Look! Look at that dog!" She laughed as if in admiration. "He ain't scared of nobody. He a big black dog." She whispered, "Sic[1] him!"

"Watch me get rid of that cur," said the man. "Sic him, Pete! Sic him!"

Phoenix heard the dogs fighting, and heard the man running and throwing sticks. She even heard a gunshot. But she was slowly bending forward by that time, further and further forward, the lid stretched down over her eyes, as if she were doing this in her sleep. Her chin was lowered almost to her knees. The yellow palm of her hand came out from the fold of her apron. Her fingers slid down and along the ground under the piece of money with the grace and care they would have in lifting an egg from under a setting hen. Then she slowly straightened up, she stood erect, and the nickel was in her apron pocket. A bird flew by. Her lips moved. "God watching me the whole time. I come to stealing."

The man came back, and his own dog panted about them. "Well, I scared him off that time," he said, and then he laughed and lifted his gun and pointed it at Phoenix.

She stood straight and faced him.

"Doesn't the gun scare you?" he said, still pointing it.

"No, sir, I seen plenty go off closer by, in my day, and for less than what I done," she said, holding utterly still.

He smiled, and shouldered the gun. "Well, Granny," he said, "you must be a hundred years old, and scared of nothing. I'd give you a dime if I had any money with me. But you take my advice and stay home, and nothing will happen to you."

"I bound to go on my way, mister," said Phoenix. She inclined her head in the red rag. Then they went in different directions, but she could hear the gun shooting again and again over the hill.

She walked on. The shadows hung from the oak trees to the road like curtains. Then she smelled wood-smoke, and smelled the river, and she saw a steeple and the cabins on their steep steps. Dozens of little black children whirled around her. There ahead was Natchez shining. Bells were ringing. She walked on.

In the paved city it was Christmas time. There were red and green electric lights strung and crisscrossed everywhere, and all turned on in the day-

---

[1] To urge to attack; a dialectical variation of "seek."

time. Old Phoenix would have been lost if she had not distrusted her eyesight and depended on her feet to know where to take her.

She paused quietly on the sidewalk where people were passing by. A lady came along in the crowd, carrying an armful of red-, green- and silver-wrapped presents; she gave off perfume like the red roses in hot summer, and Phoenix stopped her.

"Please, missy, will you lace up my shoe?" She held up her foot.

"What do you want, Grandma?"

"See my shoe," said Phoenix. "Do all right for out in the country, but wouldn't look right to go in a big building."

"Stand still then, Grandma," said the lady. She put her packages down on the sidewalk beside her and laced and tied both shoes tightly.

"Can't lace 'em with a cane," said Phoenix. "Thank you, missy. I doesn't mind asking a nice lady to tie up my shoe, when I gets out on the street."

Moving slowly and from side to side, she went into the big building, and into a tower of steps, where she walked up and around and around until her feet knew to stop.

She entered a door, and there she saw nailed up on the wall the document that had been stamped with the gold seal and framed in the gold frame, which matched the dream that was hung up in her head.

"Here I be," she said. There was a fixed and ceremonial stiffness over her body.

"A charity case, I suppose," said an attendant who sat at the desk before her.

But Phoenix only looked above her head. There was sweat on her face, the wrinkles in her face shone like a bright net.

"Speak up, Grandma," the woman said. "What's your name? We must have your history, you know. Have you been here before? What seems to be the trouble with you?"

Old Phoenix only gave a twitch to her face as if a fly were bothering her.

"Are you deaf?" cried the attendant.

But then the nurse came in.

"Oh, that's just old Aunt Phoenix," she said. "She doesn't come for herself—she has a little grandson. She makes these trips just as regular as clockwork. She lives away back off the Old Natchez Trace." She bent down. "Well, Aunt Phoenix, why don't you just take a seat? We won't keep you standing after your long trip." She pointed.

The old woman sat down, bolt upright in the chair.

"Now, how is the boy?" asked the nurse.

Old Phoenix did not speak.

"I said, how is the boy?"

But Phoenix only waited and stared straight ahead, her face very solemn and withdrawn into rigidity.

"Is his throat any better?" asked the nurse. "Aunt Phoenix, don't you hear me? Is your grandson's throat any better since the last time you came for the medicine?"

With her hands on her knees, the old woman waited, silent, erect and motionless, just as if she were in armor.

"You mustn't take up our time this way, Aunt Phoenix," the nurse said. "Tell us quickly about your grandson, and get it over. He isn't dead, is he?"

At last there came a flicker and then a flame of comprehension across her face, and she spoke.

"My grandson. It was my memory had left me. There I sat and forgot why I made my long trip."

"Forgot?" The nurse frowned. "After you came so far?"

Then Phoenix was like an old woman begging a dignified forgiveness for waking up frightened in the night. "I never did go to school, I was too old at the Surrender,"[2] she said in a soft voice. "I'm an old woman without an education. It was my memory fail me. My little grandson, he is just the same, and I forgot it in the coming."

"Throat never heals, does it?" said the nurse, speaking in a loud, sure voice to old Phoenix. By now she had a card with something written on it, a little list. "Yes. Swallowed lye.[3] When was it?—January—two-three years ago—"

Phoenix spoke unasked now. "No, missy, he not dead, he just the same. Every little while his throat begin to close up again, and he not able to swallow. He not get his breath. He not able to help himself. So the time come around, and I go on another trip for the soothing medicine."

"All right. The doctor said as long as you came to get it, you could have it," said the nurse. "But it's an obstinate case."

"My little grandson, he sit up there in the house all wrapped up, waiting by himself," Phoenix went on. "We is the only two left in the world. He suffer and it don't seem to put him back at all. He got a sweet look. He going to last. He wear a little patch quilt and peep out holding his mouth open

---

[2] After Lee's surrender to Grant on April 9, 1865, ended the Civil War, the federal government established the Freedmen's Bureau, which, among other things, created schools for blacks.

[3] A caustic solution made from leaching wood ashes with water and used with waste fat to make soap.

like a little bird. I remembers so plain now. I not going to forget him again, no, the whole enduring time. I could tell him from all the others in creation."

"All right." The nurse was trying to hush her now. She brought her a bottle of medicine. "Charity," she said, making a check mark in a book.

Old Phoenix held the bottle close to her eyes, and then carefully put it into her pocket.

"I thank you," she said.

"It's Christmas time, Grandma," said the attendant. "Could I give you a few pennies out of my purse?"

"Five pennies is a nickel," said Phoenix stiffly.

"Here's a nickel," said the attendant.

Phoenix rose carefully and held out her hand. She received the nickel and then fished the other nickel out of her pocket and laid it beside the new one. She stared at her palm closely, with her head on one side.

Then she gave a tap with her cane on the floor.

"This is what come to me to do," she said. "I going to the store and buy my child a little windmill they sells, made out of paper. He going to find it hard to believe there such a thing in the world. I'll march myself back where he waiting, holding it straight up in this hand."

She lifted her free hand, gave a little nod, turned around, and walked out of the doctor's office. Then her slow step began on the stairs, going down.

Discussion Questions

1. What is the significance of the story's title? Consider both its literal meaning and its symbolic associations. Does Phoenix Jackson follow a clearly defined path, or does she have to make her own way?
2. Discuss the story's setting by looking closely at the time, place, and social context in which the action occurs. In what way are the season and the passing of time important? What are the differences between the country and the city?
3. What is significant about Phoenix Jackson's first and last names?
4. Identify the various trials and difficulties Phoenix must overcome. How might they represent different stages of a journey or quest?
5. What is Phoenix Jackson's relationship to nature? To what extent does nature help or hinder her?
6. Phoenix has several lapses of memory and dreamlike experiences. Identify these instances, and explain what each one contributes to your understanding of both Phoenix and the story.
7. Trace the references in the story to birds, color, and time. What patterns emerge? What do these patterns contribute to the story? Do other similar patterns appear?
8. Phoenix Jackson's meeting with the young hunter is a central event in the story. In what ways is this incident important? Does the hunter kill the dog? Why does he point his gun at Phoenix? What does Phoenix's response suggest?
9. During the course of her journey, Phoenix meets three white women—the "nice lady" who ties her shoes, the office attendant, and the nurse. Explain how the women's responses to Phoenix differ. What do these responses reveal about the women themselves? about race relations? What do Phoenix's responses to them reveal about her?
10. Why do you think Welty does not mention Phoenix Jackson's return home? Do you think she returns home safely? What is significant about Phoenix's intention to buy a windmill? Do you find the ending satisfactory? Why or why not?

Research Topics

1. There has been much critical debate about whether Phoenix Jackson is a stereotype. Using the sources in this text as well as others found in the bibliography, review the different arguments concerning this issue. Then, using the story as your guide, determine whether or not you find Phoenix to be a stereotypical figure. Explain how your conclusion affects your reaction to and interpretation of the story.

2. As Welty herself has pointed out, many readers have asked whether or not Phoenix Jackson's grandson is dead. Examine what Welty has said about this topic in her essay "Is Phoenix Jackson's Grandson Really Dead?" (41–43). Next read "Life and Death in Eudora Welty's 'A Worn Path'" (45–48), the article by Roland Bartel that first discussed this issue. How relevant do you think this question is? Would knowing whether the grandson is dead or alive change the meaning of the story for you? If so, how?

3. Compare John Reid and Claudia Velasco's videocassette production *A Worn Path* to the printed story. What are the differences between the two versions? What changes are made in the film, and how effective are they? Discuss the advantages and disadvantages of watching the video as opposed to reading the text.

4. "A Worn Path" was first published in 1941. To what extent does it accurately reflect race relations in Mississippi during that pre–civil rights era? Is the story a product of a particular time and place, or could it have occurred anywhere at any time? Read Welty's essay "Must the Novelist Crusade?" (28–37). Then, in the two collections of conversations listed in the bibliography of this casebook, find several interviews in which Welty comments on social and political issues. Do you find Welty's position on these matters appropriate for a writer? Why or why not?

5. Several critics have seen a connection between the people in Welty's photographs and the characters in her stories. Examine Welty's photographs in *One Time, One Place* and in *Images in the South* edited by Bill Ferris. Find some of the articles written about Welty the photographer in the bibliography of this casebook. Then, determine what relationship exists between Phoenix Jackson and the women Welty photographed.

Secondary Sources

The eleven sources in this section provide different ways of reading and thinking about "A Worn Path." They include two essays by Welty and nine critical articles that make various kinds of comments about the story. The sources are arranged in chronological order so you can see the relationship of the critics to each other as their scholarly discussion evolves. A careful reading of these sources may suggest an idea that you can develop into a paper, or perhaps you can use the sources to support an idea you already have. Once you are familiar with the secondary material provided here, you can use the bibliography at the back of this book to extend your investigation by locating further commentary about Welty, "A Worn Path," or some of Welty's other works. Remember to document your use of words or ideas borrowed from these or any other sources. For information about documenting sources, consult the concise guide to MLA documentation provided in the Appendix of this volume.

Eudora Welty

Must the Novelist Crusade?
(1965)

Not too long ago I read in some respectable press that Faulkner would have to be reassessed because he was "after all, only a white Mississippian." For this reason, it was felt, readers could no longer rely on him for knowing what he was writing about in his life's work of novels and stories, laid in what he called "my country."

Remembering how Faulkner for most of his life wrote in all but isolation from critical understanding, ignored impartially by North and South, with only a handful of critics in forty years who were able to "assess" him, we might smile at this journalist as at a boy let out of school. Or there may have been an instinct to smash the superior, the good, that is endurable enough to go on offering itself. But I feel in these words and others like them the agonizing of our times. I think they come of an honest and understandable zeal to allot every writer his chance to better the world or go to his grave reproached for the mess it is in. And here, it seems to me, the heart of fiction's real reliability has been struck at—and not for the first time by the noble hand of the crusader.

It would not be surprising if the critic I quote had gained his knowledge of the South from the books of the author he repudiates. At any rate, a reply to him exists there. Full evidence as to whether any writer, alive or dead, can be believed is always at hand in one place: any page of his work. The color of his skin would modify it just about as much as would the binding of his book. Integrity can be neither lost nor concealed nor faked nor quenched nor artificially come by nor outlived, nor, I believe, in the long run denied. Integrity is no greater and no less today than it was yesterday and will be tomorrow. It stands outside time.

The novelist and the crusader who writes both have their own place—in the novel and the editorial respectively, equally valid whether or not the two happen to be in agreement. In my own view, writing fiction places the novelist and the crusader on opposite sides. But they are not the sides of right and wrong. Honesty is not at stake here and is not questioned; the only thing at stake is the proper use of words for the proper ends. And a mighty thing it is.

Because the printed page is where the writer's work is to be seen, it may be natural for people who do not normally read fiction to confuse novels with journalism or speeches. The very using of words has these well-intentioned people confused about the novelist's purpose.

The writing of a novel is taking life as it already exists, not to report it but to make an object, toward the end that the finished work might contain this life inside it, and offer it to the reader. The essence will not be, of course, the same thing as the raw material; it is not even of the same family of things. The novel is something that never was before and will not be again. For the mind of one person, its writer, is in it too. What distinguishes it above all from the raw material, and what distinguishes it from journalism, is that inherent in the novel is the possibility of a shared act of the imagination between its writer and its reader.

"All right, Eudora Welty, what are you going to do about it? Sit down there with your mouth shut?" asked a stranger over long distance in one of the midnight calls that I suppose have waked most writers in the South from time to time. It is part of the same question: Are fiction writers on call to be crusaders? For us in the South who are fiction writers, is writing a novel *something we can do about it?*

It can be said at once, I should think, that we are all agreed upon the most important point: that morality as shown through human relationships is the whole heart of fiction, and the serious writer has never lived who dealt with anything else.

And yet, the zeal to reform, which quite properly inspires the editorial, has never done fiction much good. The exception occurs when it can rise to the intensity of satire, where it finds a better home in the poem or the drama. Large helpings of naïveté and self-esteem, which serve to refresh the crusader, only encumber the novelist. How unfair it is that when a novel is to be written, it is never enough to have our hearts in the right place! But good will all by itself can no more get a good novel written than it can paint in watercolor or sing Mozart.

Nevertheless, let us suppose that we feel we might help if we were to write a crusading novel. What will our problems be?

Before anything else, speed. The crusader's message is prompted by crisis; it has to be delivered on time. Suppose John Steinbeck had only now finished *The Grapes of Wrath*? The ordinary novelist has only one message: "I submit that this is one way we are." This can wait. When we think of Ibsen, we see that causes themselves may in time be forgotten, their championship no longer needed; it is Ibsen's passion that keeps the plays alive.

Next, we as the crusader-novelist shall find awkward to use the very weapon we count on most: the generality. On fiction's pages, generalities clank when wielded, and hit with equal force at the little and the big, at the merely suspect and the really dangerous. They make too much noise for us to hear what people might be trying to say. They are fatal to tenderness and are in themselves non-conductors of any real, however modest, discovery of the writer's own heart. This discovery is the best hope of the ordinary novelist, and to make it he begins not with the generality but with the particular in front of his eyes, which he is able to examine.

Taking a particular situation existing in his world, and what he feels about it in his own breast and what he can make of it in his own head, he constructs on paper, little by little, an equivalent of it. Literally it may correspond to a high degree or to none at all; emotionally it corresponds as closely as he can make it. Observation and the inner truth of that observation as he perceives it, the two being tested one against the other: to him this is what the writing of a novel is.

We, the crusader-novelist, having started with our generality, must end with a generality; they had better be the same. In the place of climax, we can deliver a judgment. How can the plot seem disappointing when it is a lovely argument spread out? It is because fiction is stone-deaf to argument.

The ordinary novelist does not argue; he hopes to show, to disclose. His persuasions are all toward allowing his reader to see and hear something for himself. He knows another bad thing about arguments: they carry the menace of neatness into fiction. Indeed, what we as the crusader-novelist are scared of most is confusion.

Great fiction, we very much fear, abounds in what makes for confusion; it generates it, being on a scale which copies life, which it confronts. It is very seldom neat, is given to sprawling and escaping from bounds, is capable of contradicting itself, and is not impervious to humor. There is absolutely everything in great fiction but a clear answer. Humanity itself seems to matter more to the novelist than what humanity thinks it can prove.

When a novelist writes of man's experience, what else is he to draw on but the life around him? And yet the life around him, on the surface, can be used to show anything, absolutely anything, as readers know. The novelist's real task and real responsibility lie in the way he uses it.

Situation itself always exists; it is whatever life is up to here and now, it is the living and present moment. It is transient, and it fluctuates. Using the situation, the writer populates his novel with characters invented to express it in their terms.

It is important that it be in their terms. We cannot in fiction set people to acting mechanically or carrying placards to make their sentiments plain. People are not Right and Wrong, Good and Bad, Black and White personified; flesh and blood and the sense of comedy object. Fiction writers cannot be tempted to make the mistake of looking at people in the generality—that is to say, of seeing people as not at all *like us*. If human beings are to be comprehended as real, then they have to be treated as real, with minds, hearts, memories, habits, hopes, with passions and capacities like ours. This is why novelists begin the study of people from within.

The first act of insight is throw away the labels. In fiction, while we do not necessarily write about ourselves, we write out of ourselves, using ourselves; what we learn from, what we are sensitive to, what we feel strongly about—these become our characters and go to make our plots. Characters in fiction are conceived from within, and they have, accordingly, their own interior life; they are individuals every time. The character we care about in a novel we may not approve of or agree with—that's beside the point. But he has got to seem alive. Then and only then, when we read, we experience or surmise things about life itself that are deeper and more lasting and less destructive to understanding than approval or disapproval.

The novelist's work is highly organized, but I should say it is organized around anything but logic. Just as characters are not labels but are made from the inside out and grow into their own life, so does a plot have a living principle on which it hangs together and gradually earns its shape. A plot is a thousand times more unsettling than an argument, which may be answered. It is not a pattern imposed; it is inward emotion acted out. It is arbitrary, indeed, but not artificial. It is possibly so odd that it might be called a vision, but it is organic to its material: it is a working vision, then.

A writer works *through* what is around him if he wishes to get to what he is after—no kind of proof, but simply an essence. In practice he will do anything at all with his material: shape it, strain it to the breaking point, double it up, or use it backward; he will balk at nothing—see *The Sound and the Fury*—to reach that heart and core. But even in a good cause he does not falsify it. The material itself receives deep ultimate respect: it has given rise to the vision of it, which in turn has determined what the novel shall be.

The ordinary novelist, who can never make a perfect thing, can with every novel try again. But if we write a novel to prove something, one novel will settle it, for why prove a thing more than once? And what, then, is to keep all novels by all right-thinking persons from being pretty much alike? Or exactly alike? There would be little reason for present writers to keep on, no reason for the new writers to start. There's no way to know, but we might guess that the reason the young write no fiction behind the Iron Curtain is the obvious fact that to be acceptable there, all novels must conform, and so must be alike, hence valueless. If the personal vision can be made to order, then we should lose, writer and reader alike, our own gift for perceiving, seeing through the fabric of everyday to what to each pair of eyes on earth is a unique thing. We'd accept life exactly like everybody else, and so, of course, be content with it. We should not even miss our vanished novelists. And if life ever became not worth writing fiction about, that, I believe, would be the first sign that it wasn't worth living.

With a blueprint to work with instead of a vision, there is a good deal that we as the crusader-novelist must be at pains to leave out. Unavoidably, I think, we shall leave out one of the greatest things. This is the mystery in life. Our blueprint for sanity and of solution for trouble leaves out the dark. (This is odd, because surely it was the dark that first troubled us.) We leave out the wonder because with wonder it is impossible to argue, much less to settle. The ordinary novelist thinks it had better be recognized. Reckless as this may make him, he believes the insoluble is part of his material too.

The novelist works neither to correct nor to condone, not at all to comfort, but to make what's told alive. He assumes at the start an enlightenment in his reader equal to his own, for they are hopefully on the point of taking off together from that base into the rather different world of the imagination.

It's not only the fact that this world is bigger and that fewer constrictions apply that may daunt us as crusaders. But the imagination itself is the problem. It is capable of saying everything but no. In our literature, what has traveled the longest way through time is the great affirmative soul of Chaucer. The novel itself always affirms, it seems to me, by the nature of itself. It says what people are like. It doesn't, and doesn't know how to, describe what they are *not* like, and it would waste its time if it told us what we ought to be like, since we already know that, don't we? But we may not know nearly so well what we are as when a novel of power reveals this to us. For the first time we may, as we read, see ourselves in our own situation, in some curious way reflected. By whatever way the novelist accomplishes it—there are many ways—truth is borne in on us in all its great weight and angelic lightness, and accepted as home truth.

Passing judgment on his fellows, which is trying enough for anybody, is frustrating for an author. It is hardly the way to make the discoveries about living that he must have hoped for when he began to write. If he does not pass judgment, does this mean he has no conscience? Of course he has a conscience; it is, like his temperament, his own, and he is one hundred percent answerable to it, whether it is convenient or not. What matters is that a writer is committed to his own moral principles. If he is, when we read him we cannot help but be aware of what these are. Certainly the characters of his novel and the plot they move in are their ultimate reflections. But these convictions are implicit; they are deep down; they are the rock on which the whole structure of more than that novel rests.

Indeed, we are more aware of his moral convictions through a novel than any flat statement of belief from him could make us. We are aware in that part of our mind that tells us truths about ourselves. Yet it is only by way of the imagination—the novelist's to ours—that such private neighborhoods are reached.

There is still to mention what I think will give us, as the crusader-novelist, the hardest time: our voice will not be our own. The crusader's voice is the voice of the crowd and must rise louder all the time, for there is, of course, the other side to be drowned out. Worse, the voices of most crowds sound alike. Worse still, the voice that seeks to do other than communicate when it makes a noise has something brutal about it; it is no longer using words as words but as something to brandish, with which to threaten, brag or condemn. The noise is the simple assertion of self, the great, mindless, general self. And for all its volume it is ephemeral. Only meaning lasts.

Nothing was ever learned in a crowd, from a crowd, or by addressing or trying to please a crowd. Even to deplore, yelling is out of place. To deplore a thing as hideous as the murder of the three civil rights workers demands the quiet in which to absorb it. Enormities can be lessened, cheapened, just as good and delicate things can be. We can and will cheapen all feeling by letting it go savage or parading in it.

Writing fiction is an interior affair. Novels and stories always will be put down little by little out of personal feeling and personal beliefs arrived at alone and at firsthand over a period of time as time is needed. To go outside and beat the drum is only to interrupt, interrupt, and so finally to forget and to lose. Fiction has, and must keep, a private address. For life is *lived* in a private place; where it means anything is inside the mind and heart. Fiction has always shown life where it is lived, and good fiction, or so I have faith, will continue to do this.

A Passage to India is an old novel now. It is an intensely moral novel. It deals with race prejudice. Mr. Forster, not by preaching at us, while being passionately concerned, makes us know his points unforgettably as often as we read it. And does he not bring in the dark! The points are good forty years after their day *because of the splendor of the novel.* What a lesser novelist's harangues would have buried by now, his imagination still reveals. Revelation of even the strongest forces is delicate work.

Indeed, great fiction shows us not how to conduct our behavior but how to feel. Eventually, it may show us how to face our feelings and face our actions and to have new inklings about what they mean. A good novel of any year can initiate us into our own new experience.

From the working point of view of the serious writer of fiction, nothing has changed today but the externals. They are important externals; we may have developed an increased awareness of them, which is certainly to the good; we have at least the same capacity as ever for understanding, the same eyes and ears, same hearts to feel, same minds to agonize or remember or to try to put things together, see things in proportion with. While the raw material of our fiction is changing dramatically—as indeed it is changing everywhere—we are the same instruments of perceiving that we ever were. I should not trust us if we were not. And we do not know what is to be made out of experience at any time until the personal quotient has been added. To convey what we see around us, whatever it is, so as to let it speak for itself according to our lights is the same challenge it ever was, not a different one, not a greater one, only perhaps made harder by the times. Now as ever we must keep writing from what we know; and we must really know it.

No matter how fast society around us changes, what remains is that there is a relationship in progress between ourselves and other people; this was the case when the world seemed stable, too. There are relationships of the blood, of the passions and the affections, of thought and spirit and deed. There is the relationship between the races. How can one kind of relationship be set apart from the others? Like the great root system of an old and long-established growing plant, they are all tangled up together; to separate them you would have to cleave the plant itself from top to bottom.

What must the Southern writer of fiction do today? Shall he do anything different from what he has always done?

There have already been giant events, some of them wrenchingly painful and humiliating. And now there is added the atmosphere of hate. We in the South are a hated people these days; we were hated first for actual and particular reasons, and now we may be hated still more in some vast unparticularized way. I believe there must be such a thing as sentimental hate. Our people hate back.

I think the worst of it is we are getting stuck in it. We are like trapped flies with our feet not in honey but in venom. It's not love that is the gluey emotion; it's hate. As far as writing goes, which is as far as living goes, this is a devastating emotion. It could kill us. This hate seems in part shame for self, in part self-justification, in part panic that life is really changing.

Fury at ourselves and hurt pride, anger aroused too often, outrage at being hated need not obscure forever the sore spots we Southerners know better than our detractors. For some of us have shown bad hearts. As in the case of our better qualities, we are locally blessed with an understanding and intimate knowledge of our faults that our worst detractors cannot match, and have been in a less relentless day far more relentless, more eloquent, too, than they have yet learned to be.

I do not presume to speak for my fellow Southern writers, a group of individuals if there ever was one. Yet I would like to point something out: in the rest of the country people seem suddenly aware now of what Southern fiction writers have been writing about in various ways for a great long time. We do not need reminding of what our subject is. It is humankind, and we are all part of it. When we write about people, black or white, in the South or anywhere, if our stories are worth the reading, we are writing about everybody.

In the South, we who are now at work may not learn to write it before we learn, or learn again, to live it—our full life in the South within its context, in its relation to the rest of the world. "Only connect," Forster's ever wise and gentle and daring words, could be said to us in our homeland quite literally at this moment. And while the Southern writer goes on portraying his South, which I think nobody else can do and which I believe he must do, then if his work is done well enough, it will reflect a larger mankind as it has done before.

And so finally I think we need to write with love. Not in self-defense, not in hate, not in the mood of instruction, not in rebuttal, in any kind of militance, or in apology, but with love. Not in exorcisement, either, for this is to make the reader bear a thing for you.

Neither do I speak of writing forgivingly; out of love you can write with straight fury. It is the *source* of the understanding that I speak of; it's this that determines its nature and its reach.

We are told that Turgenev's nostalgic, profoundly reflective, sensuously alive stories that grew out of his memories of early years reached the Czar and were given some credit by him when he felt moved to free the serfs in Russia. Had Turgenev set out to write inflammatory tracts instead of the sum of all he knew, could express, of life learned at firsthand, how much less of his mind and heart with their commitments, all implicit, would have filled his stories! But he might be one of us now, so directly are we touched with a hundred and thirteen years gone by since they were first published.

Indifference would indeed be corrupting to the fiction writer, indifference to any part of man's plight. Passion is the chief ingredient of good fiction. It flames right out of sympathy for the human condition and goes into all great writing. (And of course passion and the temper are different things; writing in the heat of passion can be done with extremely good temper.) But to distort a work of passion for the sake of a cause is to cheat, and the end, far from justifying the means, is fairly sure to be lost with it. Then the novel will have been not the work of imagination, at once passionate and objective, made by a man struggling in solitude with something of his own to say, but a piece of catering.

To cater to is not to love and not to serve well either. We do need to bring to our writing, over and over again, all the abundance we possess. To be able, to be ready, to enter into the minds and hearts of our own people, all of them, to comprehend them (us) and then to make characters and plots in stories that in honesty and with honesty reveal them (ourselves) to us, in whatever situation we live through in our own times: this is the continuing job, and it's no harder now than it ever was, I suppose. Every writer, like everybody else, thinks he's living through the crisis of the ages. To write honestly and with all our powers is the least we can do, and the most.

Time, though it can make happenings and trappings out of date, cannot do much to change the realities apprehended by the imagination. History will change in Mississippi, and the hope is that it will change in a beneficial direction and with a merciful speed, and above all bring insight, understanding. But when William Faulkner's novels come to be pictures of a society that is no more, they will still be good and still be authentic because of what went into them from the man himself. Mankind still tries the same things and suffers the same falls, climbs up to try again, and novels are as true at one time as at another. Love and hate, hope and despair, justice and injustice, compassion and prejudice, truth-telling and lying work in all men; their story can be told in whatever skin they are wearing and in whatever year the writer can put them down.

Faulkner is not receding from us. Indeed, his work, though it can't increase in itself, increases us. His work throws light on the past and on today as it becomes the past—the day in its journey. This being so, it informs the future too.

What is written in the South from now on is going to be taken into account by Faulkner's work; I mean the remark literally. Once Faulkner had written, we could never unknow what he told us and showed us. And his work will do the same thing tomorrow. We inherit from him, while we can get fresh and firsthand news of ourselves from his work at any time.

A source of illumination is not dated by what passes along under its ray, is not qualified or disqualified by the nature of the traffic. When the light of Faulkner's work will be discovering things to us no more, it will be discovering *us*. Even we shall lie enfolded in perspective one day: what we hoped along with what we did, what we didn't do, and not only what we were but what we missed being, what others yet to come might dare to be. For we *are* our own crusade. Before ever we write, we are. Instead of our judging Faulkner, he will be revealing us in books to later minds.

ELMO HOWELL

Eudora Welty's Negroes: A Note on "A Worn Path"
(1970)

Eudora Welty's picture of her native Mississippi, which deserves comparison with that of William Faulkner, is remarkably free of bias or coloring, beyond the author's avowed love of all phases of life in her region. She takes no stand on topical issues, since it is part of her creed that the novelist should not crusade. For ultimately she is concerned, not just with Mississippi, but with—to use Faulkner's phrase—the human heart in conflict with itself . . . because only that is worth writing about."[1]

Consequently, she is the most catholic of writers in her approach to the variegated social scene of her state; aristocrats and poor whites, city dwellers and country people, Negroes of varying rank and condition—all are taken up, not as the representatives of groups (though they are carefully realized on the objective level), but as individuals who in some way are related to the general human predicament. Phoenix Jackson of "A Worn Path" is an aged Negro woman taken from the life in the South of a generation ago, but she is also everyman, or everywoman, who has a journey to make, a mission to accomplish, and somehow musters the courage and strength to do it. Her story is exhilarating, not because she is a Negro or a Mississippian, but because she is a fine human being.

Old Phoenix, so old that she remembers "the Surrender," lives alone with her little grandson, an invalid who is kept alive by the "soothing medicine" which she brings periodically from a doctor's office in Natchez. It is a long walk from her home on the old Natchez Trace; and the occasion of the story is one of her trips, on a bright December day just at Christmas time. Nothing in particular happens. She falls down, and a hunter—a white man—helps her up, with Phoenix managing to salvage a nickel that the man accidentally drops. In town she asks a white lady to tie her shoes, which the lady does after laying her bundles down on the sidewalk. In the doctor's office she has a lapse of memory, but the nurse knows her, brings the medicine, and gives her another nickel out of her own pocket. Phoenix says that she will buy her little grandson a toy windmill for Christmas—"He going to find it hard to believe there such a thing in the world"[2]—and then sets off on her return journey.

Phoenix's contact with the hunter and the nurses, whom Miss Welty postulates as average Southern whites, has caused some critics to interpret the story in racial terms. The town and its inhabitants, says Alfred Appel, Jr., are "presented in contrast to Phoenix," and not to the advantage of the whites, over whom Phoenix has "moral superiority." Both the white man and the nurses, not to mention the lady who ties her shoes, are tainted, in

---

[1] William Faulkner, "Speech of Acceptance Upon the Award of the Nobel Prize for Literature," *The Faulkner Reader* (New York, 1959), p. 3.

[2] Eudora Welty, "A Worn Path," *A Curtain of Green* (New York, 1941), p. 289. (Subsequent references to this work will appear in the text.)

Mr. Appel's view, merely because they are white and consequently insensitive to the higher values.[3] John Edward Hardy would go further. "It is obvious that neither of the two white women has any comprehension of what they are witnessing, that they are all but totally incapable of the human recognition that is essential to true charity." To them, the child is merely a nuisance, "a stubborn case." "Obviously, from the tone of her first inquiries, the nurse has almost hoped that this time Phoenix will tell them he is dead." As for the hunter, he is "very pleased with himself in the superior strength of his youth and whiteness." There is nowhere in modern literature, continues Mr. Hardy, "a more scathing indictment of the fool's pride of the white man in the superiority of his civilization."[4]

Readers who are insensitive to the nuances of Southern life are at a disadvantage in reading Eudora Welty, who with her feminine intuition is even closer than William Faulkner to the heartbeat of her region. Mr. Hardy, who would adjust the details of the story to fit a personal view, suggests that the incident with the white lady who ties Phoenix's shoes indicates that the white woman is too proud to refuse "the outrageous request" and that Phoenix, like other Southern Negroes, has learned "to take subtle revenge" on white people by exploiting their pride in this way. In the first place, the request is not "outrageous," at least in the country of which Miss Welty writes:[5] Phoenix is old, and her age warrants respect from both black and white. It is part of the system that older generations of Southerners subscribed to that old servants like Phoenix be accorded a special regard by the people whom they have served; the titles of "aunt" and "uncle", for example, were expressions of respect and affection and not mere patronage. Consequently, the white lady who ties Phoenix's shoes does so as a partial fulfillment of what she regards in some abstract manner as her obligation to the

---

[3] Alfred Appel, Jr., *A Season of Dreams: The Fiction of Eudora Welty* (Baton Rouge, 1965), p. 170.

[4] John Edward Hardy, "Eudora Welty's Negroes," *Images of the Negro in American Literature*, eds. Seymour L. Gross and John Edward Hardy (Chicago, 1966), pp. 227–228.

[5] The incident was taken from life. Once an old Negro woman, "with a bright, weathered face," asked Miss Welty to tie her shoes for her, and when asked about her age, said, "I was old at the Surrender." Ruth M. Vande Kieft, *Eudora Welty* (New York, 1962), p. 23. In an interview with Bill Ferris, Welty indicates that the story was based on not one but two separate instances: in one she saw an old woman walking across the horizon; in another she had a conversation with a different woman who used the line, "I was too old at the Surrender" (Prenshaw, *Conversations* 167–68).

old Negro. The fact that she has never seen her before does not matter, because it is enough that she knows that Phoenix's race has stood in a position of fealty to her own race through generations of intimate life together. Phoenix is aware of this feeling and knows that she can presume; and in this request of the white lady loaded down with Christmas parcels she is simply demanding her due, which both she and the lady understand from the long contractual relationship between the two races. The lady would have resented a similar request from another white woman—such are the intricacies of social behavior which make up a part of the fascination of Miss Welty's fiction. On the surface, the picture of old Phoenix standing on a Natchez street while a white woman ties her shoes suggests sardonic humor; but to Miss Welty it dramatizes the kindliness and intimacy which she finds among the best elements of her region.

In a critique of Miss Welty's novel *Delta Wedding,* John Crowe Ransom calls the book "a comedy of love."[6] The phrase is apt and could be applied to her work in general, for although she is aware of the substratum of evil—the cruelty that is latent in human nature—the world she portrays is essentially beneficent, because the forces that tend towards chaos are held in check by prescription and law. There is no conflict between Phoenix and the white world, and there is no hate. The nickel that she takes from the white man is not taken in revenge. The "theft" is prompted by her great need and by her love for the little boy; and even then she does not deceive herself. "God seeing me the whole time. I come to stealing." (283) When the nurse suggests a few pennies because it is Christmas, Phoenix says, "Five pennies is a nickel," which the nurse gives her. (288) Phoenix depends on these people, not for much but for a little, just as she depends on them for the medicine, which is the purpose of the trip.

As for the whites, Eudora Welty makes no effort to defend a caste society, but on the other hand she would not portray it in false colors. The whites who confront Phoenix reflect the usual attitudes of their generation towards the Negro. To the outsider, and to a later generation this attitude may appear offensive, but in the context of the story the charity of the whites, meager as it is, is proffered in kindliness and received as such.

But the story is not about the whites. It is about Phoenix; and the people she meets impinge on her consciousness hardly more than the natural phenomena that she confronts on her way to town: the trees, the sun, the

---

[6] John Crowe Ransom, "Delta Fiction," *Kenyon Review,* VIII (Summer, 1946), 503.

wind, the foot-log across the creek, and the gay Christmas lights on the Natchez streets. And in her heart there is nothing but good will for all. "Dance, old scarecrow, while I dancing with you." (279) She has fought with life and conquered it, and now in extreme old age her heart is too vast for malice, too full of love for the whole creation and in particular for the little suffering child who is her special charge.

Phoenix is a whole person, whose life, even in her lowly sphere, is completely realized. She exults in her long walk, even in its hazards, for she moves in harmony with the natural world about her, with "all you foxes, owls, beetles, jack rabbits, coons and wild animals," and the sun in the pine needles "too bright to look at, up where the wind rocked" (276). If there is any criticism of white society, it is in the mere choice of Phoenix as protagonist, rather than a white person, whose sophistication has cut him off from this basic communion with nature. Old Phoenix is a triumphant human being because of her acceptance of the conditions of life and because even at her great age, she still reflects the primal joy of creation.

Eudora Welty

"Is Phoenix Jackson's Grandson Really Dead?"
(1974)

A story writer is more than happy to be read by students; the fact that these serious readers think and feel something in response to his work he finds life-giving. At the same time he may not always be able to reply to their specific questions in kind. I wondered if it might clarify something, for both the questioners and myself, if I set down a general reply to the question that comes to me most often in the mail, from both students and their teachers, after some classroom discussion. The unrivaled favorite is this: "Is Phoenix Jackson's grandson really *dead*?"

It refers to a short story I wrote years ago called "A Worn Path," which tells of a day's journey an old woman makes on foot from deep in the country into town and into a doctor's office on behalf of her little grandson; he is at home, periodically ill, and periodically she comes for his medicine; they give it to her as usual, she receives it and starts the journey back.

I had not meant to mystify readers by withholding any fact; it is not a writer's business to tease. The story is told through Phoenix's mind as she undertakes her errand. As the author at one with the character as I tell it, I must assume that the boy is alive. As the reader, you are free to think as you like, of course: the story invites you to believe that no matter what happens, Phoenix for as long as she is able to walk and can hold to her purpose will make her journey. The *possibility* that she would keep on even if he were dead is there in her devotion and its single-minded, single-track errand. Certainly the *artistic* truth, which should be good enough for the fact, lies in Phoenix's own answer to that question. When the nurse asks, "He isn't dead, is he?" she speaks for herself: "He still the same. He going to last."

The grandchild is the incentive. But it is the journey, the going of the errand, that is the story, and the question is not whether the grandchild is in reality alive or dead. It doesn't affect the outcome of the story or its meaning from start to finish. But it is not the question itself that has struck me as much as the idea, almost without exception implied in the asking, that for Phoenix's grandson to be dead would somehow make the story "better."

It's *all right,* I want to say to the students who write to me, for things to be what they appear to be, and for words to mean what they say. It's all right, too, for words and appearances to mean more than one thing—ambiguity is a fact of life. A fiction writer's responsibility covers not only what he presents as the facts of a given story but what he chooses to stir up as their implications; in the end, these implications, too, become facts, in the larger, fictional sense. But it is not all right, not in good faith, for things *not* to mean what they say.

The grandson's plight was real and it made the truth of the story, which is the story of an errand of love carried out. If the child no longer lived, the truth would persist in the "worn-ness" of the path. But his being dead can't increase the truth of the story, can't affect it one way or the other. I think I signal this, because the end of the story has been reached before old Phoenix gets home again: she simply starts back. To the question "Is the grandson really dead?" I could reply that it doesn't make any difference. I could also say that I did not make him up in order to let him play a trick on Phoenix. But my best answer would be: "*Phoenix* is alive."

The origin of a story is sometimes a trustworthy clue to the author—or can provide him with the clue—to its key image; maybe in this case it will do the same for the reader. One day I saw a solitary old woman like Phoenix. She was walking; I saw her, at middle distance, in a winter country landscape, and watched her slowly make her way across my line of vision. That sight of her made me write the story. I invented an errand for her, but that only seemed a living part of the figure she was herself: what errand other than for someone else could be making her go? And her going was the first thing, her persisting in her landscape was the real thing, and the first and the real were what I wanted and worked to keep. I brought her up close enough, by imagination, to describe her face, make her present to the eyes, but the full-length figure moving across the winter fields was the indelible one and the image to keep, and the perspective extending into the vanishing distance the true one to hold in mind.

I invented for my character, as I wrote, some passing adventures—some dreams and harassments and a small triumph or two, some jolts to her pride, some flights of fancy to console her, one or two encounters to scare her, a moment that gave her cause to feel ashamed, a moment to dance and preen—for it had to be a *journey,* and all these things belonged to that, parts of life's uncertainty.

A narrative line is in its deeper sense, of course, the tracing out of a meaning, and the real continuity of a story lies in this probing forward. The real dramatic force of a story depends on the strength of the emotion that has set it going. The emotional value is the measure of the reach of the story. What gives any such content to "A Worn Path" is not its circumstances but its *subject:* the deep-grained habit of love.

What I hoped would come clear was that in the whole surround of this story, the world it threads through, the only certain thing at all is the worn path. The habit of love cuts through confusion and stumbles or contrives its way out of difficulty, it remembers the way even when it forgets, for a dumbfounded moment, its reason for being. The path is the thing that matters.

Her victory—old Phoenix's—is when she sees the diploma in the doctor's office, when she finds "nailed up on the wall the document that had been stamped with the gold seal and framed in the gold frame, which matched the dream that was hung up in her head." The return with the medicine is just a matter of retracing her own footsteps. It is the part of the journey, and of the story, that can now go without saying.

In the matter of function, old Phoenix's way might even do as a sort of parallel to your way of work if you are a writer of stories. The way to get there is the all-important, all-absorbing problem, and this problem is your reason for undertaking the story. Your only guide, too, is your sureness about your subject, about what this subject is. Like Phoenix, you work all your life to find your way, through all the obstructions and the false appearances and the upsets you may have brought on yourself, to reach a meaning—using inventions of your imagination, perhaps helped out by your dreams and bits of good luck. And finally too, like Phoenix, you have to assume that what you are working in aid of is life, not death.

But you would make the trip anyway—wouldn't you?—just on hope.

JEANNE R. NOSTRANDT

Welty's "A Worn Path"
(1976)

That traces of an old Norse tale appear in Eudora Welty's "A Worn Path" is not surprising to readers aware of her love of folktales and legend. The metamorphosis in her story is similar in image and theme to an old tale found in an elementary school reader used in the 1930's and '40's. Opening descriptive paragraphs of Welty's story suggest the image of a red-headed woodpecker such as those in the pinewoods of Mississippi. Closing paragraphs of the Norse legend in the *Elson Gray Basic Readers, Book Two* describe the woodpecker into which an old woman has been changed.

Critics who discuss bird imagery in "A Worn Path" focus their remarks upon the name of the character Phoenix Jackson, pointing to a rejuvenation theme or a Christ symbol. They note coincidental bird references such as the bird that flies overhead when Phoenix hides the hunter's nickel, or the tapping sound of her cane "like the chirping of a solitary little bird." But the woodpecker image can be traced more directly to the story from folklore.

The Norse legend reveals an old woman turned into a bird because of her selfishness and inhumanity to another's need; Welty inverts the legend's theme and structure to depict the humanizing of Phoenix Jackson through her charitable character. Both Phoenix and the old Norse woman appear as woodpeckers, an image Welty suggests early in her story. This image becomes a pivotal point for her inversion of the legend's theme.

In her realistic portrayal of the character, Welty's description of Phoenix's dress is similar to that of the older tale. She describes Phoenix as very old, small, and swaying from side to side in her walk, tapping an umbrella cane on the frozen earth which gives off a sound like a chirping bird. She wears a dark striped dress and a long apron of bleached sugar sacks which reach down to her shoe tops. On her head is tied a red rag, and her untied shoelaces drag behind her. The old woman of the Norse tale wears a black dress, a small white apron, and a red cap on her head. She refuses to give an old beggar one of the cakes she is baking because they get bigger and bigger no matter how small she rolls them, and she subsequently becomes smaller and smaller with each bite she takes from the cakes she kept for herself. Her arms become black wings, her nose a sharp bill, her feet sharp claws, and she hops up and down the pine trees looking for bugs and worms. The children's tale advises readers to look for her in the woods where they will recognize the black dress, white apron, and red cap on a woodpecker. The woman who would not be human is turned into a bird.

Welty's inversion of the legend's theme and central image carries the moral of "A Worn Path." At the beginning of the story Phoenix emerges from the pinewoods, the habitat of woodpeckers, as a tiny, bird-like creature. The reader follows her path on her long and arduous journey and sees the interior state of the character. As Phoenix overcomes obstacles in her quest, her dignity and humor reveal her as human, while her sacrifice and endurance show her great spirit. Whereas the old Norse woman loses her humanity by her selfishness, Phoenix gives of herself—all she has to give—and thereby gains her humanity in the eyes of the reader. The metamorphosis is from woodpecker image to human being in the Welty story, and from human being to woodpecker in the legend. The moral is embodied in the central image of both stories.

Eudora Welty professes in articles and reviews her love of folktales from her childhood reading. Whether she borrows from the Norse legend or from the oral tradition of storytelling common to the South, she consciously employs the image of the bird to emphasize the theme. The use of fairytales in the works of both Henry Green and Isak Dinesen interests her, and she writes that "throughout fiction runs the constant, casual reference to the fairy tale, for which the memory of the reader everywhere has laid up recognition" ("And They Lived Happily Ever After," *The New York Times Book Review,* November 10, 1963, p. 3). Her own early reading of legends may possibly be the seed of much of her fiction, and does seem to be the case with "A Worn Path."

ROLAND BARTEL

Life and Death in Eudora Welty's "A Worn Path"
(1977)

I have found Saralyn Daly's interpretation of "A Worn Path" to be basically sound (*Studies in Short Fiction,* 1 [Winter 1964], 133–139), but the more I teach the story the more I become convinced that an additional comment is needed to bring out the richness of the central character, Phoenix Jackson.

As most critics have noted, Phoenix Jackson's first name links her to the Egyptian myth of the bird that renews itself periodically from its own ashes.

Equally obvious is the quest motif associated with her annual journey to Natchez. What concerns me about these discussions is that they treat Phoenix Jackson as a stereotype and allow the obvious archtypal significance of her name and her journey to overshadow the uniqueness of one of the most memorable women in short fiction.

Phoenix Jackson is a very old woman who walks from the Old Natchez Trace into Natchez at Christmas time to get medicine for her grandson. Previous critics have noted the many ways in which the renewal myth applies to the frail grandmother and to the grandson for whom she undertakes the hazardous journey each year. I want to add the suggestion that the story operates on the psychological level also, that Phoenix Jackson must make the journey to sustain her own life, that her character becomes unusually poignant if we consider seriously the possibility that her grandson is, in fact, dead. The journey to Natchez then becomes a psychological necessity for Phoenix, her only way of coping with her loss and her isolation. As she says to the white hunter who twice urges her to give up the journey: "I bound to go to town, mister, the time come around" and "I bound to go on my way, mister." Having at first made the journey to save the life of her grandson, she now follows the worn path each Christmas season to save herself. Her survival depends on her going through a ritual that symbolically brings her grandson back to life.

The assumption that the grandson is dead helps to explain Phoenix Jackson's stoical behavior in the doctor's office. She displays a "ceremonial stiffness" as she sits "bolt upright" staring "straight ahead, her face solemn and withdrawn into rigidity." This passiveness suggests her psychological dilemma—she cannot explain why she made the journey. Her attempt to blame her lapse of memory on her illiteracy is unconvincing. Her lack of education is hardly an excuse for forgetting her grandson, but it goes a long way toward explaining her inability to articulate her subconscious motives for her journey.

When the nurse asks whether the grandson is dead, Phoenix suddenly remembers and then overcompensates. In her imagination she brings him back to life, her concluding comment sounding very much like the language of a person trying to revive the image of someone who has died: "I remember so plain now. I not going to forget him again, no, the whole enduring time. I could tell him from all others in creation."

The story ends with Phoenix going down the stairs. Ascending a stairway is associated in folklore and religion with entering a new level of life, with achieving one's destination. Descending a stairway has the opposite implication and has, since *Dante's Inferno,* often been associated with a descent into hell. When Phoenix ascends the stairs she knows she has reached her destination when she sees hanging on the wall the gold seal in the gold frame, "which matched the dream that was hung up in her head." After she gets the medicine from the nurse and the nickel from the attendant, she talks briefly about a paper windmill for her grandson, but then the story ends abruptly with her going down the stairs, a fact that suggests the end of her hope, possibly the end of her life. This interpretation strengthens the thematic unity and symmetry of the story by beginning and ending with references to death. At the beginning of the story Phoenix taps the frozen ground with her cane. At the end of the story, just before she goes down the stairs, she taps the wooden floor with her cane, an action reminiscent of the old man in Chaucer's *Pardoner's Tale*, who taps the earth with his cane seeking death.

Phoenix has to make herself and others believe that her grandson lives so that she can endure her hardships and her subconscious awareness of the imminence of her own death. Literally she seeks the city to give life to her grandson, but symbolically she needs the city to support her own life. Carl Jung has interpreted the city as the feminine principle in general and more specifically as a woman who cares for the inhabitants as if they were her children. When Phoenix enters the city she cannot trust her eyes, so she relies on her feet to take her to destination, another indication of the subconscious element of her journey.

If the journey is as much a necessity for the grandmother as for the grandson, then the episodes along the way take on added significance. After she crosses the creek with her eyes closed, she has a vision of a boy offering her a cake, quite possibly her deceased grandson. Her desperate need for companionship is demonstrated not only by this vision but also by her practice of talking to animals and objects, most of which she imagines rather than sees.

Phoenix Jackson thus emerges from the story as a distinctive person, a feeble old woman whose active imagination rescues her from the harshest aspects of her existence. She is driven to the necessity of inventing such details as make the last portion of her life bearable. If her grandson is dead, then the rebirth implied in her name is doubly pathetic: she unwittingly makes the journey to meet her own needs rather than her grandson's, and what begins as a life-sustaining journey seems to end in a journey of death. If the white hunter was right in saying that she hardly had enough time to return home if she started back immediately, she certainly will not make it back, literally or symbolically, after the passing of the additional time required to get to the city and the doctor's office. During the first part of the journey we get flashes of her sense of humor, but by the end of the story her senility seems to overcome her. The second sentence of the story, "Her name was Phoenix Jackson," seems to suggest by its brevity that all she has left in life is her name and all it implies. At the end of the story the impression prevails that she has risen from the ashes for the last time.

JAMES WALTER

Love's Habit of Vision in Welty's Phoenix Jackson
(1986)

Phoenix Jackson, the protagonist of Eudora Welty's "A Worn Path," is first described as coming along a path through pinewoods far out in the country near the Natchez Trace:

> She was very old and small and she walked slowly in the dark pine shadows, moving a little from side to side in her steps, with the balanced heaviness and lightness of a pendulum in a grandfather clock. She carried a thin, small cane made from an umbrella, and with this she kept tapping the frozen earth in front of her.[1]

As if her name were not signal enough of her association with time,[2] the evocation of the grandfather clock implies not only the venerableness of time as Phoenix lives it, but also its repetitive, inflexible quality. Her progression is strictly proportioned to an objective order of time to which she responds with a curious mechanical tapping that only heightens the impression of time's domineering over her actions. If the "heaviness" of the clock's

---

[1] *The Collected Stories of Eudora Welty* (New York: Harcourt Brace Jovanovich, 1980), p. 142. Future page references appear in the text.

[2] Dan Donlan, "'A Worn Path': Immortality of Structure," *English Journal* 62 (1973), 549–50, finds evidence from the meanings of the Phoenix bird in Egyptian mythology that "Old Phoenix is immortal" although she is "in death"; but he does not consider elements of perspective and structure in the story that give substance to her immortality. According to Marilyn Keys, "Worn Path: The Way of Dispossession," *Studies in Short Fiction* 16 (1979), 354–356, the Phoenix symbol was appropriated by Christian tradition to represent the resurrection of Christ. Her comparison of Phoenix's "worn path" to the Via Dolorosa of Christ's Passion, while broadly illuminating, neglects the essentially epic and comic quality of the old woman's perseverance.

descending pendulum suggests the submission of her personal time to a natural cyclic law, the "lightness" of the pendulum's upward swing almost hints of a redeeming quality of freedom in Phoenix's actions. The full sweep of the pendulum, with its upward motion incorporated periodically into a pattern of temporally dominant gravity—just as Phoenix's journey is incorporated into a landscape of winter and death—symbolically captures the full range of the "habit of love" at the heart of this story's meaning.

Atypically for a short story, the meaning of "A Worn Path" is not something discovered by a character in the story; as Louise Cowan observes, "the discovery of [Phoenix's] inner burning . . . is not . . . based on an epiphany," since the protagonist undertakes the worn path "in full awareness."[3] Already in its first two sentences, however, Welty's story deftly promotes a change in the reader's perspective that becomes, through the action's complete unfolding, a genuine deepening of knowledge. This epiphany in the reader imitates and participates in a revisioning of history like that promoted by New Testament faith: earlier events that had seemed limited to immediate and transitory significance are discovered, in time, to have been prefigurations of a hidden life whose reach and destiny continue through the present and ultimately transcend time.[4]

Despite its simplicity, or perhaps because of it, "A Worn Path" has provoked far-ranging interpretations by a number of critics who agree, at least, that in some way the worn path of Phoenix figures the path of life. According to Sara Trefman, Phoenix is "clearly a symbol of Christ" and her journey reverberates with symbols from Christian tradition.[5] Neil D. Isaacs argues that throughout the story are "allusions to and suggestions of the Christ-myth at large and the meaning of Christmas in particular"; moreover, that "the whole story is suggestive of a religious pilgrimage" by which Phoenix, "with an abiding intuitive faith, arrives at the shrine of her pilgrimage."[6] While emphasizing the resurrection aspect of Phoenix's journey and finding possible Israelite and Christian parallels for it, both these critics overlook the important motif of cyclic revolution which becomes even a structural element when Phoenix turns and begins to retrace her steps.

---

[3] "Imagination and Survival," *Dragonflies* 3 (1974), 11.

[4] See Erich Auerbach, "Figura," trans. Ralph Manheim, in *Scenes from the Drama of European Literature* (New York: Meridian, 1959), pp. 49–60.

[5] "Welty's 'A Worn Path'," *Explicator* 24 (February 1966), item 56.

[6] "Life for Phoenix," *Sewanee Review* 71 (1963), 75–81.

Another commentator who explores the path : life theme is Saralyn Daly, who accepts Ruth Vande Kieft's description of Welty's vision as "pessimistic and existential" and argues that Phoenix ("not a Christian") follows a path that leads to no certain Christian reward or promise.[7] Daly believes, rather, that the old woman proves herself a stoic who "moves through 'chaotic reality'" overcoming many obstacles, including her own naïveté, to mature in a wisdom that expects little from either nature or Christian charity.

My interpretation agrees with Isaacs' that the faith of Phoenix teleological, but I would emphasize that its constancy matures and is expressed through the mediation of her care for what is natural and temporal. And certainly Phoenix's thoughtful reading of nature's signs in a teleological light renders questionable any idea that the reality she moves in is intrinsically chaotic.

The initial description of Phoenix notes a suffusing brilliance, but its meaning remains mysterious. Although her clothing, "a dark striped dress reaching down to her shoetops, and an equally long apron of bleached sugar sacks, with a full pocket" (p. 142), minimizes her personal presence, "a golden color ran underneath" her skin and "the two knobs of her cheeks were illuminated by a yellow burning under the dark." These carefully observed visual details lure the reader into the immediate presence of Phoenix without disclosing the secret of her journey's purpose. In an essay entitled "Is Phoenix Jackson's Grandson Really Dead?" Welty recalled the experience that gave her the story:

> One day I saw a solitary old woman like Phoenix. She was walking; I saw her, at middle distance, in a winter country landscape, and watched her slowly make her way across my line of vision. The sight of her made me write the story.... I brought her up close enough, by imagination, to describe her face, make her present to the eyes, but the full-length figure moving across the winter fields was the indelible one and the image to keep, and the perspective extending into the vanishing distance the true one to hold in mind.[8]

But Welty's fictional description of her heroine does more than bring her before the reader's eyes; by a skillful shift of perspective in the first

---

[7] "'A Worn Path' Retrod," *Studies is Short Fiction* 1 (1964), 133–39. See Vande Kieft's analysis in *Eudora Welty* (New York: Twayne, 1962), esp. p. 102.

[8] *The Eye of the Story: Selected Essays and Reviews* (New York: Vintage, 1979), pp. 159–62.

two sentences, Welty transports the reader, not just from a vantage point of middle distance, but from a "far" distance to the nearness of an observer attending the approach of Phoenix along the path. By this almost imperceptible transposition, Welty quickly frees the reader from a more rationalist and urban interpretive context and inserts him into Phoenix's special world of nature, where she is "*coming* [not 'going,' as an objective reader might have expected] along a path through the pinewoods" (emphasis added). The last sensible detail in the description, her emanation of "an odor like copper" (p. 142), almost compels the reader's participation in the scene. Still, the signs and stages of her progress remain, for the reader, ambiguous, as do her "full pocket" and the "red rag" she wears on her head.

Phoenix's journey is along a path somewhat conventional for legendary questers: it goes through the thicket, up a hill and down, past the thorny bush, across the log over the creek, under the barbed-wire fence, through the "maze" of the cornfield, around the mocking scarecrow, over the whispering grass; when she finally reaches "easy going" on a familiar track, she still has to contend with the canine beast and the destructive hunter before she arrives at her goal—"Natchez shining," where Christmas bells ring and "dozens of little black children" whirl about her. Phoenix's responses to each obstacle along her path are not conventional, however; they reveal the imagination of a very unique and patient soul, capable of being fooled and even of fooling herself, but still resourceful enough to learn from her troubles and not just in spite of them.

As signs of her patience and her faith multiply, her comments to herself along the way express a preoccupation with time as a component of her journey. "Sun so high! . . . The time getting all gone here," she says in an early stage. As she bends down to drink from a hidden spring, she says, "Nobody knows who made this well, for it was here when I was born." She tells the hunter, "The time come around." And having achieved her object, she remarks, "We is the only two left in the world . . . He [Phoenix's ill grandson for whom she has travelled to town to get medicine] going to last. . . . I not going to forget him again, no, the whole enduring time. I could tell him from all the others in creation" (p 148).

Parochial though her thought may seem, Phoenix moves the reader to question his own view of history and to expand his vision to the vast sweep, from the beginning to the end, that Phoenix includes in hers. The "well" she drinks from, coeval with her very life (which, she implies, has coexisted with all creation), figures a spiritual resource within Phoenix that is something like Augustinian memory, a faculty enabling the human to know innately more than the intellect can originate or tell.[9] If Phoenix imagines herself as old as the creation and intends to remember her grandson until the resurrection (she implies this by her conviction that she will find him among "all the others" at the end of "enduring time"), then she must intuit her mortal journey as an epitome of time itself. Her essential mode of being was focussed symbolically in the "true" image of her that appeared to the writer's creative imagination: the full-length figure moving across the winter fields in a "perspective extending into the vanishing distance." This image suggests Phoenix's imitation of Christ, whose participation in a hidden totality unfolding in history is summarized in words John attributes to him: "I am Alpha and Omega" (Revelation 1:8; 22:13). At each stage of Phoenix's pilgrimage, her personal experience resonates for her with implications extending to and beyond time's borders. This mode Welty calls "the habit of love," which "cuts through confusion and stumbles or contrives its way out of difficulty, it remembers the way even when it forgets, for a dumbfounded moment, its reason for being."[10]

Seeing the evidence of this visionary power as Phoenix overcomes her hardships, the reader is gradually persuaded that her perspective is not limited, at least not so severely as that of her secular foil on her path, the white hunter. In juxtaposition, Phoenix and the hunter personify two primordially opposed positions concerning the human's relation to nature and time:

"On your way home?"
"No sir, I going to town."
"Why, that's too far! That's as far as I walk when I come out myself, and I get something for my trouble." He patted the stuffed bag he carried, and there hung down a little closed claw. It was one of the bob-whites, with its beak hooked bitterly to show it was dead. "Now you go on home, Granny!"
"I bound to go to town, mister," said Phoenix. "The time come around" (p. 145).

The hunter represents a pragmatism that proudly preys on nature for security against the revolutions of fortune and time; Phoenix, in contrast, embodies love's patience, accepting the conditions time and nature impose, yet transforming them at each turn by a spiritual vision which sees them as

---

[9] See Robert L. Montgomery, *The Reader's Eye: Studies in Didactic Literary Theory from Dante to Tasso* (Berkeley: Univ. of California Press, 1979), pp. 31–34. According to Augustine, the Divine is a presence in human memory before any conscious reflection on it.

[10] *The Eye of the Story*, p. 161.

mediators of a Divine providence—"watching me the whole time" (p. 146), she says. Even the dead, she imagines as vital and present when, in passing old boarded-up cabins, she remarks with a vigorous nod, "I walking in their sleep" (p. 144).

Both the first and the last names of the heroine are significant in "A Worn Path." While "Phoenix" figures her continuous personal renewal, "Jackson" echoes the history of the specific place in which her actions are rooted (Jackson, Mississippi, near the Natchez Trace, named after Andrew Jackson.) Welty comments elsewhere on the important role of place in self-understanding:

> One place comprehended can make us understand other places better. Sense of place gives equilibrium; extended, it is a sense of direction too. Carried off we might be in spirit, and should be, when we are reading or writing something good; but it is the sense of place going with us still that is the ball of golden thread to carry us there and back and in every sense of the word to bring us home.[11]

Phoenix Jackson's sense of her place, signalled in so many ways, is particularly emphasized by multiple references in the story to her feet, which seem to lead her along the earth almost instinctively to her destination; when she reaches the doctor's office, for example, "her feet knew to stop" (p. 147).

The key to Phoenix's sureness and largeness of vision, paradoxically, is her complete responsibility to and for temporality, her accepting and living profane time proportionate to its cyclic demands on her. She lives it, not in a romantic cult of immediacy, but carefully—in the same way she taps the frozen earth with her cane: probing, listening, seeing, listening. Although her meditative habit can cause her to appear foolish, as when a black dog rolls her in her state of abstraction into a ditch, it is also evidence of her contemplative capacity that sustains her dignity. Her eyesight may be bad, but her memory holds an image of her origin, her path and her goal.

The red rag she wears on her head, then, is, in one perspective, her tiara, signifying her sovereignty over the creatures in her domain. Like a queen, she issues commands and expects obeisance: "Please, missy, will you lace up my shoe?" she says to a city lady whose arms are filled with Christmas packages. In her relations with others, Phoenix's words and instructions are paradigmatic; she is a surprising lovely lady, imposing heroic tasks, redistributing

---

[11] "Place in Fiction," in *The Eye of the Story*, pp. 128–29.

wealth, and creating manners. Her creativity is a result of her purposeful love and her ability, after long experience, to read people and know what she can expect from them. Although she cannot read letters, she is adept at reading signs in the books of nature and history.

When Phoenix arrives at the doctor's office to obtain the medicine, she reports with a "fixed and ceremonial stiffness," "Here I be." Nearing her journey's end, however, like a quester knight she faces a last crucial test. She must answer a question put to her, but to her consternation it is not the question she expected. The attendant asks her, "What's your name? We must have your history, you know. Have you been here before? What seems to be the trouble with you?" (p. 147) All observers of Phoenix, as perhaps the reader during the early stages of her journey, assume a self-serving motive for her actions. The questions of the woman behind the desk, reiterating categorical "you's," catch Phoenix off-guard since she is not in the habit of self-concern. For a moment, as she is encouraged to consider her own troubles instead of those of her grandson, she loses her sense of mission and withdraws into rigid self-preoccupation.

Fortunately, however, a more experienced nurse asks the question, perhaps the only question, that can stir Phoenix from her paralysis: "He isn't dead, is he?" It is her quick emotion responding to the threat in this question that brings forth the meaning hidden previously in her pendulum-like walk and in the "yellow burning" beneath her dark skin. As "a flame of comprehension" flickers across her face, the burning reveals itself to be the old woman's love, now insisting on her grandson's life for all time. "He going to last," she assures all who have ears to hear her voluble recollection of her task. Her unique heroism, this scene makes clear, is in her ability to remember, against odds, the purpose which keeps her true to her path. That it is a path worn by repetition is insignificant in light of the beginning and the end Phoenix remembers for it.

The plot of "A Worn Path," analysis has shown, is not constructed according to the conventional short story model in which an ascending action builds tension, rising climactically to a *peripeteia* or reversal, followed by a denouement or untying. From the start of Welty's story there is little mystery about Phoenix's eventual success on her journey; a visible constancy in the woman convinces that she will succeed. For the reader, it is her goal that is the mystery until near the story's end—a mystery which probes and examines the reader's own ability to discern, while accompanying Phoenix, the habit of love that impels her mission.

To test the reader, Welty has planted several obstacles to recognition, such as the stereotypical features of Phoenix, common prejudices represented in the hunter and the medical attendant, and Phoenix's amnesia almost making her appear, at times, a confused and foolish old woman. As it turns out, however, while Phoenix remains steadfast in her purpose, the reader of Welty's story is made to experience, at a certain moment of the action, a revaluation of interpretive assumptions and mental habits that may have contributed to misreading. Phoenix's constancy in her role, her indefatigable charity of purpose, inspires in the reader a change of attitude, away from presumption and toward receptivity to new meanings. This kind of reading effect is clearly described by Wolfgang Iser:

> The efficacy of a literary text is brought about by the apparent evocation and subsequent negation of the familiar. What at first seemed to be an affirmation of our assumptions leads to our own rejection of them, thus tending to prepare us for a re-orientation. And it is only when we have outstripped our preconceptions and left the shelter of the familiar that we are in a position to gather new experiences. As the literary text involves the reader in the formation of illusion and the simultaneous formation of the means whereby the illusion is punctured, reading reflects the process by which we gain experience.[12]

Iser's phenomenology of reading describes an experience like the action of interpreting Biblical typology (and perhaps reveals the extent to which interpretive procedures borrowed from Biblical exegesis remain a key element in the reading of Western literature): past events first understood under the aspect of law are revisioned, in the illumination of grace, as prefigurations of present events themselves prefiguring a more perfect fulfillment yet to be enjoyed. That Phoenix displays and inspires a faith that reads created signs as prophecy of a divine intention in the world coheres, I believe, with the essentially Christian vision expressed throughout Welty's fiction.

The story of Phoenix does not end, however, at her journey's end, since there is a special reward for her constancy and her readiness to make good use of time. The nickel she wins from the medical attendant is only the profane token of her reward; its sacred element, reminding us of the profounder meaning of the Christmas event whose celebration nears, comes as a gift to her spirit:

> Then she gave a tap with her cane on the floor.
> "This is what come to me to do," she said. "I going to the store and buy my child a little windmill they sells, made out of paper. He going to find it hard

---

[12] "The Reading Process: A Phenomenological Approach," in *New Directions in Literary History,* ed. Ralph Cohen (Baltimore: Johns Hopkins, 1974), p. 141.

to believe there such a thing in the world. I'll march myself back where he waiting, holding it straight up in this hand." (p. 149)

The gift Phoenix imagines in her responsiveness to a providential prompting in time will be perfect for the child, who is confined to bed with a throat injury that vexes his breathing. If the "little windmill" will not provide literal breeze to help the child's respiration, the windmill's bright revolutions will provide the child a small share in the big turning world and a child's satisfaction in its life.[13] It will be a reflection of that good proportionality between need and provision so clear in the life Phoenix makes for herself.

The windmill, of course, repeats the motif of temporal revolution that structures this story. The journey of Phoenix, which seems to be coextensive with a larger arc of time from creation to resurrection, suggests the circularity of nature, as did the earlier comparison of her to a grandfather clock. Phoenix persists in her temporal journey because she has faith that natural processes disclose a spiritual truth. Strangely, in accepting the limitations of her physical place and time she gains in her imagination a world whose ultimate coordinates are love and eternity. Small as her world may appear, she finds it sufficiently large for her complete enactment of human responsibility.

DAVID ROBINSON

A Nickel and Dime Matter: Teaching Eudora Welty's "A Worn Path"
(1987)

Since I believe writing and reading are allied skills, I like to give essay assignments that involve careful reading. One of my most successful assignments concerns the nickel episode of Eudora Welty's story "A Worn Path," which is included in many literature textbooks. The passage is an excellent test of a student's ability to see how facts can be fitted into different interpretive

---

[13] My interpretation of the windmill, as a figure of the world's revolutions being redeemed by farsighted love, differs from Daly's, that the windmill, evoking Quixote's "undefeated madness," crystallizes a sort of "irrationality" against which Phoenix pits herself to "create" an existential meaning. Such a reading seems to wrench this gift for the child entirely out of its imagistic and dramatic context.

patterns, though some of the patterns accommodate more of the facts than others do.

The central character, Phoenix Jackson, is an old black woman on her way to Natchez at Christmas time. We know that she is poor, feeble, and nearsighted; nonetheless she is willing to face a number of obstacles—animals, a barbed-wire fence, a narrow log traversing a stream—for her mission, which is not revealed until the end of the story. The title, as well as clues throughout, suggests that her action has taken place many times before, and we finally learn that Phoenix regularly takes the "worn path" to bring back medicine for her grandson, who has swallowed lye and is evidently bedridden. The nurse who gives her the medicine asks about the child; Phoenix assures her that he is still alive, and receiving a nickel in addition to the medicine, she leaves for her home.

The passage central to my assignment appears about two-thirds of the way through the story. Momentarily distracted by a large and frightening black dog, Phoenix falls into a ditch and is unable to get up. Luckily a white hunter comes by shortly thereafter, and lifts her out. He asks where she lives; when she tells him, and mentions her destination, he replies that it is too far for her to go. She is adamant about her mission, saying, "I bound to go to town, mister. . . . The time come round"; he laughs and says, "I know you old colored people! Wouldn't miss going to town to see Santa Claus!"[1] She sees a nickel fall from the hunter's pocket, and calls his attention to the black dog that has troubled her. While the hunter is chasing the dog away, she carefully picks up the nickel and puts it in her apron pocket. The hunter returns and points his gun at her, asking if she is scared by it. She answers, "No, sir, I seen plenty go off closer by, in my day, and for less than what I done." He smiles, shoulders the gun, and remarks, "[Y]ou must be a hundred years old, and scared of nothing. I'd give you a dime if I had any money with me. But you take my advice and stay home, and nothing will happen to you." Phoenix tells him that she intends to continue her journey, and they part.

This scene is the climax of the story. Whereas up to this point Phoenix has faced physical, external obstacles, her situation here involves moral choice, as she well knows ("God watching me the whole time. I come to stealing"). The sympathy we have felt for her so far is now qualified by our sense of her wrongdoing, though we discover at the end of the story that she

---

[1] Eudora Welty, "A Worn Path," in *Collected Stories* (New York: Harcourt Brace Jovanovich, 1980), pp. 145–6. All subsequent quotations are from these pages.

intends to use this money, as well as the nickel she takes from the nurse, to buy her grandson a paper windmill as a present. One critic has accused the story of sentimentality,[2] and certainly Welty's decision to write about a poor old black woman in the South risks bathos. But this scene refutes such a judgment. In a truly sentimental tale, Phoenix would be a figure of pure goodness who would either refuse the temptation or, having taken the coin, experience remorse; she might tell the hunter that he had dropped the nickel.

The theft itself is the important issue in the scene; a number of critics have discussed its place in the story's theme of charity.[3] However, the issue my students write about is this: does the hunter know Phoenix has stolen the nickel, and if so, how *much* does he know?

When I first read the story, I was sure that he knew nothing about the theft; subsequent readings, and a number of papers by my students, have made me less sure. According to one interpretation, the entire episode is a charade performed by the hunter. One student commented, "The white man sees an opportunity for Phoenix to pick up his coin, so he gets his dog and chases after the black dog. The hunter gave Phoenix enough time to see if she was going to pick the money up and keep it for herself or return it to him."[4] Some students argue that he does not wish to insult her by offering the money outright. Certainly Welty's description of the dropping nickel is neutral enough to permit such a reading. The hunter's action would of course fit into the charity theme, and would suggest the intricacy of relations between the races. Attractive as this view is, though, objections are easy to find. For one thing, it seems odd to assume that his motive is to preserve her dignity, if she is going to feel as though she is stealing the money. Second,

---

[2] Robert Towers, "Mississippi Myths," *New York Review of Books*, 24 December 1980, pp. 30–2. In this review of Welty's Collected Stories, Towers writes, "Only one story [of the early stories], the much-admired 'A Worn Path,' strikes me as sentimental in its effort to coerce one's sympathies in behalf of the ancient, half-senile Negro woman who heroically trudges over hill and dale, past briar and stream, to get 'soothing' medicine for her little grandson from a Natchez dispensary."

[3] Alfred Appel, Jr., has argued in *A Season of Dreams: The Fiction of Eudora Welty* (Baton Rouge: Louisiana State University Press, 1965), that Phoenix's gift for the child is the antithesis of the "false" Christmas spirit in Natchez, but his claim for the falsity of the white townspeople depends upon scanty evidence. For a reply to Appel see Elmo Howell, "Eudora Welty's Negroes: A Note on 'A Worn Path,'" *Xavier University Studies*, 9 (Spring, 1970), 28–32.

[4] I am indebted to my students in English 101 and English 424 at Georgia College for permission to quote this and the other passages from their work.

the passage about the gun becomes inexplicable. Why would he point the gun at her if he wishes to conceal his knowledge? A reading that more students offer is that he is unaware at first that he has dropped the money, but sees her pick it up. Welty says nothing about what he sees while he is chasing the black dog. In this case the gun passage becomes quite clear: he points the gun at her to see if she will confess, but she does not flinch. A student wrote, "He should have known when Phoenix said, 'No, sir, I seen plenty go off closer by, in my day, *and for less than what I done.*'" Another student concluded, "He lets her keep the nickel because he admires her age and fearlessness." This interpretation is better than the previous one, since it accounts for more of the facts, while still focusing on the charity theme. (The hunter's compassion vies with his annoyance at her theft, and the former wins out.) The one difficulty with this reading is his next-to-last sentence: "I'd give you a dime if I had any money with me." This is the only explicit reference to money in the entire dialogue. Such a statement is incongruous if he knows she already has the nickel. To make the statement fit this reading, one must assume either that he means "if I had *more* money" or that he is being ironic. The former is an unlikely meaning for such an apparently direct remark; the latter is an assumption about his character which needs examining.

The sentence is less troublesome if one assumes that it means exactly what it appears to: that he doesn't know that he had any money with him. Some students doubt his good nature: "I think that if the hunter had known he would not have been as kind to her," one commented. Certainly it is a common experience for one to forget a small coin in a pocket, or for such a coin to fall through a hole. If this is what has happened, a different reading becomes possible, or even necessary, because we need a new explanation for the gun passage. Why would the hunter point the gun at her if he does not suspect her of the theft?

An answer to this must begin with consideration of an earlier exchange. After he has lifted Phoenix out of the ditch and asked her destination, the hunter says, "I know you old colored people! Wouldn't miss going to town to see Santa Claus!" We do not know at this point that Phoenix's object is to get medicine for her grandson, but the hunter's remark is nonetheless condescending—tactless even if he's only teasing. This is another reason to think he is incapable of the benevolent charade the first interpretation assumes. He means well, as his helping her out of the ditch indicates, but he is not very sensitive to her feelings. In this light we can reconsider the gun episode. A student offered this interpretation: "When the hunter had the gun pointed at the old woman, it was another of his careless pranks. He wasn't trying to scare her; he was teasing with her just as he had teased with her from the beginning of the encounter. If he had been serious about pointing the gun at the woman as a threat, he wouldn't have so soon given up the prank." If this is the case, he has been completely taken in by her misdirection of his attention, and his remark about her purpose in going to Natchez, based upon a stereotype of black people as simple and childlike, has redounded upon him: he is the one who isn't very bright. (Phoenix may even be teasing him when she says, "for less than what I done," knowing he won't understand.) The comment about the dime is further irony on Welty's part, since the hunter is unaware that he has given Phoenix some money already. The whole incident may then show Phoenix as using the man's prejudice to her advantage—exacting a fine, so to speak—and it allows us to assent to the theft. Like the other two interpretations, this assumes Welty is commenting subtly on race relations, but the position of superiority is now Phoenix's rather than the hunter's. The drawback to this reading, however, is that it may put more emphasis on the hunter's words than they will bear.

Other critics have interpreted this scene as evidence of Phoenix's refusal to be patronized, or of the hunter's prejudice,[5] but they have not sufficiently analyzed Welty's ingenuity in the whole scene. The entire complicated situation is presented in a few lines of dialogue and some descriptive passages. The scene is thus useful for showing students how a great short-story writer can create a very rich episode with a minimum of words.

NANCY K. BUTTERWORTH

From Civil War to Civil Rights
Race Relations in Welty's "A Worn Path"
(1989)

Since such seminal studies as Robert Penn Warren's "The Love and Separateness in Miss Welty" and Harry Morris's "Eudora Welty's Use of Mythology," it has become traditional to interpret Welty's characters in terms of mythological and cultural archetypes. Welty's black characters frequently

---

[5] See Appel, and Grant Moss, Jr., "'A Worn Path' Retrod," *College Language Association Journal*, 15 (December, 1971), 144–52. Moss says that the episode has been included to show her resolution rather than the hunter's prejudice, though the prejudice is also apparent. Moss also rejects the idea that Phoenix is a sentimental character.

have evoked such parallels. In addition to the obvious reference to the Egyptian resurrection myth implied by her name,[1] Phoenix Jackson in "A Worn Path" has been compared to the pagan fertility figures Kore, Demeter, and Persephone, Osiris, Attis, and Adonis, as well as Theseus and Aeneas (Ardolino 1–6); knight questers such as the Red Cross Knight and Don Quixote; Bunyan's Christian, a Magi, and Christ.[2] Little Lee Roy in "Keela, The Outcast Indian Maiden" has been likened to the archetypal scapegoat Le Roi Mehaigné, the maimed Fisher King (May), the albatross in *The Rime of the Ancient Mariner* (Warren), and American Negro folk tricksters such as Brer Rabbit (Appel, *Season* 146). Powerhouse, more simplistically, has been described as "a virtual Negro Paul Bunyan" (Appel, "Powerhouse's" 222).

Although such "superimpositions" of external ideas, as Morris terms them (40), always risk distorting the text, a majority of these mythological and symbolic readings are valid because they add resonances that enrich our understanding of the characters' roles. Welty's own comments on her use of name symbolism and the influence of remembered fairy tales and myths further support such interpretations.[3] Commentaries on her black characters, however, sometimes obfuscate more than they reveal. (One obvious reason is our sensitivity to the race issue, which has made it tempting to oversimplify the narrative events to fit our own conceptions of history and how the races ought to have behaved.)

Recent revisionist criticism, in particular, frequently falsifies Welty's portrayals of black-white relations in earlier eras. For example, John Hardy's "Eudora Welty's Negroes," in *The Image of the Negro in American Literature*,

---

[1] The earliest critical reference to the mythological phoenix is William Jones. Two interesting studies parallel Phoenix's physical description with other birds. See Donlan, who also interprets Phoenix's encounters with the small boy and the hunter as manifestations of the sun god Ra; and Nostrandt, who traces Phoenix as an inversion of an old Norse folktale in which a selfish woman is transformed into a woodpecker.

[2] Almost all of these interpretations are implicit in Isaac's seminal (though too loosely argued) study of the story. Welker and Gower (203–06) make suggestive parallels to religious questers. The most detailed study of the Christian imagery, including specific analogues to the Passion Week, is Keys (354–56). Daly offers an existentialist interpretation which views Phoenix as less like Christ and Bunyan's Christian than Don Quixote. See also Trefman.

[3] Welty, "And They Lived Happily Ever After" 3; *OWB*, esp. 8, 99. See also her *Conversations* interviews with Van Gelder, Buckley, Freeman, Gretlund, Maclay, Haller, and Jones (4, 107–08, 174, 224–25, 275, 313, and 324, respectively).

is, paradoxically, both sentimental and satirical. Although his attitude is somewhat inconsistent,[4] Hardy views Phoenix as "a saint":

> One of those who walks always in the eye of God, on whom He has set His sign, whether ordinary men are prepared to see it or not. For we realize finally that she has done nothing for herself, for her own advantage, either psychological or material. Just because sanctity is never self-regarding, she must see herself as a sinner. But in the ultimate perspective she is, by virtue of her sanctity, exempt from the usual requirements of economic and social morality. (229)

Conversely, he argues that those who fail to see her as such are the whites, and particularly the white women. He concludes that "There is nowhere in modern literature a more scathing indictment of the fool's pride of the white man in the superiority of his civilization, of his fool's confidence in the virtue of the 'soothing medicine' he offers to heal the hurts of that 'stubborn case,' black mankind" (229). John R. Cooley, in "Blacks as Primitives in Eudora Welty's Fiction," accuses Welty of failing to "develop her racial portraits with sufficient sensitivity or depth" (27) and criticizes her for creating a primitive idyll in "A Worn Path," making it "difficult to cut through the reverence and romance which cloud the story, in order to see the babe as a pathetic image of life caught in the stranglehold of white civilization." He cynically questions whether Welty intended the story as a myth of the phoenix perishing in its own ashes (24–25).

Such polemical demythologizings conflict with Welty's persistent refusal to use fiction as a platform, particularly for political or sociological issues, as well as her downplaying and even disavowal of racial implications in her stories.[5] Even in "Keela, The Outcast Indian Maiden," "Where Is the

---

[4] Hardy's treatment of blacks is difficult to understand because it is internally contradictory. Clearly he intends his treatment of Phoenix to be sympathetic (see also his comments on Welty's characters in the introduction and conclusion [221, 232]). Yet he confusingly refers to Phoenix's "outrageous request" that the white woman tie her shoes as an example of "the ways in which southern Negroes have learned to take subtle revenge on the 'superior race,' to exploit, for their own material or psychological advantage, the weaknesses of white pride" (228–29).

[5] Welty's "Must the Writer Crusade?" (*Eye* 146–58) is her most thorough discussion of what she considers the author's appropriate role in regard to morality and reforming society. For specific comments on race, see her *Conversations* interviews with Clemons, Bunting, Kuehl, Buckley, Walker, Ferris, Freeman, Gretlund, Royals and Little, Brans, and Jones (31, 48, 83–84, 99–103, 136–37, 166, 182–84, 225, 259, 299–300, and 337, respectively), as well as the preface to *The Collected Stories of Eudora Welty* (x–xi). In the Brans interview, she

Voice Coming From?" and "The Demonstrators," which treat racial interactions directly, she eschews authorial statement or facile solutions or dichotomies. Thus, although we condemn his act, we are brought to understand the mundane motives for a lower-class white's murder of a black civil rights worker in "Where Is the Voice Coming From?"; the guilt-ridden Steve and cynical civil rights worker in "Keela" and "The Demonstrators," respectively, are portrayed as ethically equivocal; and even such white characters as Max and Dr. Strickland, who attempt to mediate between the races and ameliorate oppression and illness, remain largely ineffectual. The blacks, too, range from virtuous victims to perpetrators of wanton violence, but most of them are merely traditional family members coping with tragedy as best they can. One of Welty's greatest achievements as a writer is that she refuses to rewrite history but rather presents individualized conflicts and tensions, in all of their disturbing ambiguity.

Although there have been some balanced commentaries on the race relations in "A Worn Path"—in particular, Elmo Howell's "Eudora Welty's Negroes: A Note on 'A Worn Path'"[6]—one aspect of the story that has not been adequately explored is the portrayal of Phoenix Jackson as an almost allegorical representation of black people's traits and behaviors from slave times to the story's present. Alfred Appel, Jr., has suggested such a reading when he describes the story as "an effort at telescoping the history of the Negro woman" (*Season* 166), but he doesn't develop it.

The most compelling reason for seeing Phoenix as an avatar of her race is her almost mythic age. When Phoenix asks the nurse to forgive her momentary senility, she explains, "I never did go to school, I was too old at the Surrender" (*CS* 148). If we assume that Phoenix was eighteen or more at Emancipation and posit the present action of the story to be around 1940,

---

remarks that making Phoenix black was not a deliberate decision, such as "I am now going to write about the black race. I write about all people." She continues somewhat facetiously, "I think all my characters are about half and half black aud white." Later in the same interview, however, she admits that only a black person "would be in such desperate need aud live so remotely away from help and . . . have so far to go" (*Conversations* 300). She also notes that Phoenix is a common black name (*Conversations* 51); see also Freeman's interview (*Conversations* 188). Davis (5) interestingly notes the irony in the practice of slaveholders who named slaves and other chattel for classical personages. Within a larger cultural context, he sees this practice in Welty's fiction as "both a constant reminder of the past and a testament to the capacity to turn derision into dignity."

[6] See also Vande Kieft, *Eudora Welty* (rev. ed., 140); and Moss (147–49) which asks some very difficult questions about the race issues in the story, especially regarding those readers who have been searching to find illiberal racial attitudes.

when it was written, she would be approximately 100 years old. Further corroboration for her age is afforded by her boast when dancing with the scarecrow, "I the oldest people I ever know"; the hunter also marvels that she "must be a hundred years old" (*CS* 144, 146). This extreme age serves a symbolic function of allowing her personally to have spanned the entire history of the black people from antebellum days to those just prior to the civil rights movement.

Such an interpretation requires considerable caution so as not to reduce the story to mere allegory. It is essential to emphasize—as Stella Brookes does concerning Joe Chandler Harris's Uncle Remus (47–48)—that Phoenix is not a stereotypical or stock black character but a real human portrait with a distinctive personality. In interviews and essays Welty has explained the key image that suggested the story to her imagination:

> One day I saw a solitary old woman like Phoenix. She was walking; I saw her in the middle distance, in a winter country landscape, and watched her slowly make her way across my line of vision. That sight of her made me write the story. I invented an errand for her, but that only seemed a living part of the figure she was herself: what errand other than for someone else could be making her go? (*Eye* 161)

She conflated this experience with another on the Old Canton Road when an elderly black woman stopped to talk with her; the woman's remark, "I was too old at the Surrender," Welty tells us, "was indelible in my mind" (*Conversations* 168). The nexus of Phoenix's character for Welty seems to have been her sense of urgency, her "desperate need" to reach her goal. She notes that Phoenix's "going was the first thing, her persisting in the landscape was the real thing.... The real dramatic force of a story depends on the strength of the emotion that has set it going.... What gives any such content to 'A Worn Path' is not its circumstances but its *subject:* the deep-grained habit of love" (161).

Phoenix particularizes these attributes of persistence and enduring love through her own distinct set of decorums and devotions, such as wearing tied shoes into town and her somewhat dubious adherence to the eighth commandment (although in her own estimation she "stoops" when she retrieves a dropped coin, she does not in conning a few more pennies and accepting the "charity" medicine for her grandson). Phoenix's personality also comprises a complicated mixture of shrewdness—"Five pennies is a nickel" (*CS* 149)—and childlike unself-consciousness—shown when she talks aloud to herself and warns all of the "foxes, owls, beetles, jack rabbits, coons, and wild animals" to keep out of her way (*CS* 141). Her composite of character traits is somewhat like conflating Ida M'Toy with the bird women in "A Pageant of Birds." This complexity, along with her distinctive voice and humor ("'Old woman,' she said to herself, 'that black dog come up out of the weeds to stall you off, and now there he sitting on his fine tail, smiling at you'" [*CS* 145]), keep Phoenix from falling into mere quaintness or caricature.[7]

Phoenix's individuality, though, does not preclude another, simultaneous, view of her as a symbolic representative of her race. Such an interpretation helps to elucidate otherwise confusing statements or situations in the surface narrative. For example, one of the more cryptic passages in Welty's fiction occurs when Phoenix walks "past cabins silver with weather, with the doors and windows boarded shut, all like old women under a spell sitting there," and she says, "'I walking in their sleep,' . . . nodding her head vigorously" (*CS* 144). Her strong identification with these "women" (the white woman in town who ties her shoes is termed a "lady" [*CS* 147]) suggests that they are the matriarchs of her race whose dreams she views herself as proudly carrying on. Indeed, in her own almost trancelike state, she seems to gain strength from their vicarious vision of her persisting in the landscape while they doze.

The content of Phoenix's dream becomes clearer at the conclusion of the story when she sees the gold-framed document (presumably a diploma) nailed up on the clinic wall, and the narrator asserts that it "matched the dream that hung up in her head" (*CS* 147). On the surface level, the document verifies that she has reached her specific dream or goal of obtaining the medicine ("'Here I be,' she said" [*CS* 147]), though she ironically has a memory lapse about her mission immediately afterward. On a deeper level, the diploma also seems to represent her respect for education, which is reiterated later in the scene. Wonderful pathos is evoked by the formally unschooled Phoenix wishing education for herself, her grandson, and, by implication, her people. This dream also may inform part of her faith that her grandson, though frail in body, will prevail and prosper.

Viewing Phoenix as an emblem of her people also helps to explain the title, "A Worn Path," which seems to imply that others have trod and retrod the same arduous path before her. Echoes of slave times can be heard in her chant as she heads up the hill, "Seem like there is chains about my feet, time I get this far" (*CS* 143), as well as in the images of confinement and

---

[7] See Bartel; Feld 64–65; and Robinson 24. For dissenting views, see Cooley (23) and Hardy (226).

persecution, such as the barbed-wire fence, one-armed black men, and the threatening black dog. These symbolic references could refer specifically to the difficulties encountered by the blacks, as well as more generally to any enslaved or downtrodden people from the times of the early Egyptians and Greeks (from whom her name derives) on through the twentieth century.

Finally, this reading explains a number of Phoenix's encounters with whites, both real and imaginary. On the surface level, the story consists of a simple journey composed of about twelve obstacles—external or internal—which Phoenix must overcome to obtain her goal (*Season* 167). These encounters take on deeper meaning when seen as symbolic trials or tests of her faith. Robert Welker suggests this interpretation when he refers to the "visions" which sometimes tempted wayfaring knights so as to divert them from their final purpose (203–04). Likewise, Phoenix is tempted at numerous points to forestall her journey, as exemplified by the scene in which she marches across the hollow log, "like a festival figure in some parade," and then hallucinates a little boy bringing her a slice of marble cake which she finds "acceptable" (*CS* 143).

If taken literally, this vision makes little sense; however, it makes a great deal of sense if we see it as a symbolic role reversal in which Phoenix is tempted to accept the dream—the marble cake—rather than the reality of economic equality. This scene bears much resemblance to the parallel one in town when Phoenix requests the nice-smelling white lady to tie her shoes for her, which Hardy so incorrectly interprets as an "outrageous request," one of "the ways in which southern Negroes have learned to take subtle revenge on the 'superior' race, to exploit, for their own material or psychological advantage, the weakness of white pride" (228–29). On the simplest level, both scenes involve wish-fulfillment fantasies—one imaginary and the other realized—in which Phoenix probably does gain psychological pleasure from being waited upon by those whom she previously served. However, in neither does she seem vindictive toward the whites; she merely accepts with dignity what she considers her "due" (Howell 30–31; Robinson 26; and Dazey 92–93). Further, both situations carry a covert danger; for if Phoenix were to remain eating imaginary marble cake or allowing others to care for her, she would not complete her necessary journey.

Phoenix's vulnerability is also made explicit in the scene just prior to the hunter's entrance. Evoking her earlier hallucinations or misperceptions of reality, the setting is imbued with a fairy tale aura: a road which cuts "deep, deep ... down between high green-colored banks" of the swamp, with live oaks meeting overhead, making it "as dark as a cave." The sleeping alligators and Cerberus-like black dog which suddenly rears up out of the weeds suggest covert dangers and unprovoked violence which catch her unawares: "She was meditating, and not ready, and when he came at her she only hit him a little with her cane. Over she went in the ditch, like a little puff of milkweed" (*CS* 145). Her inability to help herself is shown by her drifting into a dream of rescue.

Perhaps the most troubling incident in the whole story concerns her encounter with the young white hunter. At first he appears to be sympathetic as he helps her out of the ditch. Yet almost immediately the situation takes on uncomfortable undertones in the reversal of usual youth-age decorums when the hunter cheerily condescends to her as "Granny" and swings her through the air like a child. His apparent charity of dropping the nickel is also belied by his later assertion that he would give her a dime, if he had "*any money*" with him (*CS* 146, emphasis added).[8] Finally, the tone darkens with the implications of his hunting bobwhites—both Phoenix and the grandson are linked with frail birds[9]—and his seemingly sadistic act of turning his gun on her.

It is difficult not to condemn the hunter's behavior (Welty herself refers to him as a "really nasty white man" [*Conversations* 335]).[10] One way of gaining more perspective on his behavior is to interpret this scene broadly as an allegory of the racial stances of the early twentieth century. All of the hunter's actions can be explained in terms of accepted social behavior of the rural South in the 1930s and 1940s, which would have allowed a young white man—a simple "red neck" hunter—some degree of domineering byplay with the curious old black woman. Welty does not distort the man's

---

[8] This scene is analyzed in great detail by Robinson (25–26).

[9] Ardolino (8) relates the dove symbolism with Song of Solomon 2:10–13; Welker and Gower (204–05) also notes New Testament birds to which Welty may have been alluding. Throughout Welty's fiction birds seem to be signs of beneficence. See, for example, the scene in "Keela, The Outcast Indian Maiden" in which at the moment when Little Lee Roy recognizes Steve, "a sparrow alighted on his child's shoe" (*CS* 43), and the conclusion of "The Demonstrators" in which Dr. Strickland watches the hen and the cock and peacefully recalls how his estranged wife's "eyes would follow the birds when they flew across the garden" (*CS* 621), as well as "A Pageant of Birds."

[10] Casty (6) captures the dualism of the hunter well, seeing him as exemplifying "the imperfect mixture that is mankind." See also Moss 149–50 and Robinson 24–27. Cooley lamentably claims that the "white reader may identify himself with the hunter" (24). Recent studies of race relations in Welty's fiction, particularly Vande Kieft on "The Demonstrators" and "Where Is the Voice Coming From?" and Coulthard's study of "Keela, The Outcast Indian Maiden," represent perceptive and balanced treatments of the complex and tragic issue of racism.

realistic responses to Phoenix, much as, two decades later, she similarly refuses to pretty up the depiction of the equivalent lower-class white city dweller who murders a black civil rights worker (Medgar Evers) in "Where Is the Voice Coming From?"

More specifically, each of the characters' actions in this scene symbolically represents a particular stage in the pre–civil rights era treatment of blacks. For example, for an indeterminate time before the hunter's arrival, Phoenix waits patiently, merely dreaming of salvation. At one point she reaches up her hand expectantly, "but nothing reached down and gave her a pull" (*CS* 145). After the zeal of Reconstruction, which Phoenix missed out on because she was too old to be educated, a period of indifference to blacks' welfare persisted well into the early decades of the twentieth century. When the hunter finally arrives, Phoenix uses her vulnerability, lying flat on her back "like a June-bug waiting to be turned over" (*CS* 145), to obtain her simple need of being helped out of the ditch. Likewise, when the blacks so desperately required help out of the social, educational, and economic ditch, whites finally reached out a hand to aid them, though only perhaps because they appeared so helpless. The next stage is symbolized by Phoenix's having to grovel on her knees for the nickel, which the hunter avers he does not have. The hunter's threatening act of pointing his gun at her and his false advice—"stay home, and nothing will happen to you" (*CS* 146)—seem prophetic of southern whites' stance during the mid-fifties when blacks began to demand equal opportunities and dignity. Had Phoenix given in to this temptation to remain passive, she would not have obtained the much-needed medicine. Finally, the hunter fails to comprehend the dire necessity of her mission, mistakenly believing she is merely going to see Santa Claus. He is not, in a last analysis, so much malicious as insensitive (Robinson 24).

The final scene at the clinic has also drawn considerable commentary on the failure of charity—in the sense of the Latin *caritas* or Christian love.[11] Yet to see the white attendant and nurse merely as representing the callous welfare state is simplistic. The attendant, who does not know Phoenix's case, displays a clinical sort of charity, dispensed without care or personalization: "A charity case, I suppose" (*CS* 147). Yet it is noteworthy that at the end of the story she offers Phoenix a small personal gratuity

---

[11] Hardy (227–29) presents the most scathing interpretation of their actions. See also Appel, *A Season of Dreams* 16; and Cooley 24. Welker and Gower (205) offer a necessary corrective that "all Christians, through Grace, are 'charity cases'"; the "obstinate case," they further argue, suggests Original Sin, "the nature of the human condition."

for Christmas. The nurse does act impatiently when Phoenix lapses into senility, but only after five patient attempts to elicit the needed information regarding the grandson.

This scene focuses two of the most significant motifs of the story: Phoenix's unreserved love for her grandson and her hope for his future. The slightly humorous suspense afforded by her momentary lapse of memory functions to undercut the tendency to sentimentalize a tragic situation. When she finally remembers, Phoenix expresses one of the most powerful definitions of Christian love imaginable: "I not going to forget him again, no, the whole enduring time. I could tell him from all the others in creation" (*CS* 148). She is also adamant in her faith that, despite his seeming frailty, he is going to survive. The flame, bird, and windmill (Isaacs 81; Ardolino 7) imagery in the final scene reinforces the virtuous cycle by which she keeps her grandson alive through her persistent care; his need likewise gives her a reason to live. To overlook the real suffering in both their lives is to distort. Yet to interpret this scene cynically, as Cooley does, as the blacks swallowing the lye (lie) of racist condescension and occasional charity (24)—or to view Phoenix as some sort of misguided Don Quixote flapping at imaginary windmills (Daly 138)—misses the point that Phoenix, in her slow, plodding, and often interrupted course, has overcome every temptation and obtained her goal.

Thus, the truth of the racial interactions in "A Worn Path" lies somewhere between Hardy's, Cooley's, and Appel's encomiums of the blacks and excoriations of the whites and Howell's almost complete exoneration of both:

> There is no conflict between Phoenix and the white world, and there is no hate. . . . The whites who confront Phoenix reflect the usual attitudes of their generation toward the Negro. . . . [T]he charity of the whites, meager as it is, is proffered in kindliness and received as such. (Howell 31; see also Vande Kieft, *Eudora Welty* 140)

Whereas the former interpretations are too polemical, the latter is perhaps overly sanguine. The story does portray interracial tension and misunderstanding, if not overt conflict. To obtain her meager needs, Phoenix has to remain in her subservient role as requester. Although she avoids the more obvious near-parodic ploys, such as Uncle-Tom obsequiousness or Sambo antics, she does rely—consciously or unconsciously—on her shrewdness, senility, and even minor thievery. The whites also evince at least degrees of insensitivity toward Phoenix, but seemingly more out of callous incomprehension than deliberate cruelty. Finally, however, the mythic aura of the story mitigates the impact of these political issues, allowing the reader to apprehend Phoenix whole, as no single character within the story does.

ELAINE ORR

"Unsettling Every Definition of Otherness":[1] Another Reading of Eudora Welty's "A Worn Path"
(1992)

Eudora Welty's "A Worn Path," first published in 1941, is one of her most widely read stories. But to date, it has not received a critical reading that questions the interpretation of Phoenix Jackson offered by the white attendant at the end of the story. Phoenix is "a charity case" (282). Given the story's "thick" rendering of Phoenix and the textual evidence that the attendant is an unreliable interpreter, this absence of different readings is puzzling.[2] We should not fail to notice that Welty's verbose and inventive protagonist is herself immediately silenced when she is so summed up by her "superior." Why?

Through careful attention to the narrative itself—an attention that leads us to deconstruct the authoritative and delimiting perspectives offered by the white characters and to reconstruct an excessive subjectivity emerging among Phoenix, the narrator's voice, and the path—this essay seeks to break the critical silence surrounding this often-read story. My argument is that the text figures the writing process, that much more than a character sketch, "A Worn Path" is a complex analogy of fabulation—of invention, discovery, and subjective expansion. Far from resting on stereotypes, the story plays upon our "knowledge" of "others" to resist the "wornness" of old scripts. Phoenix's traits—her blackness, femaleness, age, and apparent

---

[1] I borrow this phrase from Teresa de Lauretis's essay.

[2] See Clifford Geertz for a discussion of "thick" and "thin" descriptions. "Thick" descriptions pay attention to webs of signification and layers of complexity.

poverty—are riddles told by the author to challenge the reader both to unlearn and to relearn, that is, to enter the process of creation.

A scene from the middle of the story suggests the complex "re-figuring" of Phoenix and her path that the text requires:

> Then she gave a little cry and clapped her hands and said, "Git on away from here, dog! Look! Look at that dog!" She laughed as if in admiration. "He ain't scared of nobody. He a big black dog." She whispered, "Sic him!"
> "Watch me get rid of that cur," said the man. "Sic him, Pete! Sic him!"
> Phoenix heard the dogs fighting, and heard the man running and throwing sticks. She even heard a gunshot. But she was slowly bending forward by that time, further and further forward, the lids stretched down over her eyes, as if she were doing this in her sleep. Her chin was lowered almost to her knees. The yellow palm of her hand came out from the fold of her apron. Her fingers slid down and along the ground under the piece of money with the grace and care they would have in lifting an egg from under a sitting hen. Then she slowly straightened up, she stood erect, and the nickel was in her apron pocket. A bird flew by. Her lips moved. "God watching me the whole time. I come to stealing." (279–80)

In this passage, Phoenix Jackson creates a fictive diversion by improvising upon her knowledge of the white male character she confronts—of his penchant for bravado and of *his* fictions about her. While he appears the authority (certainly the interrogator), she employs his definitions and rewrites them as riddles, thus deconstructing his privilege and (if we are good enough readers) reconstructing her own subjectivity.

Having (somewhat miraculously, since she is earlier described as nearly blind) spotted a nickel which has fallen "out of the man's pocket onto the ground" (279), she invents a competition between the dogs (his dog and the "big black" stray that surprises her, causing her to fall into a ditch). With the slim thread of her story, Phoenix draws the man off in chase and retrieves his money for herself. This brief but effective fiction within the fiction reveals Phoenix's identity as a self-conscious fabulist (something different from what the hunter thinks she is: a self-forgetful old woman) with a penchant for re-creation (making up stories) rather than resolution.

James Walter has suggested that the story's simplicity is misleading and argues that Welty "tests" the reader by requiring "a revaluation of interpretive assumptions and mental habits" (83). I agree, and yet it seems to me that Walter and others have underread the story's complex, even contradictory signs, in particular, the interrelated tracings of race, class, and gender that Welty crisscrosses in Phoenix's journey.³ Though most of the narrative renders her trek, critics often depend upon the story's penultimate and stereotypical moment—Phoenix's securing of the "soothing medicine" (283)—to provide unity or closure to this "dark" character and typically "feminine" tale.

A representative reading is offered by Ruth M. Vande Kieft, who writes that "there are no significant barriers to the expressive love of old Phoenix." Comparing her to Dilsey in *The Sound and the Fury*, Vande Kieft suggests that Phoenix is "a completely and beautifully harmonious person," whose journey is undertaken with a "clear object—her grandson" (29). Similarly, John Hardy has proposed that Phoenix does "nothing for herself, for her own advantage" (229); and John R. Cooley has interpreted "A Worn Path" as a primitive idyll (24–25) that fails its black character in "sensitivity or depth" (27).⁴ Vande Kieft's reading appears to overlook the complexities of the story while Hardy and Cooley, in analyzing race and not gender, seek a unified understanding of the story's meaning. Though these critics differ on the question of the story's success (some praise Welty for its harmony and pathos; others criticize its romantic tendency), they appear to agree with Granville Hicks's summary of its plot: in the "simple". . . story, 'A Worn Path,' there is nothing at all except the details of an old Negro woman's journey to the city to get medicine for her grandson" (262).

Other critics have hinted at a more complex reading. Nancy K. Butterworth, for example, suggests that Phoenix "is not a stereotypical or stock black character" (167), yet her reading supports the "charitable" view of Phoenix that the white community in the text finds acceptable: Phoenix's "purpose" arises out of "unreserved love for her grandson" (171). When she "obtains her goal" (171), it is none other than the goal of self-sacrifice. Robert H. Brinkmeyer's view is more instructive; he views Welty's writing as revealing "an openness to otherness" (69) that is expansive and expanding

---

³ Feminist scholarship on Welty does exist, beginning with Peggy W. Prenshaw's "Woman's World, Man's Place: The Fiction of Eudora Welty." More recently, Patricia Yaeger's "'Because a Fire Was in My Head': Eudora Welty and the Dialogic Imagination" performs a feminist reading of Welty. However, this most-often anthologized story of Welty's continues to be read thematically and traditionally.

⁴ Cooley does say that Welty creates "an ironic contrast between the primitivism whites assume to characterize blacks, and the somewhat more detailed portraits revealed by [the writer]" (90), but he views the story as ultimately failing to present a complex subject. In his reading, the romantic, idyllic tendencies in "A Worn Path" are too strong and seduce both writer and reader.

rather than conclusive. His analysis of Welty's nonfiction prose can be applied to this story, which does not conclude. Contrary to most critics' assumptions, the reader does not, in fact, know where Phoenix is going at the "end" any more than the hunter (or the reader either, for that matter) knows why she is going to town in the "middle." Once we read our own hegemonic tendencies in the white characters' "reasoning" about Phoenix's trip, we realize that the text authorizes no "other" reason for her journey, no reason that makes her "other" and hence decipherable and defined.

We see an example of the text's refusal to authorize universal readings in Welty's elaborate description of Phoenix's scooping up of the coin while the hunter is off after the dogs; here we can read both the erasure of the hunter's signs (his "reason") and the writing of undecidable possibilities. Phoenix and the narrator emerge in this passage as unsettling subjects who steal not only money but stories. If this is a crucial moment in the text, as I am suggesting, we are faced with a subject (Phoenix and the writer's art) always in the making, a subject exceeding the boundaries of our expectations. By metaphorically connecting the hunter with the hen (Phoenix takes his money with "the grace and care [she] would have [used] in lifting an egg from under a sitting hen" [280]), Welty playfully "crisscrosses" genders, subverts white male authority, and suggests her own writerly deftness (hence the need for readerly invention in response). As I have already suggested, Phoenix's theft challenges the framing designation—"charity case"—that many past readings have assumed as *the* authoritative comment in this story.[5] She takes or makes up what she needs.

Phoenix's diversion of the hunter and her theft of his money illustrate the text's metaphorical challenge to all hegemonic definitions, all unitary readings. In the narrative doubling of a woman writer telling the story of a woman inventing a (devious) story, "A Worn Path" excessively re-presents the "defian[t] . . . act of woman writing" otherwise (Meese 131), creating "a space of contradictions," or "the consciousness of 'something else'" (de Lauretis 144–45). In this case, "A Worn Path" surpasses the phallic and supremacist definitions it includes and opens windows to contradiction and paradox.

Even in her own comments about the story, Welty is contradictory (see *Eye* 161), for she implies both that the story is about the path (the process)

---

[5] John Hardy suggests that the white women in the story have no "comprehension of what they are witnessing" (227). I agree. And yet I do not find a very compelling rereading of Phoenix in his essay.

and that it is about Phoenix's going out for another (the goal). I read the story as tracing Phoenix's marginalized selves in order to celebrate the woman writer's fabular (nonunitary) pleasure, which defies enclosure.[6] Welty herself remarks upon the story in this way:

> In the matter of function, old Phoenix's way might it even do as a sort of parallel to your way of work if you are a writer of stories. The way to get there is the all-important, all-absorbing problem, and this problem is your reason for undertaking the story. . . . Like Phoenix, . . . you . . . us[e] inventions of your imagination, perhaps helped out by your dreams and bits of good luck. (Eye 162)

From misleading the hunter to conjuring up marble cake, Phoenix "help[s herself] out by [her] dreams and bits of good luck." Rather than classify Phoenix "a charity case," a more appropriate response to the story, then, is to "us[e] inventions of [our own] imagination," following the contradictions, the "unclassified" play that the journey affords us in our reading.

Welty begins her narrative with contradictions, insisting from the beginning that we "fill in," invent with her, imagine possibility within paradox. For example, in the first paragraph, Phoenix is described as "old" and "very old"; she is "small" and carries a "small cane" that makes the sound "of a solitary little bird" (273). Yet in naming her protagonist after the mythical phoenix (an ancient Egyptian, hence non-Christian, symbol of *kingly* cremation and rebirth) and having her appear in December (the time of the Winter Solstice, when according to folk tradition, the Witch Destroyer and Regeneratrix appears, a witch whose "nose is hooked like the beak of a bird" [Gimbutas 209–10]), Welty immediately complicates her own representation.[7] These mythical contradictions are followed by homelier textual ones. For example, Welty describes her protagonist as "neat and tidy" (273), and yet Phoenix walks all the way to town with her shoe untied. Her gait is compared to the balance of a pendulum in a grandfather clock, and she crosses a log with her eyes shut, but she is at critical moments quite "unbalanced." She is nearly blind, as evidenced when she is fooled by the scarecrow, yet she sees a nickel fall from the hunter's pocket (and knows that it is a nickel, not

---

[6] I am indebted to a number of feminist critics for theories of women's writing that inform my reading of Welty, in particular, Patricia Yaeger, Susan Winnett, and Hélène Cixous.

[7] The December context has generally been read as authorizing a more Christian thematics in spite of Phoenix's name and the clear non-Christian mythological ties. See Gimbutas, especially chapter 18.

another coin). To herself, she thinks, "I the oldest people I ever know" (277), yet the narrator describes her at one point as "stretching her fingers like a baby" (276). She appears dominated by time, yet she often dreams, and as the windmill at the story's end suggests, is more like the wind, now gusting, now still, than she is inflexible or constant. She is both simple and wise, marginalized within the social fields she traverses and yet mysteriously beyond the boundaries drawn by her social superiors. She is poor, but her face is superior to jewels.

As textual contradiction, Phoenix herself "shake[s] up the ... communities which do not acknowledge the excluded margins" (Bauer 13). Within the story, her encounters with the hunter and the larger white middle-class community illustrate both her marginality (as female, black, old, and poor) and the unsettling that occurs when her presence challenges that community's "readings" of her. If "it is not a writer's business to tease" (*Eye* 159), it certainly *is* a writer's business to give us new knowledge of human possibilities, to invent metaphors that complicate "worn" knowledge. In this sense, the "worn path" that must be overcome in this story is not Phoenix's but ours, the worn path of old readings, tried and untrue assumptions.

Audre Lorde describes some of these assumptions when she writes, "Somewhere, on the edge of consciousness, there is ... a *mythical norm,* which each one of us within our hearts knows '... is not me.' In america [sic], this norm is usually defined as white, thin, male, young, heterosexual, christian [sic], and financially secure" (116). Along the worn path, it is, of course, the hunter, not Phoenix, who appears as a fit hero for the American adventure.[8] He, the narrator tells us, is "a white man ... a hunter, a young man, with his dog on a chain" and a gun (278). As we have already seen, Phoenix is almost shrunken with age and apparently "poor"; her only weapon is a walking stick made from an old umbrella which she waves before her like a wand. In setting up this contrast, Welty's text certainly challenges assumptions about the hero. What readers have missed is the story's thoroughgoing deconstruction of familiar models, even the models we have employed to understand the heroine.

The hunter's authoritative voice is unequivocal, assumes privilege, and conveys a belief in the literal power of his words. When he tells Phoenix to

---

[8] According to Leslie Fiedler, "westering, in America, means leaving the domain of the female" (60), by which, of course, he means, the domestic, what has already been tamed. This location, the hearth and home, appears trivial when compared with all that lies west of the Mississippi. See his *The Return of the Vanishing American,* especially the page cited. I am indebted to Annette Kolodny for the location of this passage.

"stay home" so that "nothing will happen to [her]" (indeed!) (280), he seems to expect that his command will literally turn her around. Phoenix's speech, on the other hand, suggests a playful and deviant use of language. Creating riddles and playing with others' fictions about her, she is able to continue on her way despite the hunter. Like the character of the fool, who appears foolish only to the literal-minded, her language "serves to defamiliarize the conventions which have been accepted as 'natural,' as myth" (Bauer 13). And as John Hardy notes, "[T]he habit of mythologizing the lives of Negroes [sic], . . . is one of the best established and most effective methods that the white man [sic] has devised for denying them full status in his cultural community" (226). Feminist writers have said as much about patriarchal mythologizing of women. Thus, Phoenix's play is seriously aimed, and at a fairly daunting set of canons. If there is purpose in this tale it is not to appease us through mere repetition of myth but to unsettle us through iconoclastic reversals and inventions. Phoenix, who appears simple, may not be; her path, which seems necessarily eclipsed by the hunter's may be of greater magnitude than he can imagine, and her purposes, which he and the nurse neatly categorize, may be far more mysterious and regenerative than are our associations with the traditional hero or heroine.

When the hunter learns that Phoenix is "bound to go to town" (279), he immediately declares it unmanageable *for her* since the trek is *equal* to the distance he normally travels. "Why, that's too far," he argues, and then boasts while patting the bag of game he carries: "'When I come out myself, . . . I get something for my trouble'"(279). Phoenix's understanding of his "sport" is signaled when the narrator shows us "a little closed claw. . . . one of the bob-whites, with its beak hooked bitterly to show it was dead" (279). The hunter's "gaming" is not playful but conclusive and, as Butterworth notes, sadistic. The hunter assumes that Phoenix goes out with similar goals when, actually, she goes out not to bring things to a close, but to see what she can *make* of things, what she can *make up*. By analogy, Welty's writing does not conclusively frame the charitable heroine. Both writer and character initiate discourse as a form of play. Later, in town, for example, Phoenix approaches a well-to-do woman and asks for help tying her shoe, but no careful reader will believe Phoenix could not tie her own shoes. Rather, she wants to see what her talk will do, just as Welty does.

The hunter's condescension is reflected in past readings (and parodied in the shoe-tying episode) that preclude the possibility of Phoenix's self-conscious and self-interested play with language. Robert L. Phillips, Jr., for example, denies the possibility that Phoenix is aware of the manifold dimensions of language when he writes, "In 'The Worn Path' the rich texture of allusion and symbol is there for the reader and the critic to enjoy." Phoenix, he argues, "is not aware that she is acting out patterns as ancient as the imagination. She knows only what she sees and feels to be important" (60). But why can we not imagine that Phoenix is linguistically skilled? Earlier, facing a "field of dead corn," she whispers to herself, "'Through the maze now'"(276), thus playfully exchanging the words maze/maize. Indeed, she appears to illustrate the double consciousness and duplicitous use of language that W. E. B. DuBois postulated for African Americans, developed, he proposed, through their negotiation with white authority. Feminist theorists have similarly pointed to women writers' studied use of "doubletalk," a subversive speech appearing to say one thing when really another meaning is intended.[9] Phoenix's playful skill with language allows her to transform herself from "subject into object into subject," a fabular talent that "grounds [her] different relation . . . to consciousness, and to knowing" (de Lauretis 119). Analogically, she is a figure for Welty's writing, for a subversive feminist knowledge that unravels worn assumptions and weaves new visions, for example, of woman's identity as evolving out of self-interested fabular play rather than self-forgetful abnegation.

Indeed, as Hardy and Butterworth have shown, Welty warns the reader against the obvious (or merely a literal reading) by parodying the all-too-predictable hero and his (self-)definition of the quest. One must be young, strong, and male to set out on the hunt, and the guiding maxim is this: one goes out with an eye toward the goal—toward the kill, no less. The gun, which the young hunter soon exhibits, connects the intention of his language with his assured and literal result. Though we may quickly recognize Welty's play at the hunter's expense, previous readings have not recognized Phoenix's (and the narrator's) play at ours. For most readers desire closure and ends; and while some critics have scoffed at the hunter's definition of those ends, others have "swallowed" the "soothing medicine" of feminine self-sacrifice as an appropriate and noble "end" for Phoenix or, if they

---

[9] Sandra Gilbert and Susan Cubar comment upon the use of "doubletalk" among women writers. "With only one language at their disposal, women writers in England and America had to be . . . adept at doubletalk. . . . We shall see . . . that in publicly presenting acceptable facades for private and dangerous visions women writers have long used a wide range of tactics to obscure but not obliterate their most subversive impulses" (74). Annis Pratt has noted that "many women [writers] have even succeeded in hiding the covert or implicit feminism in their books from themselves. . . . As a result we get explicit cultural norms superimposed upon an authentic creative mind in the form of all kinds of feints, ploys, masks and disguises embedded in the plot structure and characterization" (183).

have rejected the medicine for themselves, have assumed that the writer accepts it.[10]

Like the hunter, readers do not know Phoenix's "purpose" yet and have been reading this outing as more or less plotless, a "simple" story lacking sufficient motivation and purpose. We are trained as the hunter is toward greater expediency than Phoenix seems capable of. The hunter jumps to a second conclusion, since he finds a motivation that he can understand so necessary: "'I know you old colored people!'" he remarks, "'Wouldn't miss going to town to see Santa Claus'" (279).

Actually, like Christmas Jenny in Mary Wilkins Freeman's story by that name, Phoenix is closer to *being* Santa Claus (in her mysterious capacities) than she is likely to be his devotee. She is a blend of biblical and mythical figures, all feminized through their association with Phoenix herself,[11] while most of her antagonists are masculinized (the dead trees, the snake, the scarecrow, the dog). Clearly, she is the phoenix, who rises from her own ashes (thus one who is ageless and self-inventing), but also a female Aaron (when her cane/staff appears to be coming to life), a wiser Eve (when she hopes to avoid the snake "coming around that tree" [276]), and the sibyl (in her frequent "dreams" and meditations, some of which are not revealed to us). The succession of mythic female characters suggests the story's less-worn path, its bringing of the traditionally marginal to center and simultaneous decentering of the reader through the character of Phoenix. She is a subject we cannot "pen" down according to any "other" definition or stereotype, even, as we will see, according to the type of "the good mother."

In his reinscription of Phoenix according to the limits of *his* imagination—as quaint, childlike, and needy—the hunter is the unimaginative reader who reads not to entertain something new but to confirm what he already knows. Phoenix appears aware of his limitations when she responds to his questions about her age and origin. "'You can't even see it from here'" (279), she replies to the question about where she lives. And when she answers "'No telling'" (279) to his question about her age, she plays both with her own deviance (she will not tell him) and with the possibility that she is

---

[10] Vande Kieft's and Cooley's readings may serve as representative examples, Vande Kieft finding in the medicine authority for reading Phoenix heroically and Cooley refusing to take the "soothing medicine" as it merely glosses the pain of the black race in America rather than healing it.

[11] When critics have read this story "religiously," they have tended to define Phoenix's character in the masculinist imagery of a Christ figure.

ageless, that she is mysteriously outside of or beyond his measured time. Indeed, the narrative seems to suggest that Phoenix's context is not small at all; it only appears that way to the hunter, who is limited by his self-referential language. Her origins as well as her destination are "beyond" the hunter, perhaps literally, certainly figuratively and symbolically. Like Pilate in Toni Morrison's *Song of Solomon*, Phoenix is presented as one who cannot be understood by those who imagine that they already know her. The "golden color" that runs underneath her skin and her "eyes . . . blue with age" (274) are signs of her mystery, pointed to by Welty but not at all "read" by those whom Phoenix encounters on her way.

When Phoenix creates the fictive diversion of the dogs, the hunter's "knowledge," not merely his physical prowess, is questioned. This (black female) character's detouring of the hunter breaks the frame of the (white) masculine myth and reveals it as a literary convention. Indeed, as Phoenix negotiates her way around the hunter and his commanding language/commanding gun/authoritative tradition, she lifts her skirts and walks out of his picture into another space, "a space of contradictions, in the here and now, that need[s] to be affirmed but not resolved" (de Lauretis 144). Tracing out the process of writing with the extended metaphor of Phoenix's journey, Welty affirms a knowledge of uncertainties, a revisionist practice of looking at the "other" in order to rename and expand the self, not to rename and delimit those "others."

But Phoenix has not yet escaped all "framing." When she arrives in town and enters the doctor's office, we are finally given a "reason" for this trek. Phoenix is a grandmother whose sick grandson needs the "soothing medicine" for which she has come. As the nurse remarks: "'Oh, that's just old Aunt Phoenix, . . . *She doesn't come for herself*—she has a little grandson. She makes these trips just as regular as clockwork. She lives away back off the Old Natchez Trace'" (282, italics mine). The nurse, of course, is another reader/interpreter like the hunter, but now Welty sharpens the critique of hegemonic definition (clearly inscribed in Phoenix's meeting with the hunter) by revealing the uncharitable authority of white women in relation to Phoenix. Hardy correctly calls the scene a "scathing indictment of the fool's pride of the white man [sic] in the superiority of his civilization" (229).

Are we to believe that Phoenix does not come for herself? In *The Eye of the Story*, Welty's only definitive answer to the question of whether the boy is dead is this: "*Phoenix is alive*" (160). Thus while Phoenix's encounter with the hunter initiates the story's critique of the well-worn path of racist and masculinist definitions, the encounter with the "professional" women in the office sharpens the review by dramatizing the racism and classism that inform the white women's "charitable" understanding of Phoenix. Like the racism and sexism of the hunter, the classism and racism of the white women are dead languages (the ashes) in Welty's text, played upon by Phoenix to call forth a new alphabet, a new text of emerging subjectivity, of coming to life through invention.

The white women's knowledge depends on and subsumes some "other," someone who "I am not." It deadens relationship through dependence on static categories. Like the hunter, these women read Phoenix stereotypically, never imagining that she might deviate from their prescription. Profiting from their alliance with the white male doctor, they have escaped certain material oppressions of patriarchy (they will, for example, be rewarded materially for their work outside the domestic sphere), yet they expect Phoenix to act humbly and always out of love. She is (their) servant. Or as Bell Hooks remarks in her description of white feminists, "they are the 'hosts,' [we/black women/Phoenix are the] guests" (53), in other words, the other, the foreigner.

The acceptable motivation of a black woman's maternal love—a part of the mythology of the "superhuman black woman"[12]—might be *a* reason Phoenix comes to town but it is not her defining reason. Said differently, Phoenix does not come to be herself merely through bearing the medicine but through her fabulous thought. She is primarily the woman who journeys and thinks rather than the woman who bears.[13] She lives (as a text does) through her constant telling and retelling. Welty's narrative represents these "feminine" contradictions, though most readers resist reading them, concluding (unitarily) that this good woman's story can finally be understood as really being about maternal charity.

But as soon as the nurse provides herself (us?) with an "acceptable" reason for Phoenix's journey, Welty erases it. Phoenix forgets why she came: "The old woman sat down, bolt upright in the chair. . . . as if she were in armour" (282). The static and constricting definition given to Phoenix is imagistically conveyed in her body; as a charity case, she loses all agency, all fluidity. She is no longer the graceful writer of her path. Perhaps her forgetfulness is simply old age (but can we ignore the name Phoenix even in the

---

[12] See Hooks, especially page 13.

[13] I draw this distinction from Paula Gunn Allen, who, in writing about the mythology of the Keres Indians, describes the "basic idea of the Creatrix as She Who Thinks rather than She Who Bears." "In this epistemology," she writes, "the perception of female power as confined to maternity is a limit on the power inherent in femininity" (24).

most literal of readings), or perhaps the boy *is* dead and she is momentarily ashamed for having troubled the nurse (again to read this way, we must forget the numerous mythical allusions in the text and ignore the playful and resonant language Phoenix has spoken throughout the story). More likely, the erasure is not forgetfulness at all but self-consciousness—Phoenix's self-conscious resistance to the erasure of her subjectivity and Welty's self-conscious refusal to author-ize her character (her own writing) as "other."

Like the hunter, the attendant "reads" Phoenix quickly: "'A charity case,'" she "supposes" (282). Her immediate sizing up reveals stereotypical attitudes toward Phoenix's race and class. On the one hand, the attendant reads her blackness as meaning she requires charity (thus blackness and poverty are conflated). On the other hand, readers have "supposed" that the statement is the key to understanding the story: Phoenix's story is *about* charity, about her (*grand*)motherly love for a child. The white women's overdetermined "reading" of Phoenix reveals their actual complicity in the simple story that makes every woman Mary or Eve. But Phoenix's response again casts doubt on such simple readings. Here she employs silence rather than narrative invention to rebel against white and male "author-izations" of her journey as (m)other.

Phoenix refuses to answer in the way that the attendant requires. Even when the nurse, who "knows" Phoenix, enters the story, Phoenix does not comply with the script the nurse supplies. She is still silent, though finally she does "remember" her purpose. Still, the slippage between the nurse's prescriptive view and Phoenix's deviant silence provokes us into thought. Such fictional play reevaluates the traditional procedures of communication—here between a white woman and a black woman, where the black participant is expected simply to say "yes"—and releases us from established patterns. Phoenix provokes the nurse, who warns that she "mustn't take up our time this way" (283), actually pleading that Phoenix stay with the frayed script of black/white (also self/other) relations with which both are familiar. But Welty erases that old "dialogue" and shows that it is indeed the ever-emerging path that matters, that Phoenix's fabulous journey beyond the familiar and outside the boundaries of our previous knowledge is her reason for coming (*Eye* 162). "The deep-grained habit of love" (*Eye* 161) is Phoenix's habit of self-invention and Welty's writerly habit of empathy, of extending her knowledge not by defining the "other" but by redefining herself in relation to others, what Vande Kieft correctly refers to as Welty's "power to 'slip into' people whose lives and social and economic situations differed greatly from her own" (140).

Clearly a thoughtful readerly pause will make more of Phoenix's pause than mere forgetfulness. Middle- and upper-class white women have often escaped the requirements of "pure" motherly love in part by hiring black women to mother their children and clean their houses. The pause in Welty's text exposes the white women's assumptions as their own fictional construction. Their identifying statements—statements identifying Phoenix, that is—are not Phoenix's, and in her pause, she (along with Eudora Welty) erases them. In the absence of identification (foreigners and "others" must be identified), readers may bridge the gap by holding on tenaciously to *their* need for Phoenix's charity (for her being a charity case) or they can imaginatively reconstruct the subjectivity of the fabulator that Phoenix has played with throughout her journey. Such a reconstruction offers a fruitful opportunity for speaking the contradictory subject that emerges when we read Welty and Phoenix Jackson as (metaphorical) writer(s). This move, initiated by Welty and expansively rewritten in our reading may allow us to do what Valerie Smith says we must: "develop a mode of self-evaluation, and sustain a dialogue with those [black and white feminists] involved in related enterprises" (56–57). Welty expands her writing self through fabulating this African American woman. The writer and her subject are both related and distinct. As the "'Inappropriate/d Other,'" the metaphorical subject arising between Phoenix and Welty "moves about, with always at least two/four gestures: that of affirming 'I am like you' while pointing insistently to the difference; and that of reminding 'I am different' while unsettling every definition of otherness arrived at" (Trinh T. Minha-ha, qtd. in de Lauretis 144).

When Phoenix does finally answer the nurse, she actually overanswers in a self-effacing response that is another parody of readers' unimaginative expectations. Begging forgiveness, Phoenix offers this life history: "'I never did go to school, I was too old at the Surrender." Then she adds, 'I'm an old woman without an education. It was my memory fail me'" (283). Alluding to the Civil War, Phoenix fulfills the image the nurse has of her. She promises not to forget again (that she should be subservient and/or that she has come for the boy).

Welty's overwriting of this passage, coming just on the heels of the underwriting of the narrative pause, again disconcerts our reading. Having created a spirited and inspiriting character, she belittles her beyond recognition. But the writing here merely mimics the white women's language. We have actually left Phoenix's text (her criss-crossing, difficult, interesting path) and embarked upon the nurse's sterile path of self-denunciation, a path she marks for Phoenix-as-(m)other, not for herself.

We are given a final sign of Phoenix's refusal to stay in her place, however, when, after gaining the nurse's approval, she cunningly pockets another nickel before leaving. She reminds us of her encounter with the hunter and of her subversion of his authority. Though she plans to buy a windmill for the boy, there is no evidence that she plans to go "straight" home. Instead, the quixotic image clearly suggests the fabulous subject Welty has been tracing. Through Phoenix's play, which crosses the established field of power between whites and blacks, between those upstairs and those down (Welty's clear imaging of the race/class hierarchy), the character has re-created herself linguistically (the phoenix!). We may assume she is going home, but there is no evidence in the story. Instead, I suggest she will move as she has throughout, beyond us, always re-marking the space of contradiction, the open ending.

The story's parodic or "non-sensical" (because inconclusive) character interrogates our attempt to find an all-encompassing truth in fiction and in particular our propensity to identify feminine truth as motherly love exclusive of self-interest or African American identity as auxiliary to white ideologies of wealth, conquest, and leisure. By refusing to stay in its place, to abide by any definition of otherness, the story offers no conclusions, only complications and deferrals. Not only the image of the hunter but that of the (black) mother is momentarily disestablished. What is left is the path/tracing and Phoenix/Welty upon it. Zigzagging in our reading of her, Phoenix recalls the goddess whose symbol is the zigzag, the image of water (Gimbutas 19). Her play with many selves—adventurer, fool, mother, inventor, comic—is like Welty's expansive writing which will not allow us to conclude but moves back and forth upon itself. When Phoenix refuses to stay in (her) place, defying the hunter who misreads her and would send her home (to the house) as well as the attendant and nurse who misname her a "charity case" (and thus would send her back to the type of "angel in the house" so familiar to women writers and feminist readers, white and African American alike), Phoenix/Welty generates a story that gets away from us (because we are inclined like those others to underread). If we follow Phoenix's path, however, (that is, Welty's writing), we are able to "see meaning in what previously has been empty space" (Showalter, qtd. in Gilbert and Gubar 75). Appealing to a feminized past through the character of Phoenix, Welty generates her playful, evasive, stubborn, and fabulous writing *selves*. Certainly, she is not a "charity case." Crossing boundaries with Phoenix, she does not create a type but shows her process of invention and her determined erasing of those myths which keep all emerging subjects penned in or up.

At last, we can read Phoenix's mothering but now through the defamiliarization brought about by parody which, as Patricia Waugh says, allows new and more authentic forms of the subject to be released (see especially 65). Phoenix herself crosses self-interest with other interest. When she claims that she will remember the boy "the whole enduring time" (284), she hints at something that past readings have not noticed: that she chooses him, as a fiction perhaps, but nevertheless as willfully desired.

Phoenix's desire to mother as she will rather than according to definition recalls the Goddess Creatrix, the source (of fictions as well as lives). As Marija Gimbutas reminds us, early Goddess Creatrix images were bird-woman hybrids (3–18). More than fertility goddesses, these beings were beings of thought, of intellect, as well as of body. Like Phoenix, readers who remember the complexity of this other past, will learn to make their (textual) ways *like a mother,* by hook or by crook, writing and erasing, always interested and self-conscious, and always tracing the complexities of (self- and other-) love.

Works Consulted

Allen, Paula Gunn. "Grandmother of the Sun." *Weaving the Visions: New Patterns in Feminist Spirituality.* Ed. Judith Plaskow and Carol P. Christ. San Francisco: Harper, 1989. 22–28.

Bauer, Dale M. *Feminist Dialogics: A Theory of Failed Community.* Albany: State U of New York P, 1988.

Brinkmeyer, Robert H. "An Openness to Otherness: The Imaginative Vision of Eudora Welty." *Southern Literary Journal* 20.2 (1988): 69–80.

Butterworth, Nancy K. "From Civil War to Civil Rights: Race Relations in Welty's 'A Worn Path.'" *Eudora Welty: Eye of the Storyteller.* Ed. Dawn Trouward. Kent State UP, 1989. 165–72.

Cixous, Hélène. "The Laugh of the Medusa." *New French Feminisms: An Anthology.* Ed. Elaine Marks and Isabelle de Courtivron. New York: Schocken, 1981. 245–64.

Cooley, John R. "Blacks as Primitives in Eudora Welty's Fiction." *Ball State University Forum* 14 (1973): 20–28.

de Lauretis, Teresa. "Eccentric Subjects: Feminist Theory and Historical Consciousness." *Feminist Studies* 16.1 (1990): 115–50.

DuBois, W. E. B. *The Souls of Black Folk.* Millwood, NY: Kraus Thomson, 1973.

Fiedler, Leslie A. *The Return of the Vanishing American.* New York: Stein & Day, 1968.

Freeman, Mary E. (Wilkins). "Christmas Jenny." *A New England Nun and Other Stories.* 1891. Ridgewood, NY: Gregg, 1967.

Geertz, Clifford. *The Interpretation of Cultures.* New York: Basic, 1973.

Gilbert, Sandra M., and Susan Gubar. *The Madwoman in the Attic.* New Haven, CT: Yale UP, 1979.
Gimbutas, Marija. *The Language of the Goddess.* San Francisco: Harper, 1989.
Hardy, John Edward. "Eudora Welty's Negroes." *Images of the Negro in American Literature.* Ed. Seymour Gross and John Edward Hardy. Chicago: U of Chicago P, 1966. 221–32.
Hicks, Granville. "Eudora Welty." *Critical Essays on Eudora Welty.* Ed. W. Craig Turner and Lee Emling Harding. Boston: G.K. Hall, 1989. 259–67.
Hooks, Bell. *Feminist Theory: From Margin to Center.* Boston, MA: Southend, 1984.
Lorde, Audre. *Sister Outsider: Essays and Speeches by Audre Lorde.* Trumansburg, NY: Crossing, 1984.
Meese, Elizabeth A. *Crossing the Double-Cross: The Practice of Feminist Criticism.* Chapel Hill: U of North Carolina P, 1986.
Morrison, Toni. *Song of Solomon.* New York: Knopf, 1977.
Phillips, Robert L., Jr. "A Structural Approach to Myth in the Fiction of Eudora Welty." *Eudora Welty: Critical Essays.* Ed. Peggy Whitman Prenshaw. Jackson: UP of Mississippi, 1979. 56–67.
Pratt, Annis V. "The New Feminist Criticisms: Exploring the History of the New Space." *Beyond Intellectual Sexism: A New Woman, A New Reality.* Ed. Joan I. Roberts. New York: McKay, 1976.
Prenshaw, Peggy W. "Woman's World, Man's Place: The Fiction of Eudora Welty." *Eudora Welty: A Form of Thanks.* Ed. Louis Dollarhide and Ann J. Abadie. Jackson: UP of Mississippi, 1979. 46–77.
Smith, Valerie. "Gender and Afro-Americanist Literary Theory and Criticism." *Speaking of Gender.* Ed. Elaine Showalter. New York: Routledge, 1989.
Vande Kieft, Ruth M. *Eudora Welty: Revised Edition.* Boston: Twayne, 1987.
Walter, James. "Love's Habit of Vision." *Journal of the Short Stories in English* 7 (1986): 77–85.
Waugh, Patricia. *Metafiction: The Theory and Practice of Self-Conscious Fiction.* New York: Methuen, 1984.
Welty, Eudora. *The Eye of the Story: Selected Essays and Reviews.* New York: Random, 1977.
———. "A Worn Path." *A Curtain of Green.* Garden City, NY: Doubleday, 1941. 273–85.
Yaeger, Patricia. "'Because a Fire Was in My Head': Eudora Welty and the Dialogic Imagination." *PMLA* 99 (1984): 955–73.
———. *Honey-Mad Women: Emancipatory Strategies in Women's Writing.* New York: Columbia UP, 1988.

James Robert Saunders

*"A Worn Path": The Eternal Quest of Welty's Phoenix Jackson
(1992)

Of all the ingenious stories written by Eudora Welty over the past half century, it is perhaps "A Worn Path" that is most intriguing in terms of its ability to defy simple explanation. In a relatively early essay entitled "Life for Phoenix," Neil Isaacs manages to conclude that "the whole story is suggestive of a religious pilgrimage, while the conclusion implies that the return trip will be like the journey of the Magi, with Phoenix following a star (the marvelous windmill) to bring a gift to the child (medicine, also windmill)" (77). Indeed the tale is in some sense, to use Isaacs' word, "suggestive" of a religious quest. The story begins conspicuously on a cold December morning, and just as quickly we are made aware that there is an old black woman "coming along a path through the pinewoods" (59). We observe her as she negotiates a series of obstacles in that wilderness on her way to Natchez, Mississippi, presumably to pick up some medicine for her grandson who, according to the nurse's calculation near the story's end, had swallowed a certain amount of lye two or three years earlier. Elaborating further on the biblical analysis, Isaacs interprets:

> there are references to the Eden story (the ordering of the species, the snake in summer to be avoided), to the parting of the Red Sea (Phoenix walking through the field of corn), to a sequence of temptations, to the River Jordan and the City of Heaven (when Phoenix gets to the river, sees the city shining, and hears the bells ringing; then there is the angel who waits on her, tying her shoes), to the Christ-child in the manger (Phoenix describing her grandson as 'all wrapped up' in 'a little patch quilt . . . like a little bird' with 'a sweet look'). (77)

All things considered, Isaacs' analogies are quite astute and provide us with the basis for a most interesting perspective: Phoenix Jackson is involved in that crucial search for meaning in life that is founded on basic Christian principles and designed, upon completion, to provide her with life-giving sustenance. Even if she is, due both to her advancing years and the nature of her difficult mission, about to die by the story's end, it is only so that life might be affirmed through acquisition of the medicine her grandson needs.

Nevertheless, Roland Bartel specifies the story's uncertain ending as indicative of something much more pessimistic. Entitling his brief explication "Life and Death in Eudora Welty's 'A Worn Path,'" he urges us to "consider seriously the possibility that her grandson is, in fact, dead" (289). Presumably the lye that had been swallowed earlier was fatal, and now Phoenix has become engaged in a self-sacrificing ritual that carries her painfully over hills and through cave-like woods to get the "soothing medicine" that can only serve as a reminder of defeat. Commenting on what might be the significance of her name, Bartel continues, "If her grandson is dead, then the rebirth implied in her name is doubly pathetic: she unwittingly makes the journey to meet her own needs rather than her grandson's, and what begins as a life-sustaining journey seems to end in a journey of death" (290). Bartel argues vehemently for the prospect that Phoenix is just "a feeble old woman whose active imagination rescues her from the harshest aspects of her existence" (290). But by the time she has acquired her medicine, which is the purpose of her mission, she must (as Bartel has deduced) turn her limited sights toward returning home. The story ends with Jackson walking out of the doctor's office, and then "her slow step began on the stairs, going down" (68). Conveyed in that very last line of the story is the sense that Jackson had expended practically all of her energy on the journey and thus might not be able to make it back to her grandson even if he is alive. At one point, on her way to the doctor's office, she is shown lying in the midst of the wilderness flat on her back, unable to rise until a helpful hunter approaches to lend a hand, and yet there was a certain crispness in her response when that hunter had asked what she was doing there. "Lying on my back like a June-bug waiting to be turned over" (63) is what she says, and while a june bug in such a situation is not necessarily doomed, it is Bartel's belief that senility is setting in for Jackson and "she has risen from the ashes for the last time" (290).

In arriving at his conclusion Bartel rightfully draws on the Egyptian legend of the phoenix. One would be remiss not to do so in light of the protagonist's first name. However, whereas Bartel is somehow able to see the phoenix as indicative of Phoenix Jackson's ultimate demise, it is more appropriate to remember that the phoenix legend has its origin in an area of the world known as the "cradle of civilization" and also most appropriate to consider that Welty might intend for us to combine the legend with her story to unveil a process that goes on into infinity. The *Encyclopedia Britannica* describes the phoenix as

> a fabulous bird connected with the worship of the sun especially in ancient Egypt and in classical antiquity. It was known to Hesiod, and descriptions

of its appearance and behavior occur in ancient literature sporadically, with variations in detail, from Herodotus' account of Egypt onward. The phoenix is said to be as large as an eagle, with brilliant scarlet and gold plumage and a melodious cry. Only one phoenix exists at any time. It is very long-lived; no ancient authority gives it a life span of less than 500 years; some say it lives for 1,461 years (an Egyptian Sothic Period): an extreme estimate is 97,200. As its end approaches the phoenix fashions a nest of aromatic boughs and spices, sets it on fire, and is consumed in the flames. From this pyre miraculously springs a new phoenix.

Besides sharing that amazing bird's name, Phoenix resembles it in other ways. She "was an old Negro woman with her head tied in a red rag" (59). The color of that head apparel cannot be accepted as coincidental; recall the scarlet plumage of the ancient bird. Remember, as well, how that creature from antiquity is able to recreate itself by casting its body into a self-made fire. When asked the gripping question of whether or not her grandson is alive or dead, there has to come "a flicker and then a flame of comprehension" (67) before the author's Phoenix can respond—after what amounts to some sort of mystical conversion—that "he is just the same" (67). The nurse has asked six times about the condition of her grandson before Phoenix was inclined to answer. Perhaps we should accept this as an indication of senility. The protagonist herself subsequently begs forgiveness, explaining, "I never did go to school, I was too old at the Surrender . . . I'm an old woman without an education. It was my memory fail me" (67). We can believe that is the proper explanation or we can wonder, instead, how anyone forgets the purpose of so long and tedious a quest. During that nurse's interrogation, "Phoenix only waited and stared straight ahead, her face very solemn and withdrawn into rigidity" (66) as if bracing herself against the onslaught of suspicion. She apologizes as most any black person of her day would have done in that situation, but she never once denies the nature of her function.

Critic Grant Moss insists that Welty refused to use black dialect so that she might add "to the universality of her main character and her story as a whole" ("Retrod" 151). He goes on to say:

> It could have easily been an old white woman in the same circumstances as those of old Phoenix who set out that December morning on a journey to town on a mission like that of Old Phoenix. It could have been an old Czechoslovakian, Greek, or German peasant woman, who, in her own country, went across fields, through woods, over a stream, painfully into a village for the same purpose yesterday, or long ago, or ages ago. But it happened to be an old woman whom Miss Welty identifies as a Negro woman. (145)

Certainly, there have been other old women in various times and places who have merited the rendering of a tale so that the world will not forget their vast accomplishments. But to believe that Phoenix Jackson just "happened to be" an old black woman is to ignore an all-too-vital aspect of our nation's history. She, in particular, has been as crucial an element in the development of moral fiber as anything one might imagine.

William Faulkner was aware of this phenomenon, and while he portrayed the effects of a disappearing wilderness, the breakdown of the family, and the haunting shadows of the Civil War, he also left us Dilsey to evaluate. One watches in awe at the overwhelming chaos of *The Sound and the Fury* while she, quite naturally, takes the idiot Compson child "to the bed and drew him down beside her and she held him, rocking back and forth, wiping his drooling mouth upon the hem of her skirt" (395). It is that frightened, whining retarded child of the Compsons who represents what is most pitiable about us, and it is Dilsey who caters to him as though he were the most important. Before accepting this comparison between the two black women (Faulkner's Dilsey and Welty's Phoenix), however, it is apropos to examine what some might call a marked distinction. Benjy is not even Dilsey's child while Phoenix's grandchild has evidently swallowed lye; negligence would seem to be a factor in the latter case. What happened to the grandson's parents? How did he come to be in Jackson's charge? Still, however we might resolve this issue in our minds, whether parental absence is due to fate or the parents' fault, Phoenix is just as prepared to meet the challenge.

There is no need to limit ourselves to Dilsey as we search for adequate comparisons. Margaret Walker's *Jubilee* is a celebration of this spirit. Based on the life of Walker's maternal great-grandmother, Margaret Duggans Ware Brown, the novel serves to chronicle the life and times of its main character, Vyry, who, like Phoenix and so many others, was born into slavery but given the chance to see her race evolve away from that degrading institution. What makes Vyry different from any other character in that novel is how she is able to be consistent in the retention of humanistic values in spite of how circumstances resulting from the Civil War tear at the hearts of other southern victims until their stability is utterly destroyed. While others flee in the face of the Union surge, Vyry remains behind with the enfeebled Miss Lillian for the simple reason that her former mistress needs her most. Later in the book, as she and her newfound husband search during the bitter Reconstruction era for a home from which they will not be driven, she responds to a young white man who instinctively appeals to her in time of crisis. In that "I reckon I can be a granny in a pinch" chapter, the young man pleads, "Oh lady, help me please, my wife's having a baby, please come in quick" (359), and within a matter of moments we hear Vyry, who had only become a mother recently herself, comforting the stranger's pregnant wife, "Now lie still on your back and I'll hold your knees for you and when you feels the pain again, close your mouth and grit your teeth and bear down hard like you is on the pot" (359). An hour later, that "granny in a pinch" had "cleaned the baby and dressed him, and left the mother, clean and comfortable, ready for sleep" (360). Rejecting the father's offer of payment, that "granny" nevertheless promises to return the next morning to make sure that complications don't occur. She was, in words written by Walker that smack of what might be Welty's theme, "touched with a spiritual fire and permeated with a spiritual wholeness that had been forged in a crucible of suffering" (407). Once again, the Egyptian phoenix comes to mind as Walker adds how her protagonist was

> only a living sign and mark of all the best that any human being could hope to become. In her obvious capacity for love, redemptive and forgiving love, she was alive and standing on the highest peaks of her time and human personality . . . unlettered and untutored, she was nevertheless the best true example of the motherhood of her race, an ever present assurance that nothing could destroy a people whose sons had come from her loins. (407)

Such laudatory words serve as a fitting tribute to the humble figure of a woman who inhabits the pages of Walker's novel as well as the texts of other writers who have rendered their interpretations of this special type of character and what her presence means.

For Welty, the character epitomizes three important things. To begin with, Phoenix is a gifted child of nature. "Far out in the country" (59) is the place from which she comes and, as she travels over her path toward the city of Natchez, elements of nature caress her along the way. Struggling on an incline, she remarks to herself, "Something always take a hold of me on this hill—pleads I should stay" (60). It is possible that this "something" is the strain that going uphill poses, but it is more than likely that the very woods are reaching out to one who is their own. Going down the hill, her skirts get caught on a thorny bush; nimble fingers free them time and time again. "It was not possible to allow the dress to tear" (60), our narrator says. Only, we are not really sure if it is nimble fingers that will absolutely not allow it or the thorny bush itself which will not harm the garments of an essential sister. Such a theory is not outlandish considering the author's use of personification to achieve the desired spiritual effect. She transcends a barbed-wire fence, and big "dead trees, like black men with one arm, were standing in the purple stalks of the withered cotton field" (61). Soon after, she thinks back to the previous summer when snakes were in abundance, and she is grateful as she passes through that old cotton and the dead corn that "whispered and shook and was taller than her head" (61). Just as those dead trees—which are indeed only dead in the strictly biological sense—have waved her by with their one-armed communal greeting, the dead corn stalks must rise to guide her through. "Thorns, you doing your appointed work" (60), Phoenix maintained earlier. Those sharp protrusions, harmful as they are to some, have helped this story's traveler to proceed on her precisely ordained course.

Mere human vision would not have been sufficient for the journey. In fact, before traversing a narrow log that had been laid across a creek, Phoenix actually closed her eyes and then "leveling her cane fiercely before her, like a festival figure in some parade, she began to march across" (61). The cane she brandishes has particular significance, for having once been an umbrella that shielded humans from the elements of nature, it now facilitates communion, and in the still air of the winter Phoenix taps this vital instrument upon the frozen earth to produce a sound that is "meditative like the chirping of a solitary little bird" (59). Once she arrives at the log, a bridge that nature has provided, she can "march" across without even looking until she has reached the other side. On she marches through some areas that have no path at all, but she continues "parting her way from side to side with the cane, through the whispering field" (62).

Shortly thereafter, Phoenix takes advantage of a trail that has been left by wagon wheels.

> She followed the track, swaying through the quiet bare fields, through the little strings of trees silver in their dead leaves, past cabins silver from weather, with the doors and windows boarded shut, all like old women under a spell sitting there. "I walking in their sleep," she said, nodding her head vigorously. (62)

The going has gotten somewhat easier upon this encountering of places where humankind has been before, but those were also special human beings not so much detached from nature as they were from a surrounding modern world. The "quiet bare fields," "trees silver in their dead leaves," and "cabins silver from weather" are "all like old women under a spell sitting there." "I walking in their sleep," the traveler speaks in curious phraseology that serves to show how her communion carries on.

Other fiction writers have employed this theme. In Alice Walker's *The Color Purple*, as Celie learns to love herself, she comes to include the air and birds and trees. In fact, we don't know what to think exactly as, after a rather lengthy process of self-actualization, she concludes, "I knew that if I cut a tree, my arm would bleed" (203). That she has become in tune with nature is quite evident, but even more intriguing is how she and nature are one and the same. Again, in Toni Morrison's *Song of Solomon* we are witness to a character, Pilate, who is so close to nature that she is apart from others in the world. There were no street lights in her part of town and no electricity or gas in her quaint home. She and her daughter "warmed themselves and cooked with wood and coal, pumped kitchen water into a dry sink through a pipeline from a well and lived pretty much as though progress was a word that meant walking a little farther on down the road" (27). We learn, furthermore, that on the edge of town her "house sat eighty feet from the sidewalk and was backed by four huge pine trees, from which she got the needles she stuck into her mattress" (27). Certainly, it can be argued that those circumstances of adulthood are unusual until we learn "how she loved, as a girl, to chew pine needles and as a result smelled even then like a forest" (27).

Yes, a child who eats of trees will smell like trees; it might have been a matter of no more or less than that. But Celie and Pilate, as well as Welty's Phoenix, are endowed with special power so that even when a "flashing" nickel falls from the hunter's pocket, Phoenix's "fingers slid down and along the ground under the piece of money with the grace and care they would have in lifting an egg from under a setting hen" (64). However, at this point it is no longer Phoenix who is acting, for she simply "stood erect, and the nickel was in her apron pocket" (64). A bird conspicuously flies overhead and we are made to know that this is not just thievery, in the sense of some outrageous crime, but a certain kind of natural redistribution that has taken place between the hunter who shoots bobwhites and Welty's keeper of the woods. It was Harper Lee, speaking through the voice of Atticus Finch, who had warned, "it's a sin to kill a mockingbird" (*Mockingbird* 94). "All they do is sing their hearts out for us" (94), Miss Maudie adds. Anyone who has heard the melodious calling of the bobwhite bird knows how it would be should they become extinct. Their greatest "crime," like that of the mockingbird, lies in the singing that makes them the hunters' prey. In "A Worn Path" it becomes a phoenix burden to avenge, at least in some small way, the "bitter" fate.

Somewhat similarly, Phoenix is the designated protector of another worthy innocent. Isaacs sees her grandson as symbolic of the Christ child, and this is understandable. That grandson with the "sweet look" *was* capable of infinite suffering. Moreover, Phoenix is shown declaring to the doctor's nurse that she "could tell him from all the others in creation" (67). But there is a difficulty in that strictly theological approach. In an analysis of Flannery O'Connor's "The Artificial Nigger," Louis Rubin remembers a comment made by O'Connor during a symposium at Wesleyan College in Macon, Georgia. O'Connor had regretfully conveyed, "So many students approach a story as if it were a problem in algebra; find x and when they find x they can dismiss the rest of it" ("Company" 133). Agreeing with that statement on literary limitation, Rubin proposes, "What we need is criticism that will explore the complexity of the work, and not merely seek to use it to make theological observations" (134). Even with writers who come from areas of strong religious background, there is a danger in the rendering of biblical perspective. Like O'Connor, Welty hails from the southern Bible Belt where such considerations are quite necessary; yet, this does not mean Phoenix must be Moses and her grandson, by biblical comparison, is absolutely Christ. The meaning behind the grandson will not be so easy to uncover.

While there is also a bit of difficulty in taking literally everything an author says about her work, it will perhaps be helpful to examine what Welty says about this story as a means to analyze the second thing that Phoenix might epitomize. Bartel has placed much emphasis on the question of whether or not the grandson is alive, and in her essay entitled "Is Phoenix Jackson's Grandson Really Dead?" Welty reveals that as the question she is asked most often through the mail. This is how she chooses to respond:

> The grandson's plight was real and it made the truth of the story, which is the story of an errand of love carried out. If the child no longer lived, the truth would persist in the "wornness" of the path. But his being dead can't increase the truth of the story, can't affect it one way or the other. I think I signal this, because the end of the story has been reached before old Phoenix gets home again: she simply starts back. To the question "Is the grandson really dead?" I could reply that it doesn't make any difference. I could also say that I did not make him up in order to let him play a trick on Phoenix. But my best answer would be: "*Phoenix is alive.*" (160)

There is some hesitancy on the part of Welty as she provides this explanation. As to that question concerning the possibility of the grandson's death, she answers, "I *could* reply that it doesn't make any difference" and "I *could* also say that I did not make him up in order to let him play a trick." Such ambivalence makes us inclined to take to heart what she had said some twenty years before in another piece, dated 1955, entitled "Writing and Analyzing a Story." Then she had asserted, "I never saw, as reader or writer, that a finished story stood in need of any more from the author" (107). Nevertheless one tends to accept what she does say in later years about her complex story. What interest could she have had in tricking Phoenix? Furthermore, it must not be too critical whether the grandson is alive or dead; the story has been most effective at the same time that we do not know. Welty directs our focus, instead, to the fact that Phoenix is alive and has been successful in her errand carried out in love. Without love, Phoenix could not have made the arduous journey along that route toward Natchez for the grandson's medicine. Vyry is gifted with a spirit that is just the same. Margaret Walker's character professes:

> God knows I ain't got no hate in my heart for nobody. If I is and doesn't know it, I prays to God to take it out. I ain't got no time to be hating. I believes in God and I believes in trying to love and help everybody, and I knows that humble is the way. I doesn't care what you calls me, that's my doctrine and I'm gwine preach it to my childrens, every living one I got or ever hopes to have. (406)

One remembers the sometimes torturous position of black women during slavery and wonders how those conditions could have nurtured such a doctrine. In the midst of slavery, and for years beyond, there have been solitary women, black and oppressed though they might have been, who where rightfully declared as mothers to a world. We see the situation yet again in Langston Hughes' autobiographical novel *Not Without Laughter*, where the child is raised by a grandmother who offers him this lesson:

> "White peoples maybe mistreats you'n hates you, but when you hates 'em back, you's de one what's hurted, 'cause hate makes yo' heart ugly—that's all it does. It closes up de sweet door to life an' makes ever'thing small an' mean an' dirty. Honey, there ain't no room in de world fo' hate, white folks hatin' niggers, an' niggers hatin' white folks. There ain't no room in this world fo' nothin' but love, Sandy chile. That's all they's room fo'—nothin' but love." (182)

Only pages into the novel, we become aware of that grandmother's altruistic character. A cyclone rages and not long after, she has ventured out to see where she is needed. The narrator informs, "All the neighborhood, white or colored, called his grandmother when something happened" (9). As was the case with Walker's Vyry and Welty's Phoenix, Hughes' old black woman "always came" although, just as with Vyry, "Sometimes they paid her and sometimes they didn't" (10). The capacity for endless love is compensation in itself; it is the only fuel these women need to journey. We can believe what Welty says: whether or not the grandson in her story is alive or dead, it is the memory of love that keeps old Phoenix going.

This process of keeping on is the third important thing that Phoenix epitomizes. It was the white hunter who had warned her, "you take my advice and stay home, and nothing will happen to you" (65). There is enough of an understanding between the hunter and the woman for him to be genuinely concerned; he had helped her off her back and shared a word or two. But he cannot comprehend it all. "You must be a hundred years old, and scared of nothing" (65), he admires. More than likely, the second part of what he says is true; however, the matter of her age is not so simple when we contemplate that she has always been around to do her duty. Whether it be 500 or 97,200 years ago that her initial trek began, the phoenix represents unqualified persistence.

Another white character in the story is caught between comprehension and naivete with regard to Welty's austere grandmother. Clearly, the woman with the Christmas packages has an edge on others; note how Phoenix is able to pick her from the throng. Furthermore, this stranger "gave off perfume like the red roses in hot summer" (65). The signal harkens back to nature, and Phoenix asks, "Please, missy, will you lace up my shoe?" (65). "Can't lace 'em with a cane" (65), that old black woman further emphasizes. A good question to ask is why Phoenix won't just sit down on a bench, release the cane, and tie the shoes herself? That stranger does not think about this possibility; she merely ties the shoes out of respect. Beyond this, it would be too much to ask that the white shopper ascertain the value of the makeshift cane and comprehend why Phoenix will not let it go.

It is only after Phoenix makes it to the doctor's office that she encounters one who is obdurate. "Speak up, Grandma" (66), the white attendant is immediately brusque. She demands to know the older woman's name, but before Phoenix can even answer, the attendant is demanding once again. "What seems to be the trouble with you?" (66). Bothered none at all, Phoenix merely twitches and remains intent on fulfilling her great mission. Just as that attendant is at the point of losing all patience, screaming, "Are you deaf?" (66), the white nurse comes right in to show compassion. "We won't keep you standing after your long trip" (66) she consoles. Even as that nurse prods our traveler with questions about her grandson's condition, she does so with an air of gentleness. "You musn't take up our time this way, Aunt Phoenix" (67) is the most insistent that the nurse will get before Phoenix, with a hint of recognition, finally responds. What Phoenix recognizes is that the nurse is in possession of some understanding of her journey. In what might at first seem to be a matter-of-fact reply, the nurse allows, "Throat never heals, does it?" (67). If the throat has *never* healed, why is it that Phoenix only needs to make the trip but once at the exact same time each year? She actually becomes a symbol for the world to see, a model of determination. And the gesture is not lost, for the attendant who had been unkind before now offers Phoenix money; this in itself does not present solution (recall the nickel Phoenix picked up from the hunter) but it does give hope for the future as it will go toward the purchase of a windmill (or star) upon which wishes can be made.

During the time that Welty's story was created, such hope may well have been a rare commodity. There was no formal integration, and atrocities such as those involving Emmett Till, Michael Schwerner, Andrew Goodman, and James Chaney were yet to come. Mississippi, with its incomparable natural beauty, has been plagued with stigmas far back into time. The city of Natchez, toward which old Phoenix journeys, has itself been belabored with a brutal past.

When the nurse declares to Phoenix, "it's an obstinate case" (67), she does not just mean to say that the grandson's ailment is persistent. One remembers the autobiographical *I Know Why the Caged Bird Sings*, where Maya Angelou tells us the story of a childhood toothache. With the nearest black dentist twenty-five miles away in Texarkana, the burden falls on Annie Henderson, one more black grandmother, to try and get a white dentist to see Angelou right there in Stamps, Arkansas, where the author was being reared. At that white dentist's office, Henderson is insistent but the practitioner responds, "Annie, you know I don't treat nigra, colored people" (159). The grandmother implores again; the dentist says, "I don't treat colored people" (160). Finally the old black woman resorts to calling in a debt, reminding Dr. Lincoln, "seems like maybe you owe me a favor or two" (160), and as the dentist reddens, we conjure up the past. It is the same past Faulkner could not do without, and so he dedicated *Go Down, Moses* to his mammy, Caroline Barr, who incidently lived to be a hundred too. It is a past filled with mammies who had provided for white children better than they did their own, giving love and dedication even when almost every circumstance dictated otherwise. In Welty's story the doctor would probably not, even in that era of house calls, have gone to a black home; furthermore, a black child would probably not have had access to his facility. But still, Phoenix comes to get the medicine and the nurse reminds, "The doctor said as long as you came to get it, you could have it" (67). Phoenix Jackson will continue to come in, her quest far too important to just end. In her essay entitled "Is Phoenix Jackson's Grandson Really Dead?" the artist shifts attention to a mighty cause. "The path is the thing that matters" (162) she has said, and we must suspect that the patient traveler can trod this way until the end of time.

Works Consulted

Angelou, Maya. *I Know Why the Caged Bird Sings.* 1970. New York: Bantam, 1977.
Bartel, Roland. "Life and Death in Eudora Welty's 'A Worn Path.'" *Studies in Short Fiction* 14 (1977): 288–90.
Faulkner, William. *Go Down, Moses.* 1942. New York: Vintage, 1973.
———. *The Sound and the Fury.* 1929. New York: Modern Library, 1956.
Hughes, Langston. *Not Without Laughter.* 1930. New York: Macmillan, 1969.
Isaacs, Neil. "Life for Phoenix." *Sewanee Review* 71 (1963): 75–81.
Lee, Harper. *To Kill a Mockingbird.* 1960. New York: Popular Library, 1962.
Morrison, Toni. *Song of Solomon.* 1977. New York: Signet, 1978.
Moss, Grant. "'A Worn Path' Retrod." *CLA Journal* 15 (1971): 144–52.
"Phoenix." *Encyclopedia Britannica.* 1971 ed.
Rubin, Louis D., Jr. "Flannery O'Connor's Company of Southerners or, 'The Artificial Nigger' Read as Fiction Rather Than Theology." *Flannery O'Connor Bulletin* 6 (1977): 47–71. Rpt. in *A Gallery of Southerners.* Ed. Louis D. Rubin. Baton Rouge: Louisiana State UP, 1982. 115–34.
Walker, Alice. *The Color Purple.* 1982. New York: Pocket, 1985.
Walker, Margaret. *Jubilee.* 1966. New York: Bantam, 1980.
Welty, Eudora. "How I Write." *Virginia Quarterly Review* 31 (1955): 240–51. Rpt. as "Writing and Analyzing a Story." *The Eye of the Story.* Ed. Eudora Welty. New York: Random, 1978. 107–15.
———. "Is Phoenix Jackson's Grandson Really Dead?" *Critical Inquiry* 1 (1974): 219–21. Rpt. in Welty, *The Eye of the Story.* 159–62.
——— "A Worn Path." *Atlantic Monthly* 167 (1941): 215–19. Rpt. in Welty, *Thirteen Stories.* New York: Harcourt, 1977. 59–68.

Joseph H. Gardner

Errands of Love: a Study in Black and White
(1993)

In a justly celebrated essay, first published in *Critical Inquiry,* September 1974, Eudora Welty revealed that the one question she most often receives from both students and teachers who have discussed her well-known and well-loved story "A Worn Path" in their classes is this: "Is Phoenix Jackson's grandson really *dead*?"[1] The rest of the essay is devoted to showing why the

---

[1] Eudora Welty, "Is Phoenix Jackson Really Dead?" *Critical Inquiry* I (1974), 219–221. Subsequently cited as *CI.*

question is irrelevant and why readers' absorption with it deflects from the story's central theme, a theme Welty then discusses with moving eloquence There is, however, another question that can be legitimately asked of the story, a question whose answer reveals much about the concerns of the story itself, the nature of Welty's artistry, and some of the unconscious cultural assumptions that lie behind both: "Why is Phoenix Jackson black?"

For some, the question may be more than a little disturbing, especially if it is taken to suggest some unstated allegation of an underlying racism in a work whose appeal to "liberal" moral and cultural values is, and has been, strong, ever since its appearance in *A Curtain of Green and Other Stories* in 1941. The "liberal" response might well be that this question is also irrelevant, even insulting, both to Welty and to those readers on whom the tale has had a profound effect. Such readers might argue that while Phoenix's age, her frailty, her poverty, and the remoteness of her dwelling are all essential to the development of the story's plot and theme, her race is not. She could just as easily have been a Mexican *campesina*, a Scottish crofter, or a "poor-white" Southern sharecropper for that matter. Neither the power of her love nor the emotional force of the story would be diminished. Such a response is undoubtedly socially correct. It is also critically wrong. For the facts of the matter are that Welty *chose* to make Phoenix Jackson black and that her blackness is an integral part of the story's development and its impact on the reader.[2]

Other readers might respond to the question by saying that Phoenix Jackson is black because the *real* Phoenix was black, citing Welty's assertion that the origin of "A Worn Path" came from an incident in real life: "One day I saw a solitary old woman like Phoenix. She was walking; I saw her, at middle distance, in a winter landscape, and watched her slowly make her way across my line of vision. That sight of her made me write the story" (*CI,* 220). A nitpicker might observe that when Welty states the old woman was "like Phoenix" she is not necessarily indicating that the woman was black, but there is no need to pick such nits. The "real" Phoenix has nothing to do with it. I take it as axiomatic that art is not life and that, because the artistic process involves the constant making of choices, we may legitimately assume that there is a reason for every element in the artifact, a reason that the artifact itself and the circumstances of its production (biographical, cultural,

---

[2] In an interview with Jo Brans, November 1980, Welty acknowledges as much. "I don't think that story would be the same story with a white person." Peggy Whitman Prenshaw, *Conversations with Eudora Welty* (New York: Washington Square Press, 1985), 334–35. Subsequently cited as Prenshaw.

historical and so forth) are expected to provide. We are back again to the central fact that Welty *chose* to make Phoenix Jackson black. The reasoning behind the choice is both conscious and unconscious. It has to do with what Welty has identified as the "subject" of her story, with the mode in which she chose to present that subject, and with many deep-seated, and largely unexamined, attitudes towards blacks in American culture.

In the 1974 essay, Welty is quite explicit in stating the "subject" she wished to set forth. It is, she says, "the deep-grained habit of love" that motivates Phoenix's journey and sustains her through all its uncertainties and dangers (*CI*, 221). Elsewhere in the essay, she characterizes "A Worn Path" as "the story of an errand of love" and indicates that, for her at least, the "truth of the story" is the truth of Phoenix's love as revealed by the "wornness" of her path (*CI*, 220). Welty's language itself reveals that she conceives the story to be concerned with universals, with indeed the greatest universal of them all. It is also clear from her description of the story's origin that, from the very beginning, she wished to write it in such a way as would fully convey and underscore her sense of its universality. The passage quoted earlier continues, "I invented an errand for her, but that only seemed a living part of the figure she was herself; what errand other than for someone else could be making her go? And her going was the first thing, her persisting in her landscape was the real thing, and the first and the real were what I wanted and worked to keep" (*CI*, 220). Just below the surface of Welty's words is the clear intimation that in seeing a solitary old woman slowly making her way across a desolate winter landscape she experienced the sense of having a vision of something archetypal. Deeper below that same surface is the revelation of a series of extraordinary assumptions, most of them involving the race of her protagonist.

The most obvious of these assumptions is that the woman's errand is "an errand of love": "what errand other than for someone else could be making her go?" Such an assumption may be a reflection of a fundamental optimism about human nature and motives, but in the working out of the story itself, it also leads to Phoenix Jackson's blackness. Deeply engrained in American culture is the figure of a middle-aged or older black woman as the most powerful locus of sustaining maternal love and nurture the culture can imagine. Phoenix Jackson is no "Mammy" (even though the white hunter she encounters calls her "Granny"), but she is surely yet another manifestation of the American archetype embodied elsewhere in such figures as Faulkner's Dilsey, Berenice Sadie Brown in McCullers' *Member of the Wedding* or even Lena Younger in Hanson's *A Raisin in the Sun*.

Reference to Faulkner points to another of Welty's unconscious, but nonetheless extraordinary, assumptions. What was "the real thing"—that is, the universal, archetypical thing—in Welty's vision was her sense of the old woman's "persisting in her landscape." Two elements of that sense are worth noting. One is that it predicates Phoenix's blackness in the immediate Faulknerian sense: "They endure." The other is that, like Faulkner, and like America itself, Welty assumes that blacks, somehow or other, are closer to the universal and archetypal—that is, to the mythic—than whites. Indeed, assertions about their persistence and endurance are, in large part, reflections of that potentially racist assumption. And since Welty conceived her story in terms of the universal, the archetypal, and the mythic ("Phoenix rose"), it follows that Phoenix Jackson would be black. Archetype shades into stereotype.

The origin of the stereotype lies in the Rousseauistic myth of the "Noble Savage" as tempered by and acclimated to the ironies of American social history. The subjugation and exploitation of blacks, from slavery to the present, depended (and depends) in part, upon the white conception of them as an "uncivilized," primitive, and therefore inferior race. But that same presumed primitiveness can also be made into a token of superiority. Since it places blacks outside the confines of Western, European "civilization," it thereby frees them from its discontents, especially the burden of loneliness and guilt occasioned by its egotistical empirical rationalism and its acquisitive materialism. Blacks therefore become, in the American imagination, capable of an unselfish, self-sacrificing love inconceivable among "uptight," skeptical and self-centered whites, and closer to the magical powers and forces of a beneficent "Nature."

Expressions of such assumptions range from the banality of Walt Disney's Uncle Remus with cutesy cartoon bluebirds flitting around his head, to the power of Mrs. Stowe's vision of a black Christ crucified between two slaves and her concomitant hope that Liberia will save the world. Uncle Remus's closeness to the "critters" is a function of his inability to speak "civilized," "Standard English"; Mrs. Stowe sees a white world so corrupted by what she calls "the system," (i.e., that cold rationalism and calculating materialism of which the institution of chattel slavery is merely a symptom), that only the rebirth of a purified Christianity in the untainted reaches of exotic, primitive Africa can redeem it.[3] When, in "Livvie," Welty sets out to retell the myth of Demeter, she does so with an all-black cast of characters;

---

[3] See especially George Shelby's "letter to one of his friends" in Chapter XLIII and Mrs. Stowe's own "Concluding Remarks" in Chapter XLV. Harriet Beecher Stowe, *Uncle Tom's Cabin; or Life Among the Lowly* (Boston and Cleveland: John P. Jewett & Co., 1852).

Powerhouse, in the story by that name, is given mythic stature by being portrayed as a man in close touch with the supernatural "powers" of daemonic creativity. In a marvelous exercise in multiple ironies called "The Revenge of Hannah Kemhuff," Alice Walker presents a highly sophisticated and "civilized" young black woman engaged in anthropological fieldwork who helps destroy a hated white by playing upon the white woman's deep-seated belief that black "rootworkers" do indeed have powers beyond the understanding of white skepticism and science.

In her presentation of Phoenix Jackson, Welty draws directly on such cultural assumptions. It is more than a simple matter of her talking to the "critters" or mistaking a scarecrow for a "haint." One notes, for example, such passages as her explanation of her dazed state when she finally reaches the doctor's office: "'I never did go to school. I was to old at the Surrender,' she said in a soft voice. 'I'm an old woman without an education. It was my memory fail me.'"[4] The passage does more than simply verify Phoenix's longevity. For Phoenix to refer to Appomattox and the fall of the Confederacy as "the Surrender" is to transfer it from the historical into a mythic realm and to carry Phoenix, as its namer and rememberer, along with it. She may be "an old woman without an education," but the entire story is devoted to showing her wisdom, a primal folk wisdom uncompromised by the rationalism of the European (i.e., white) Enlightenment and unsullied by the pseudo-sophistication of white technology. Hence her illiteracy is part and parcel of her "persisting in her landscape" as something timeless and elemental. Although she seeks the medicine produced by the white man's science, she herself lives in an animistic, magic realm, where thorn bushes are possessed of volition and birds are divine messengers come to tell her of her peccadilloes (*Stories*, 143 and 146). For her to journey into the white man's city is to move not only into the realm of rationalist science and technology, but also into the realm of a younger, alien, and, ultimately banal, myth: "In the paved city it was Christmas time" (*Stories*, 146). The juxtaposition of "paved" and "Christmas" is perfect for Welty's purposes. Phoenix comes from an older (and hence, by implication, more authentic), more elemental and archetypal world. When the white hunter suspects that she is going to town to see Santa Claus, we are meant to feel the full force of the irony in his patronizing affront to her mythic dignity.[5]

---

[4] Eudora Welty, *The Collected Stories of Eudora Welty* (New York and London: Harcourt, Brace, Jovanovich, 1980), 148. Subsequently cited as *Stories*.

[5] One also notes that the hunter uses his gun—another product of white technology—to kill the creatures Phoenix talks to.

It is not surprising, therefore, that almost all commentators on "A Worn Path," black and white, comment on its mythic patterns and allusions. One black critic, for example, notes that although Phoenix undergoes the "trial" of crossing a stream by means of a fallen log and wanders through the "maze" of the cornfield on her quest for the golden seal on the doctor's diploma in its golden frame, hers is not the story of the initiation of the mythic hero: "Old Phoenix has . . . reached full archetypal potential at the beginning of her story. . . . [She] is in direct communication with 'sunward forces' and with all of nature. . . . Phoenix needs no psychic growth, no initiation; she is possessed of the inner ordering of her existence, devoid of the egocentric, primitive in her ability to love another better than herself, in harmony with external nature, and at the height of her archetypal pattern of greatness."[6] The telling word here, of course, is "primitive"; that is to say, "black." A moment spent considering the phrase beginning "primitive in her ability" will reveal just how extraordinary and telling the assumptions behind it are.

The degree to which the peculiar power of "A Worn Path" depends upon the racial stereotype which associates Phoenix Jackson's blackness with her mythic stature can be seen by comparing it to essentially the same "subject,"—an "errand of love" performed for a sick child. Alice Walker's "Strong Horse Tea," far from striving for the eternal and archetypal, is purposefully grounded in the particular and temporal and told in terms of the most unrelenting naturalism. In Walker's story the protagonist, Rannie Toomer, is a black unwed mother whose baby, Snooks, is dying of pneumonia. Rannie entreats a white mailman to send a doctor from town to the isolated cabin where she lives, but the mailman, frightened by Rannie's blackness, repulsed by her odor and too unconcerned to bother, simply passes the message on to a rootworker who lives down the road. Realizing there is no hope of obtaining a "real" doctor and desperate for her child's survival, Rannie attempts to fill the "witch's" prescription that the child be given "strong horse tea." After chasing a mare through the mud of a rain-soaked field, she finally succeeds in catching its urine in a plastic boot. Plugging a leak in the boot with her mouth, she staggers back toward the house where, the reader knows, her baby lies dead. Speculations about an author's motives are always fruitless, but if Walker had intended systematically to turn Welty's story inside out, she could not have done a more thorough job.

---

[6] Zelma Turner Howard, *The Rhetoric of Eudora Welty's Short Stories* (Jackson, MS: University and College Press of Mississippi, 1973), 71–72.

Comparison of the two works, therefore, will show what happens when an essentially white myth is reinterpreted from the point of view of a black sense of reality.

One might begin with the two protagonist's names. "Phoenix Jackson," in its allusiveness, not only gives us our major clue to its possessor's mythic dimension, but is also pleasantly quaint and rolls euphoniously off the tongue. Welty herself has indicated she chose the name for both reasons (Prenshaw, 56 and 209). "Rannie Toomer," on the other hand, is purposefully ugly and "common," the kind of black name that generates the refined scorn of middle-class whites. One notes that the mailman makes his own assumptions about her name, repeatedly referring to her as "Rannie Mae." That she has named her baby "Snooks" only serves to confirm the reader's response to "Rannie."

Phoenix Jackson exists in a bright, sunlit landscape, stark in its winter outlines, yet sparkling with frost: "the sun made the pine needles almost too bright to look at" (*Stories*, 142). The coronas of light surrounding the objects drawing Phoenix's eye give a sense of divine lustration; the rime on the frozen ground shimmers with dewy magic. There is no enchantment in Rannie Toomer's world, only coldness, wet, and mud. The rain falls against her face "with the force of small hailstones." The elements greet her with the full fury of their hostility: "Thunder rose from the side of the sky like tires of a big truck rumbling over rough dirt road. Then it stood a split second in the middle of the sky before it exploded like a giant firecracker, then rolled away again like an empty keg." Rannie can only huddle, dripping, under a tree, "hoping not to be struck."[7] Similarly, if Phoenix, like Disney's Uncle Remus, talks to the critters, Rannie's separateness from the hostile world of animals and the "animalistic" nature of her impoverished existence are both established in one stroke; "Animals lived there in the pasture all around her house, and she and Snooks lived in it" (*In Love*, 93).

Welty continually emphasizes Phoenix's beauty and dignity. Everything about her is "all neat and tidy," as even her physical appearance serves to reveal her mythic stature: "Her skin had a pattern all its own of numberless branching wrinkles . . . but a golden color ran underneath, and the two knobs of her cheeks were illumined by a yellow burning under the dark. Under the red rag her hair came down on her neck in the frailest of ringlets, still black, and with an odor like copper" (*Stories*, 142). Rannie Toomer, on the

---

[7] Alice Walker, *In Love and Trouble* (New York and London: Harcourt, Brace, Jovanovich, 1973), 96. Subsequently cited as *In Love*.

other hand, is homely, dirty, and wet. Our first glimpse of her in the story's second sentence shows her "gazing into the low fire, her long crusty bottom lip hanging." The mailman thinks she smells "like a wet goat" (*In Love,* 88 and 92).

While, as Welty notes in her essay, Phoenix suffers "some jolts to her pride," she also has "some flights of fancy to console her" and "a moment to dance and preen" (*CI,* 221). In other words, she catches her skirt in a thorn bush, is knocked over by a dog, envisions a child offering her a slice of marble-cake, and waltzes with a scarecrow. Rannie, on the other hand, knows only misery, degradation, and pain. Her only consoling "flight of fancy" is that a doctor is on his way, a fantasy mocked by the older, more experienced rootworker with bitter irony: "'White mailman, white doctor,' she chanted skeptically, under her breath, as if to banish spirits" (*In Love,* 89). If there are spirits in Rannie's world, they are, ironically, human, malignant, and white.

Phoenix's encounter with the white hunter is, perhaps, her moment of greatest danger, danger that begins to dissolve when he treats her with patronizing amusement. Welty skillfully manipulates ironies when the hunter waltzes with Phoenix just as she had earlier danced with the scarecrow—and the ironies all go against the hunter. The scene also allows Welty to add another facet to Phoenix's mythic stature as she becomes B'rer Rabbit the trickster, outwitting and gaining revenge on the oppressor Fox. Her momentary shame at pocketing his nickel is removed immediately when he tells he would give her a dime "if I had any money with me" (*Stories,* 146). The scene prepares us for the ensuing episode when she "stiffly" insists that the office attendant give her another nickel instead of a few pennies (*Stories,* 148–49). Paradoxically, her doing so affirms her dignity rather than denying it.

Phoenix's encounter with the hunter is paralleled in Walker's text by Rannie's encounter with the mailman. Far from being amused by her, the mailman views Rannie only with revulsion. Contemptuous of her dull-witted ignorance, rendered uneasy by her blackness and her bedraggled homeliness, repulsed by the foulness of her breath, and offended by her smell, he hardly wants to dance. Frightened and angered by her desperation, he patronizes her dilemma: "Well, ah, *mighty* sorry to hear 'bout that little fella" (*In Love,* 92). And ultimately he betrays her.

As noted earlier, Phoenix is illiterate, but her illiteracy functions positively to place her in the timeless world of the honored "folk," a world of magic and mythic wisdom. She may seek the white man's medicine, but she herself lives in an animistic world where even a passing bird can serve as a divine messenger sent to scold her (*Stories*, 146). In full touch with natural powers, she becomes the focus of white veneration. Although Welty has denied the tradition that the episode in which Phoenix asks a white Christmas shopper to tie her shoe laces for her is based upon a "real life" incident in which an elderly black made a similar request of her (Prenshaw, 334), the tradition is symbolically appropriate. Throughout the tale one has the sense of something extraordinary taking place: an author kneeling down in her own fiction to pay homage to her own creation.

No one kneels before Rannie Toomer. Like Phoenix, she, too, is illiterate, but her illiteracy reveals only her ignorance, not a fund of folk wisdom. If she is wise, it is only in her rejection of powerworking: "I don't believe in none of that swamp magic. All the old home remedies I took when I was a child come just short of killing me" (*In Love*, 88). Indeed, her desperation in seeking a "REAL doctor" (*In Love*, 91) and her horror at realizing the mailman's betrayal gives the story its heartwrenching power. The whole tale insists upon the bitter irony that Rannie sets out on her "errand of love" for the only remedy she can get. Nor does her illiteracy earn her veneration. The mailman feels nothing but contempt for her inability to understand the advertising circulars that are her only mail. Appropriately enough, however, he himself shares assumptions similar to those that lie behind Welty's story: "He half believed with everybody else in the county that the old blue-eyed black woman possessed magic. Magic that if it didn't work on whites probably would on blacks" (*In Love*, 92).

Finally, Welty insists, both in the tale and in her essay about it, on the purity of Phoenix's "deep-grained habit of love." Although, as Phoenix explains to the nurse, she and her grandson "is the only two left in the world" (*Stories*, 148), it is also clear that the grandson is Phoenix's world. Hence the profoundly moving optimism of both essay and tale:

> The habit of love cuts through confusion and stumbles or contrives its way out of difficulty, it remembers the way even when it forgets, for a dumbfounded moment, its reason for being. The path is the thing that matters.
> (*CI*, 221)

Walker, on the other hand, while equally insistent upon the strength of Rannie's love for her baby and her paradoxical dignity and heroism in sticking desperately to a "path" that drenches her body with cold rain, coats her with mud, and fills her mouth with horse urine, makes that love a matter of more mixed motives: Rannie, she tells us, "was not married. Was not pretty. Was not anybody much. And he was all she had" (*In Love*, 88).

It all boils down to what you know. Walker and Welty first met in the summer of 1973. In her account of the interview, Walker notes that she felt curiously relaxed in Welty's home and wonders if that relaxation "means something terrible," given

> how different we are—in age, color, in the directions we have had to take in this life.... For this *is* Mississippi, U.S.A., and black, white, old, young, Southern black and Southern white—all these labels have meaning for a very good reason: they have effectively kept us apart, sometimes brutally. So that, although we live in the same town, we inhabit different worlds.... Though we are both writers, writing in some cases from similar experiences, and certainly from the same territory, we are more strangers, because the past will always separate us; and because she is white and not young, and I am black and not old (Prenshaw, 145–146).

Accordingly, despite her "relaxation," Walker gives a distinct edge to many of her questions, especially those that implicitly contrast Welty's experiences with those of such black writers as Langston Hughes, Zora Neale Hurston, and Richard Wright. Perhaps the same edge lies behind what, for the purposes of this essay, is her central question: "Over the years have you known any black women? Really known them?" (Prenshaw, 151).

In a sense, Walker had already implied an answer to that question in her remarks about white women and black women necessarily being strangers to each other. It is precisely because Welty is outside the world of black women that she can envisage a Phoenix Jackson in all her mythic grandeur. Walker, writing from inside that world, sees Rannie Toomer in all her heartbreaking reality.

Sample Student Research Paper

Daniel Collins
English 201
Professor Smith
January 30, 1996

   And Again She Makes the Journey:
Character and Act in Eudora Welty's "A Worn Path"

  For almost sixty years, Eudora Welty's "A Worn Path," the tale of Phoenix Jackson, an elderly African-American woman traveling on foot to the city of Natchez to obtain medicine for her sick grandson, has been the subject of much critical interpretation. Critics have speculated on the meaning of the many death and rebirth symbols, including the scarecrow, which the old woman perceives as a ghost; the buzzard who watches her travel; the skeleton-like branches that reach out to slow her; and her first name, Phoenix. From the study of these symbols, several critics have agreed that the theme of the story is some variation on "the path of life" (Walter 49). It is certainly true, as such interpretations imply, that during her journey Phoenix Jackson struggles through difficult terrain and encounters many dangers, and that despite these obstacles, she continues on her quest However, it is neither the quest itself nor the symbols associated with it that is the story's primary focus; what is most important is Phoenix Jackson's character and her act of making the journey.

Background establishes basic view of other writers

Thesis statement

Collins 2

Eudora Welty discusses the characterization of Phoenix Jackson in a videotaped interview. In the interview Welty acknowledges that Jackson's first name refers to a mythical bird that dies and is reborn every five hundred years. She explains, however, that despite her symbolic name, the character is a complex being with human frailties and emotions (Henley).

First major point

Phoenix Jackson has a number of physical frailties that challenge her ability to perform daily tasks. Because of her age, she has failing eyesight, which distorts her perception of the objects she encounters during her journey. For instance, Phoenix mistakes a patch of thorns for "a pretty little *green* bush," and she believes a scarecrow is the ghost of a man (Welty 18). Likewise, her ability to walk is limited, so she uses an old umbrella as a cane; at one point she seems unable even to bend down to tie her shoes. Because of these physical disabilities, readers might expect her to fail in her attempt to reach town, for as Phoenix herself says early in the journey, "The time getting all gone here" (Welty 17). And as the hunter later tells her when he learns where she is going, "Why that's too far!" (Welty 19). So what gives Phoenix Jackson the energy and endurance for the journey? The question can best be answered by looking at the inner qualities of the woman: although Jackson's body is weak, she has great spiritual and emotional strength.

First supporting example

Phoenix Jackson's spiritual strength comes from her oneness with nature and her belief in God. This oneness with nature, claims James Saunders, helps her overcome the environmental dangers that she encounters (90). Because Phoenix Jackson is "a gifted child of nature," her impaired vision, although it slows her down, does not stop her, for as Sanders explains, "mere human vision would not have been sufficient for the journey" (91). Instead of allowing her failing vision to restrict her actions, Phoenix Jackson relies on her spiritual connection with nature; thus, she warns various animals, "Keep out from under these feet" (Welty 16). Additionally, she exhibits her spiritual strength through her belief in God--a quality seen when she refers to God watching her steal the hunter's nickel. *[Second supporting example]*

Phoenix Jackson's spiritual strength is complemented by her emotional strength, for as Elmo Howell notes, Phoenix accepts "the conditions of life" (41). Her love for her grandson forces her to endure any difficulty and to defy any personal danger. Thus, throughout her journey, Phoenix demonstrates fearlessness and selflessness. For example, when the hunter threatens her with his gun, she tells him that she has faced worse dangers. Even after stealing and receiving nickels, she does not consider her own needs, but is inspired to buy something to delight her grandson--a paper windmill. "This is what come to me to do" (Welty 23), she tells the nurse. *[Third supporting example]*

Collins 4

In her video interview, Eudora Welty explains **Second major point** how she came to create Phoenix Jackson--outwardly frail and inwardly strong. Welty tells how she noticed an "old lady" slowly making her way across a "silent horizon," driven by an overwhelming determination to reach her destination; as Welty says, "She had a purpose" (Henley). Welty created Phoenix Jackson in the image of this determined woman. In order to emphasize the character's strength, Welty had her make the journey to get medication for her grandson. Because the act had to be performed repeatedly, the journey became a ritual that had to be completed at all costs. Thus, as Welty explains in her interview, the act of making the journey is the most important element in the story (Henley).

In order to convey the significance of the **Supporting material** journey, Welty focuses her story on the process of the journey. For this reason, readers are given little information about the daily life of the boy and his grandmother, or about the illness for which the boy is being treated. Regardless of the boy's condition--or even whether he is alive or dead--Jackson must complete her journey (Henley). The nurse's statement--"The doctor said as long as you came to get it [the medicine], you could have it" (Welty 22)--reinforces the ritualistic nature of Jackson's journey, a journey that Roland Bartel, a critic who thinks the grandson is dead, suggests is a "subconscious" act (46). Thus, Phoenix Jackson cannot answer the nurse's questions because she does not consciously know what compels her to make the journey. According to Welty, the character's silence and disorientation can also be attributed to her relief upon completing the ritualistic journey (Henley). Despite her difficulties and momentary confusion, Phoenix Jackson accepts time's "cyclic demands on her" (Walter 53) and will undoubtedly again follow the ancient path to Natchez when "the time come around" (Welty 19).

Clearly, the interaction of character (Phoenix Jackson) and act (the ritual journey in search of medication) are the most important aspects of Welty's story. By relying heavily on the characterization of Phoenix Jackson and by detailing the trouble she has during her ritual journey to town, Welty emphasizes how spiritual and emotional strength can overcome physical frailty and how determination and fearlessness can defeat any danger. These moral messages become clear by the time Phoenix reaches the doctor's office. The image of the elderly woman determinedly walking across the horizon, the image that prompted Welty's writing of the story, remains in the minds of the readers, and significantly, it is the final image of the videotaped version of "A Worn Path."[1]

Restatement thesis and review of major points

Summarizing image

                                              Collins 6
                     Note
¹Unlike the written version of "A Worn Path,"
the video of the short story ends not at the
doctor's office but with a vision similar
to the one that inspired Welty to write the
story--the elderly black woman silently walking along the horizon at dusk.

Works Cited

Bartel, Roland. "Life and Death in Eudora Welty's 'A Worn Path.'" Sarcone 45-48.

Henley, Beth. <u>Interview with Eudora Welty.</u> Dir. John Reid and Claudia Velasco. Videocassette. Harcourt, 1994.

Howell, Elmo. "Eudora Welty's Negroes: A Note on 'A Worn Path.'" Sarcone 37-41.

Sarcone, Elizabeth, ed. <u>The Harcourt Brace Casebook Series in Literature: "A Worn Path."</u> Fort Worth: Harcourt, 1997.

Saunders, James Robert. "'A Worn Path': The Eternal Quest of Welty's Phoenix Jackson." Sarcone 86-97.

Walter, James "Love's Habit of Vision in Welty's Phoenix Jackson." Sarcone 48-56.

Welty, Eudora. "A Worn Path." Sarcone 16-23.

<u>"A Worn Path"</u> By Eudora Welty. Dir. John Reid and Claudia Velasco. Perf. Cora Lee Day and Conchita Ferrell. Videocassette. Harcourt, 1994.

Bibliography

Works by Eudora Welty

SHORT STORY COLLECTIONS

Welty, Eudora. *The Bride of the Innisfallen.* New York: Harcourt, 1955.
———. *A Curtain of Green and Other Stories.* New York: Doubleday, 1941.
———. *The Collected Stories of Eudora Welty.* New York: Harcourt, 1980.
———. *The Golden Apples.* New York: Harcourt, 1949.
———. *The Wide Net and Other Stories.* New York: Harcourt, 1943.

NOVELS

Welty, Eudora. *Delta Wedding.* New York: Harcourt, 1946.
———. *Losing Battles.* New York: Random, 1970.
———. *The Optimist's Daughter.* New York: Random, 1972.
———. *The Ponder Heart.* New York: Harcourt, 1954.
———. *The Robber Bridegroom.* New York: Doubleday, 1942.

ESSAYS AND BOOK REVIEWS

Welty, Eudora. *The Eye of the Story: Selected Essays and Reviews.* New York: Random, 1978.
———. *A Writer's Eye: Collected Book Reviews.* Ed. Pearl Amelia McHaney. Jackson: UP of Mississippi, 1994.

CHILDREN'S BOOKS

Welty, Eudora. *The Shoe Bird.* 1964. Jackson: UP of Mississippi, 1993.

Autobiography, Biography, and Interviews

Black, Patti Carr. *Eudora.* Jackson: Mississippi Department of Archives and History, 1984.

Ferris, Bill, ed. *Images of the South: Visits with Eudora Welty and Walker Evans.* Memphis: Center for Southern Folklore, 1977.

Jones, John Griffin, ed. *Mississippi Writers Talking: Interviews with Eudora Welty, Shelby Foote, Elizabeth Spencer, Barry Hannah, Beth Henley.* Jackson: UP of Mississippi, 1982.

Kreyling, Michael. *Author and Agent: Eudora Welty and Diarmuid Russell.* New York: Farrar, 1991.

Laskin, David. *A Common Life: Four Generations of American Literary Friendship and Influence.* Hanover: UP of New England, 1996.

Percy, Walker. "Eudora Welty in Jackson." *Shenandoah* 20 (Spring 1969): 37–38.

Phillips, Robert L., Jr., ed. "III. A Time and a Place." In *Mississippi Writers in Context: Transcript of* A Climate for Genius, *A Television Series.* Jackson: Mississippi Library Commission, 1976. 35–49.

Polk, Noel. "Welty, Eudora: 1909–." *Lives of Mississippi Authors, 1817–1967.* Ed. James B. Lloyd. Jackson: UP of Mississippi, 1981. 459–64.

Prenshaw, Peggy Whitman, ed. *Conversations with Eudora Welty.* Jackson: UP of Mississippi, 1984.

———. "Eudora Welty." *The History of Southern Literature.* Ed. Louis D. Rubin, Jr. Baton Rouge: Louisiana State UP, 1985. 470–75.

———, ed. *More Conversations with Eudora Welty.* Jackson: UP of Mississippi, 1996.

Welty, Eudora. *One Time, One Place: Mississippi in the Depression; A Snapshot Album.* 1971. Rev. ed. Jackson: UP of Mississippi, 1996.

———. *One Writer's Beginnings.* Cambridge: Harvard UP, 1984.

Criticism and Commentary

BOOKS AND COLLECTIONS

Appel, Alfred, Jr. *A Season of Dreams: The Fiction of Eudora Welty.* Baton Rouge: Louisiana State UP, 1965.

Bloom, Harold, ed. *Eudora Welty: Modern Critical Views.* New York: Chelsea House, 1986.

Brown, Julie, ed. *American Women Short Story Writers: A Collection of Critical Essays.* New York: Garland, 1995.

Bryant, J. A., Jr. *Eudora Welty*. Minnesota American Writers Series. Minneapolis: U of Minnesota P, 1968. Rev. and rpt. in *Seven American Women Writers of the Twentieth Century*. Minneapolis: U of Minnesota P, 1977.

Carson, Barbara Harrell. *Eudora Welty: Two Pictures at Once in Her Frame*. Troy, NY: Whitson, 1992.

Champion, Laurie, ed. *The Critical Response to Eudora Welty's Fiction*. Westport: Greenwood, 1994.

Desmond, John F., ed. *A Still Moment: Essays on the Art of Eudora Welty*. Metuchen: Scarecrow, 1978.

Devlin, Albert J. *Eudora Welty's Chronicle: A Story of Mississippi Life*. Jackson: UP of Mississippi, 1983.

———, ed. *Welty: A Life in Literature*. Jackson: UP of Mississippi, 1987.

Dollarhide, Louis, and Ann J. Abadie, eds. *Eudora Welty: A Form of Thanks*. Jackson: UP of Mississippi, 1979.

Evans, Elizabeth. *Eudora Welty*. New York: Ungar, 1981.

Greenberg, Martin, Charles G. Waugh, and Frank McSherry. *Civil War Women: The Civil War Seen Through Women's Eyes in Stories by Louisa May Alcott, Kate Chopin, Eudora Welty, and Other Great Woman Writers*. New York: Simon, 1990.

Gretlund, Jan Nordby. *Eudora Welty's Aesthetics of Place*. Newark: U of Delaware P, 1994.

Gygax, Franziska. *Serious Daring from Within: Female Narrative Strategies in Eudora Welty's Novels*. New York: Greenwood, 1990.

Harrison, Suzan. *Eudora Welty and Virginia Woolf: Gender, Genre, and Influence*. Baton Rouge: Louisiana State UP, 1997.

Howard, Zelma Turner. *The Rhetoric of Eudora Welty's Short Stories*. Jackson: UP of Mississippi, 1973.

Isaacs, Neil D. *Eudora Welty*. Austin: Steck-Vaughn, 1969.

Johnston, Carol Ann. *Eudora Welty: A Study of the Short Fiction*. New York: Twayne, 1997.

Kreyling, Michael. *Eudora Welty's Achievement of Order*. Baton Rouge: Louisiana State UP, 1980.

MacNeil, Robert. *Eudora Welty: Seeing Black and White*. Jackson: UP of Mississippi, 1990.

Manning, Carol S., ed. *The Female Tradition in Southern Literature*. Urbana: U of Illinois P, 1993.

———. *With Ears Opening Like Morning Glories: Eudora Welty and the Love of Storytelling*. Westport: Greenwood, 1985.

Manz-Kunz, Marie Antoinette. *Eudora Welty: Aspects of Reality in Her Short Fiction*. Bern: Francke Verlag, 1971.

Mortimer, Gail L. *Daughter of the Swan: Love and Knowledge in Eudora Welty's Fiction*. Athens: U of Georgia P, 1994.

Prenshaw, Peggy Whitman, ed. *Eudora Welty: Critical Essays*. Jackson: UP of Mississippi, 1979.

———, ed. *Thirteen Essays Selected from* Eudora Welty: Critical Essays. Jackson: UP of Mississippi, 1983.

Randisi, Jennifer Lynn. *A Tissue of Lies: Eudora Welty and the Southern Romance.* Washington, D.C.: UP of America, 1982.

Schmidt, Peter. *The Heart of the Story: Eudora Welty's Short Fiction.* Jackson: UP of Mississippi, 1991.

Skaggs, Merrill Maguire. *The Folk of Southern Fiction.* Athens: U of Georgia P, 1972.

Trouard, Dawn, ed. *Eudora Welty: Eye of the Storyteller.* Kent: Kent State UP, 1989.

Turner, W. Craig, and Lee Emling Harding, eds. *Critical Essays on Eudora Welty.* Boston: Hall, 1989.

Vande Kieft, Ruth M. *Eudora Welty.* 1962. Rev. ed. Boston: Twayne, 1987.

Westling, Louise Hutchings. *Eudora Welty.* Totowa, NJ: Barnes, 1989.

———. *Sacred Groves and Ravaged Gardens: The Fiction of Eudora Welty, Carson McCullers, and Flannery O'Connor.* Athens: U of Georgia P, 1985.

Weston, Ruth D. *Gothic Traditions and Narrative Technique in the Fiction of Eudora Welty.* Baton Rouge: Louisiana State UP, 1994.

Articles

Allen, John Alexander. "Eudora Welty: The Three Moments." *Virginia Quarterly Review* 51.4 (Autumn 1975): 605–27. Rpt. in Desmond 12–34; rev. and rpt. in Champion 254–71.

———. "The Other Way to Live: Demigods in Eudora Welty's Fiction." Prenshaw, *Critical Essays* 26–55. Rpt. in Prenshaw, *Thirteen Essays* 26–55.

Arnold, Marilyn. "'The Magical Percussion': Eudora Welty's Human Recital on Art and Time." *Southern Humanities Review* 23 (Spring 1989): 101–18.

Barbat, Damon L. "Facts of Domesticity in Eudora Welty's Fiction." *Southern Studies* 24.3 (Fall 1985): 326–42.

Belshes, Alan T. "A Treasury Most Dear: The Use of Memory in Eudora Welty's Early Short Stories." *Notes on Mississippi Writers* 20.1 (1988): 9–15.

Binding, Paul. "Mississippi and Eudora Welty." *Separate Country: A Literary Journey Through the American South.* 1979. 131–48. 2nd ed. London: Paddington, 1988. 109–29.

Bolsterli, Margaret Jones. "'Bound' Characters in Porter, Welty, McCullers: The Prerevolutionary Status of Women in American Fiction." *Bucknell Review* 24 (1978): 95–105.

———. "Woman's Vision: The Worlds of Women in *Delta Wedding, Losing Battles,* and *The Optimist's Daughter.*" Prenshaw, *Critical Essays* 149–56. Rpt. in Prenshaw, *Thirteen Essays* 56–70.

Bradford, M. E. "Miss Eudora Welty's Picture Book." *Mississippi Quarterly* 26 (1973): 659–62.

Branson, Stephanie. "Ripe Fruit: Fantastic Elements in the Short Fiction of Ellen Glasgow, Edith Wharton, and Eudora Welty." Brown 61–71.

Brinkmeyer, Robert H., Jr. "An Openness to Otherness: The Imaginative Vision of Eudora Welty." *Southern Literary Journal* 22.2 (Spring 1988): 69–80.

Brookhart, Mary Hughes. "Do You Know This Author? Eudora Welty According to the Handbooks and Histories." *Eudora Welty Newsletter* 16 (Winter 1992): 6–11.

Brooks, Cleanth. "Eudora Welty and the Southern Idiom." Dollarhide and Abadie 3–24.

Bryant, James A., Jr. "Eudora Welty." *Fifty Southern Writers after 1900*. Ed. Joseph M. Flora and Robert Bain. New York: Greenwood, 1987. 516–25.

Bukoski, Anthony. "Facts of Domesticity in Eudora Welty's Fiction." *Southern Studies* 24 (Fall 1985): 326–42.

Burgan, Mary. "The 'Feminine' Short Story in America: Historicizing Epiphanies." Brown 267–80.

Burger, Nash K. "Eudora Welty's Jackson." *Shenandoah* 20 (Spring 1969): 8–15.

Buswell, Mary Catherine. "The Love Relationships of Women in the Fiction of Eudora Welty." *West Virginia University Bulletin Philological Papers* 13 (Dec. 1961): 94–106.

Butters, Ronald R. "Dialect at Work: Eudora Welty's Artistic Purposes." *Mississippi Folklore Register* 16.2 (Fall 1982): 33–39.

Byrne, Bev. "A Return to the Source: *The Robber Bridegroom* and *The Optimist's Daughter*." *Southern Quarterly* 24 (Spring 1986): 74–85. Rpt. in Turner and Harding 248–58.

Caldwell, Price. "Sexual Politics in Welty's 'Moon Lake' and 'Petrified Man.'" *Studies in American Fiction* 18 (Autumn 1990): 171–81.

Capers, Charlotte. "Eudora Welty: A Friend's View." Dollarhide and Abadie 129–35.

Carr, Duane. "Eudora Welty: The Dispossessed as Malevolent Simpleton." *A Question of Class: The Redneck Stereotype in Southern Fiction*. Ed. Duane Carr. Bowling Green, OH: Bowling Green State UP, 1996. 113–123.

Carson, Barbara Harrell. "Eudora Welty's Tangled Bank." *South Atlantic Review* 48 (Nov. 1983): 1–18. Rpt. in *Two Pictures* 29–50.

Carter, Thomas. "Rhetoric and Southern Landscapes." *Accent* 15 (1955): 293–97.

Chaffee, Patricia. "Houses in the Short Fiction of Eudora Welty." *Studies in Short Fiction* 15 (Winter 1978): 112–14.

Chronaki, Bessie. "Eudora Welty's Theory of Place and Human Relationships." *South Atlantic Bulletin* 43 (May 1978): 36–44.

Clark, John R., and William E. Morris. "Ah, Similitudo! Notes on Southern Humor." *Mississippi Folklore Register* 17.2 (Fall 1983): 67–80.

Coldwell, Joan. "The Beauty of Medusa." *English Studies in Canada* 11.4 (Dec. 1985): 422–37.

Cooley, John R. "Blacks and Primitives in Eudora Welty's Fiction." *Ball State University Forum* 14 (Summer 1973): 20–28.

Daniel, Robert. "The World of Eudora Welty." *Hopkins Review* 6 (Winter 1953): 49–58. Rpt. in *Southern Renascence: The Literature of the Modern South*. Ed.

Louis D. Rubin, Jr., and Robert Jacobs. Baltimore: Johns Hopkins UP, 1953. 306–15. Rev. and rpt. as "Eudora Welty: The Sense of Place" in *South: Modern Southern Literature in Its Cultural Setting.* Ed. Louis D. Rubin, Jr., and Robert D. Jacobs. New York: Doubleday, 1961. 276–86.

Davis, Charles E. "Eudora Welty's Blacks: Name and Cultural Identity." *Notes on Mississippi Writers* 17.1 (1985): 1–8.

———. "The South in Eudora Welty's Fiction: A Changing World." *Studies in American Fiction* 3 (Autumn 1975): 199–209.

Dean, Patricia Elder. "Eudora Welty's Onomastic Art." *Places, Pets and Charactonyms. Papers of North Central Names Institute.* Ed. Lawrence E. Seits and Jean Divine. Sugar Grove, IL: Waubonsee Community College, 1982. 90–96.

Devlin, Albert J. "Eudora Welty's Historicism: Method and Vision." *Mississippi Quarterly* 30 (Spring 1977): 213–34.

———. "Eudora Welty's Mississippi." Prenshaw, *Critical Essays* 157–78. Rpt. in Prenshaw, *Thirteen Essays* 98–119. Rev. and rpt. in Devlin, *Chronicle* 3–40.

———. Jackson's Welty." *Southern Quarterly* 20 (Summer 1982): 54–91.

———. "The 'Spell' of Jackson: Eudora Welty's Childhood Stories." *Southern Literary Journal* 21.2 (Spring 1989): 5–16.

Direnc, Dilek. "Eudora Welty on Writing an American Quilt: Justifying Women's Work in the American Literary Canon." *Centennial Review* 40.3 (Fall 1996): 587–600.

Dollarhide, Louis. "Eudora Welty." *Mississippi Short Story Writers.* Jackson: Mississippi Library Commission, 1976. n.p.

Drake, Robert Y., Jr. "Comments on Two Eudora Welty Stories." *Mississippi Quarterly* 13 (Summer 1960): 123–31.

———. "Eudora Welty's Country—and My Own." *Modern Age* 23 (Fall 1979): 403–09.

———. "The Reasons of the Heart." *Georgia Review* 11 (1957): 420–26.

Eichelberger, Julia. "From Medusa to Sibyl: Welty's Art as Cultural Critique." *Mississippi Quarterly* 46.2 (Spring 1993): 299–304.

Eisinger, Chester E. "Eudora Welty and the Triumph of the Imagination." *Fiction of the Forties.* Chicago: U of Chicago P, 1963. 258–83.

———. "Traditionalism and Modernism in Eudora Welty." Prenshaw, *Critical Essays* 3–25. Rpt. in Prenshaw, *Thirteen Essays* 120–29.

Elder, Walter. "That Region." *Kenyon Review* 17 (1955): 661–70.

Evans, Elizabeth. "Eudora Welty: The Metaphor of Music." *Southern Quarterly* 20 (Summer 1982): 92–100.

Felheim, Marvin. "Eudora Welty and Carson McCullers." *Contemporary American Novelists.* Ed. Harry T. Moore. Carbondale: Southern Illinois UP, 1964. 41–53.

Fleischauer, John F. "The Focus of Mystery: Eudora Welty's Prose Style." *Southern Literary Journal* 5.2 (Spring 1973): 64–79.

Flower, Dean. "Eudora Welty Come from Away." *Hudson Review* 38 (1985): 473–80.

French, Warren. "'All Things Are Double': Eudora Welty as a Civilized Writer." Prenshaw, *Critical Essays* 179–88. Rpt. in Prenshaw, *Thirteen Essays* 120–29.

Fuller, Danielle. "'Making a Scene': Some Thoughts on Female Sexuality and Marriage in Eudora Welty's *Delta Wedding* and *The Optimist's Daughter*." *Mississippi Quarterly* 48.2 (Spring 1995): 291–318.

Glenn, Eunice. "Fantasy in the Fiction of Eudora Welty." *A Southern Vanguard*. Ed. Allen Tate. New York: Prentice, 1947. 78–91.

Gossett, Louise Y. "Violence as Revelation: Eudora Welty." *Violence in Recent Southern Fiction*. Durham: Duke UP, 1965. 98–117.

Gretlund, Jan Nordby. "A Neighborhood Voice: Eudora Welty's Sense of Place." *Dolphin* 20 (Spring 1991): 99–107.

———. "Out of Life into Fiction: Eudora Welty and the City." *Notes on Mississippi Writers* 14 (1982): 45–62.

———. "The Terrible and the Marvelous: Eudora Welty's Chekhov." Trouard, *Eye* 107–18.

Griffith, Albert J. "Henny Penny, Eudora Welty, and the Aggregation of Friends." Prenshaw, *Critical Essays* 83–92.

———. "The Poetics of Prose: Eudora Welty's Literary Theory." Desmond 51–62.

Gross, Seymour L. "Eudora Welty's Comic Imagination." *The Comic Imagination in American Literature*. Ed. Louis D. Rubin, Jr. New Brunswick: Rutgers UP, 1973. 319–28.

Hardy, John Edward. "The Achievement of Eudora Welty." *Southern Humanities Review* 2 (Summer 1968): 269–78.

———. "Eudora Welty's Negroes." *Images of the Negro in American Literature*. Ed. Seymour L. Gross and John Edward Hardy. Chicago: U of Chicago P, 1966. 221–32.

———. "Marrying Down in Eudora Welty's Novels." Prenshaw, *Critical Essays* 93–119. Rpt. in Prenshaw, *Thirteen Essays* 71–97.

Harris, Jerry. "The Real Thing: Eudora Welty's Essential Vision." Desmond 1–11.

Harrison, Suzan. "The Other Way to Live: Gender and Selfhood in *Delta Wedding* and *The Golden Apples*." *Mississippi Quarterly* 44 (Winter 1990–91): 49–67.

Hicks, Granville. "Eudora Welty." *College English* 14 (Nov. 1952): 69–76. Rpt. in Turner and Harding 259–67.

Hinton, Jane L. "The Role of Family in *Delta Wedding*, *Losing Battles* and *The Optimist's Daughter*." Prenshaw, *Critical Essays* 120–31.

Hoffman, Frederick J. "Eudora Welty and Carson McCullers." *The Art of Southern Fiction: A Study of Some Modern Novelists*. Carbondale: Southern Illinois UP, 1967. 51–73.

Holder, Alan. "'It Happened in Extraordinary Times': Eudora Welty's Historical Fiction." *The Imagined Past: Portrayals of Our History in Modern Literature*. Lewisburg, PA: Bucknell UP, 1980. 125–46.

Howell, Elmo. "Eudora Welty and the City of Man." *Georgia Review* 33 (Winter 1979): 770–82. Rpt. in Turner and Harding 268–79.

———. "Eudora Welty and the Use of Place in Southern Fiction." *Arizona Quarterly* 28 (Autumn 1972): 248–56. Rpt. in Champion 247–253.
Inge, M. Thomas. "Eudora Welty's Comic Sensibility." *Faulkner, Sut, and Other Southerners: Essays in Literary History.* West Cornwall, CT: Locust Hill, 1992. 163–69.
Isaacs, Neil D. "Four Notes on Eudora Welty." *Notes on Mississippi Writers* 2 (Fall 1969), 42–54.
Jones, Alun. "A Frail Travelling Coincidence: Three Later Stories of Eudora Welty." *Shenandoah* 20 (1969): 40–53. Rpt. in Turner and Harding 181–92.
———. "The World of Love: The Fiction of Eudora Welty." *The Creative Present.* Ed. Nona Balakian and Charles Simmons. New York: Doubleday, 1963. 175–92.
Jones, William M. "Growth of a Symbol: The Sun in Lawrence and Eudora Welty." *University of Kansas City Review* 26 (Oct. 1959): 68–73.
———. "Name and Symbol in the Prose of Eudora Welty." *Southern Folklore Quarterly* 22 (Dec. 1958): 173–85. Rpt. in Champion 173–85.
Kates, Carolyn J. "Apollo and Dionysus: The Mysterious Duality of Eudora Welty's Fiction." *Notes on Mississippi Writers* 22.1 (1990): 1–13.
Kerr, Elizabeth M. "The World of Eudora Welty's Women." Prenshaw, *Critical Essays* 132–48.
Kreyling, Michael. "The Natchez Trace in Eudora Welty's Fiction." *Southern Quarterly* 29.4 (1991): 161–70.
———. "Subject and Object in *One Writer's Beginnings.*" *Mississippi Quarterly* 39 (Fall 1986): 627–38. Rpt. in Devlin, *A Life* 212–24.
———. "Words into Criticism: Eudora Welty's Essays and Reviews." Prenshaw, *Critical Essays* 411–22. Rpt. in Prenshaw, *Thirteen Essays* 224–35.
Landess, Thomas H. "The Function of Taste in the Fiction of Eudora Welty." *Mississippi Quarterly* 26 (Fall 1973): 543–57.
Levy, Helen Fiddyment. *Fiction of the Home Place: Jewett, Cather, Glasgow, Porter, Welty, and Naylor.* Jackson: UP of Mississippi, 1992.
MacKethan, Lucinda H. "To See Things in Their Time: The Act of Focus in Eudora Welty's Fiction." *American Literature* 50 (May 1978): 258–75. Rpt. in *The Dream of Arcady.* Baton Rouge: Louisiana State UP, 1980. 181–206.
Marrs, Suzanne. "Eudora Welty's Photography: Images into Fiction." Turner and Harding 280–96.
———. "Eudora Welty: The Southern Context." *Perspective on the American South* 4 (1987): 19–38.
———. "The Metaphor of Race in Eudora Welty's Fiction." *Southern Review* 22.4 (Autumn 1986): 697–707.
Masserand, Anne M. "Eudora Welty's Travellers: The Journey Theme in Her Short Stories." *Southern Literary Journal* 3 (Spring 1971): 39–48.
McAlpin, Sara. "Family in Eudora Welty's Fiction." *Southern Review* 18.3 (1982): 480–94. Rpt. in Champion 299–311.

McMillan, William. "Circling-In: The Concept of Home in Eudora Welty's *Losing Battles* and *The Optimist's Daughter.*" Desmond 110–17.
Meese, Elizabeth A. "Constructing Time and Place: Eudora Welty in the Thirties." Prenshaw, *Critical Essays* 401–10.
Meyers, Susan L. "Dialogues in Eudora Welty's Short Stories." *Notes on Mississippi Writers* 8 (Fall 1975): 51–57.
Moreland, Richard C. "Community and Vision in Eudora Welty." *Southern Review* 18.2 (Winter 1982): 84–99.
Morris, Harry C. "Eudora Welty's Use of Mythology." *Shenandoah* 6 (Spring 1955): 34–40.
Mortimer, Gail L. "'The Way to Get There': Journeys and Destinations in the Stories of Eudora Welty." *Southern Literary Journal* 19.2 (Spring 1987): 61–69.
Neault, D. James. "Time in the Fiction of Eudora Welty." Desmond 35–50.
Opitz, Kurt. "Eudora Welty: The Order of a Captive Soul." *Critique* 7 (Winter 1964–65): 79–91.
Phillips, Robert L. "A Structural Approach to Myth in the Fiction of Eudora Welty." In Prenshaw, *Collected Essays* 56–67.
Pickett, Nell A. "Colloquialism as a Style in the First-Person Narrator Fiction of Eudora Welty." *Mississippi Quarterly* 26 (Fall 1973): 559–76.
Pitavy-Souques, Daniele. "A Blazing Butterfly: The Modernity of Eudora Welty." *Mississippi Quarterly* 39 (Fall 1986): 537–60. Rpt. in Devlin, *A Life* 113–38 and in Johnston 179–200.
———. "On Suffering and Joy: Aspects of Storytelling in Welty's Short Fiction." Trouard, *Eye* 142–50.
Polk, Noel. "Water, Wanderers, and Weddings: Love in Eudora Welty." Dollarhide and Abadie 95–122.
———. "Welty, Eudora: 1909–." *Lives of Mississippi Authors, 1817–1967.* Ed. James B. Lloyd. Jackson: UP of Mississippi, 1981. 459–64.
Pollack, Harriet. "On Welty's Use of Allusion: Expectations and Their Revision in 'The Wide Net,' *The Robber Bridegroom,* and 'At the Landing.'" *Southern Quarterly* 29.1 (Fall 1990): 5–31. Rpt. in Champion 312–334.
———. "Words Between Strangers: On Welty, Her Style, and Her Audience." *Mississippi Quarterly* 39 (Fall 1986): 481–505. Rpt. in Devlin, *A Life* 54–81.
Prenshaw, Peggy Whitman. "The Antiphonies of Eudora Welty's *One Writer's Beginnings* and Elizabeth Bowen's *Pictures and Conversations.*" *Mississippi Quarterly* 39 (Fall 1986): 639–50. Rpt. in Devlin, *A Life* 225–37.
———. "Cultural Patterns in Eudora Welty's *Delta Wedding* and 'The Demonstrators.'" *Notes on Mississippi Writers* 3 (Fall 1970): 51–70.
———. "Southern Ladies and the Southern Literary Renaissance." Manning, *Female Tradition* 73–88.
———. "Woman's World, Man's Place: The Fiction of Eudora Welty." Dollarhide and Abadie 46–77.
Price, Reynolds. "A Form of Thanks." Dollarhide and Abadie 123–28.

Randisi, Jennifer L. "Eudora Welty and the Fairy Tale." *Southern Literary Journal* 23.1 (1990): 30–44.

Robinson, Clayton. "Faulkner and Welty and the Mississippi Baptists." *Interpretations: Studies in Language and Literature* 5 (1973): 51–54.

Romines, Ann. "How Not to Tell a Story: Eudora Welty's First-Person Tales." Trouard, *Eye* 94–104.

———. "The Power of the Lamp: Domestic Ritual in Two Stories by Eudora Welty." *Notes on Mississippi Writers* 12 (Summer 1984): 1–4.

Rupp, Richard H. "Eudora Welty: A Continual Feast." *Celebration in Postwar American Fiction 1945–1967*. Coral Gables: U of Miami P, 1970. 59–75.

Schmidt, Peter. "Sibyls in Eudora Welty's Stories." Trouard, *Eye* 78–93.

Semel, Jay M. "Eudora Welty's Freak Show." *Notes on Contemporary Literature* 3.3 (1973): 2–3.

Shinn, Thelma J. *Radiant Daughters: Fictional American Women*. Contributions in Women's Studies. Westport: Greenwood, 1986.

———. "The Wheel of Life: Eudora Welty and Gloria Naylor." *Women Shapeshifters: Transforming the Contemporary Novel*. Ed. Thelma J. Shinn. Westport: Greenwood, 1996. 19–40.

Siegal, Carol. "Floods of Female Desire in Lawrence and Eudora Welty." *D. H. Lawrence's Literary Inheritors*. Ed. Keith Cushman and Dennis Jackson. New York: St. Martin's, 1991. 109–30.

Simpson, Lewis P. "The Southern Aesthetic of Memory." *Tulane Studies in English* 23 (1978): 207–27.

Sleeth, Ronald E. "Concepts of Space and Time in the Fiction of Eudora Welty." *Iliff Review* 41.3 (Fall 1984): 31–35.

Smith, Jon. "The Welty Boom!" *Contemporary Literature* 36.3 (Fall 1995): 553–69.

Smith, William Jay. "Precision and Reticence: Eudora Welty's Poetic Vision." Dollarhide and Abadie 78–94. Rpt. in *Ontario Review* 9 (Fall–Winter 1978–79): 59–70.

Spacks, Patricia Meyer. "Gossip and Community in Eudora Welty." In Bloom 155–62.

Sullivan, Walter. *A Requiem for the Renascence: The State of Fiction in the Modern South*. Mercer University Lamar Memorial Lectures. No. 18. Athens: U of Georgia P, 1976. 41–49, 51–58.

Tarbox, Raymond. "Eudora Welty's Fiction: The Salvation Theme." *American Imago* 29 (Spring 1972): 70–91.

Tedford, Barbara Wilkie. "West Virginia Touches in Eudora Welty's Fiction." *Southern Literary Journal* 18 (Spring 1986): 40–52.

Towers, Robert. "Mississippi Myths." Rev. of *The Collected Stories*. *New York Review of Books* 4 Dec. 1980: 30–32.

Trouard, Dawn. "Diverting Swine: The Magical Relevancies of Eudora Welty's Ruby Fisher and Circe." Champion 335–55.

Vande Kieft, Ruth M. "Eudora Welty: The Question of Meaning." *Southern*

Quarterly 20.4 (Summer 1982): 24–39. Rev. as "Further Reflections on Meaning in Eudora Welty's Fiction" in Turner and Harding 296–309.

———. "Eudora Welty: Visited and Revisited." *Mississippi Quarterly* 39 (Fall 1986): 455–79. Rpt. in Devlin, *A Life* 27–53.

———. "Looking with Eudora Welty." Prenshaw, *Critical Essays* 423–44. Rpt. in Prenshaw, *Thirteen Essays* 236–57.

———. "The Love Ethos of Porter, Welty, and McCullers." Manning, *Female Tradition* 235–58.

———. "The Vision of Eudora Welty." *Mississippi Quarterly* 26 (1973): 517–45.

Vaschenko, Alexandr. "That Which 'The Whole World Knows': Functions of Folklore in Eudora Welty's Stories." *Southern Quarterly* 32 (Fall 1993): 9–15.

Wages, Jack D. "Names in Eudora Welty's Fiction: An Onomatological Prolegomenon." *Love and Wrestling, Butch and O.K.* Ed. Fred Tarpley. Publication 2. South Central Names Institute. Commerce, TX: Names Institute P, 1973. 65–72.

Waid, Candace. "Eudora Welty." *Modern American Women Writers.* Ed. Lea Beachler and A. Walton Litz. New York: Scribner's, 1991. 521–38.

Warren, Robert Penn. "The Love and the Separateness in Miss Welty." *Kenyon Review* 6 (Spring 1944): 246–59. Rev. and rpt. as "Love and Separateness in Eudora Welty" in *Robert Penn Warren: Selected Essays.* New York: Random, 1958. 156–69. Rpt. with original title in Turner and Harding 42–51 and in Johnston 158–68.

Watkins, Floyd C. "Eudora Welty's Natchez Trace in the New World." *Southern Review* 22.4 (Autumn 1986): 708–26.

Westling, Louise Hutchings. "Eudora Welty's Sacramental Vision." *The Green Breast of the New World: Landscape, Gender, and American Fiction.* Ed. Louise Hutchings Westling. Athens: U of Georgia Press, 1996. 125–47.

———. "Fathers and Daughters in Welty and O'Connor." Manning, *Female Tradition* 110–24.

———. "The Loving Observer of *One Time, One Place.*" *Mississippi Quarterly* 39 (Fall 1986): 587–604. Rpt. in Devlin, *A Life* 168–87.

———. "Toward a Feminine Sublime." *Gender and Theory: Dialogues on Feminist Criticism.* Ed. Linda Kauffman. Oxford, UK: Blackwell, 1989. 191–212.

Weston, Ruth. "Eudora Welty as Literary Agrarian." *Southern Literary Journal* 28.1 (Fall 1995): 144–48.

———. "Images of the Depression in the Fiction of Eudora Welty." *Southern Quarterly* 32.1 (Fall 1993): 80–91.

———. "Review Essay: Welty Studies in the 1990s." *South Central Review* 14.2 (Summer 1997): 45–55.

Wolff, Sally. "Eudora Welty's Autobiographical Duet: *The Optimist's Daughter* and *One Writer's Beginnings.*" *Located Lives: Place and Idea in Southern Autobiography.* Ed. J. Bill Berry. Athens: U of Georgia P, 1990. 78–92.

———. "Eudora Welty's Nostalgic Imagination." *Since Flannery O'Connor: Essays on the Contemporary American Short Story.* Ed. Loren Logsdon and Charles W. Meyer. Macomb: Western Illinois U, 1987. 45–53.

Yaeger, Patricia, S. "'Because a Fire Was in My Head': Eudora Welty and the Dialogic Imagination." *PMLA* 99 (Oct. 1984): 955–73. Rev. and rpt. in Devlin, *A Life* 139–67 and in Johnston 201–24.

A CURTAIN OF GREEN AND OTHER STORIES, 1941

Bogan, Louise. "The Gothic South." Rev. of *A Curtain of Green. Nation* 6 Dec. 1941: 572. Rpt. in Turner and Harding 17–18 and in Champion 355–36.

Boyle, Kay. "Full-Length Portrait." Rev. of *A Curtain of Green. New Republic* 24 Nov. 1941: 707. Rpt. in Champion 33–34.

Brantley, Frederick. "*A Curtain of Green:* Themes and Attitudes." *American Prefaces* 7 (Spring 1942): 241–51.

Bryant, J. A., Jr. "The Recovery of the Confident Narrator: *A Curtain of Green* to *Losing Battles.*" Prenshaw, *Critical Essays* 68–82. Rpt. in Prenshaw, *Thirteen Essays* 56–70.

Burgess, Cheryll. "From Metaphor to Manifestation: The Artist in Eudora Welty's *A Curtain of Green.*" Trouard, *Eye* 133–41.

Carson, Gary. "The Romantic Tradition in Eudora Welty's *A Curtain of Green.*" *Notes on Mississippi Writers* 9 (Fall 1976): 97–100.

———. "Versions of the Artist in *A Curtain of Green:* The Unifying Imagination in Eudora Welty's Early Fiction." *Studies in Short Fiction* 15 (Fall 1978): 421–28.

Cooley, John R. "Eudora Welty." *Savages and Naturals: Black Portrayals by White Writers in Modern American Literature.* Newark: U of Delaware P, 1982. 124–37.

Fialkowski, Barbara. "Psychic Distances in *A Curtain of Green:* Artistic Success and Personal Failures." Desmond 63–70.

Griffin, Robert J. "Eudora Welty's *A Curtain of Green.*" *The Forties: Fiction, Poetry, Drama.* Ed. Warren French. Deland, FL: Everett, 1969. 101–110.

Kreyling, Michael. "Modernism in Welty's *A Curtain of Green and Other Stories.*" *Southern Quarterly* 20 (Summer 1982): 40–53. Rpt. in Turner and Harding 18–30.

Peterman, Gina D. "*A Curtain of Green:* Eudora Welty's Auspicious Beginning." *Mississippi Quarterly* 46.1 (1992–93): 91–114.

Porter, Katherine Anne. "Introduction." *A Curtain of Green.* Garden City: Doubleday, 1941. ix–xix. Rpt. as "Introduction" to *Selected Stories of Eudora Welty.* New York: Random, 1954. xi–xxiii. Rpt. in *The Day Before.* New York: Harcourt, 1952. 101–08. Rpt. in Johnston 151–57.

"LILY DAW AND THE THREE LADIES"

Drake, Robert Y., Jr. "Comments on Two Eudora Welty Stories." *Mississippi Quarterly* 13 (Summer 1960): 123–31.
McDonald, W. U., Jr. "Artistry and Irony: Welty's Revisions of 'Lily Daw and the Three Ladies.'" *Studies in American Fiction* 9 (Spring 1981): 113–21.
Weston, Ruth D. "American Folk Art, Fine Art, and Eudora Welty: Aesthetic Precedents for 'Lily Daw and the Three Ladies.'" Trouard, *Eye* 3–13.

"A PIECE OF NEWS"

Brooks, Cleanth, and Robert Penn Warren. "Interpretation." *Understanding Fiction*. New York: Appleton, 1943. 143–46. Rev. and rpt. in *Understanding Fiction* 2nd ed. 1959. 128–33. Rev. and rpt. in *The Scope of Fiction*. Ed. Brooks and Warren. New York: Appleton, 1960. 108–113.
Hollenbaugh, Carol. "Ruby Fisher and Her Demon-Lover." *Notes on Mississippi Writers* 7 (Fall 1974): 63–68.

"PETRIFIED MAN"

Arnold, St. George Tucker, Jr. "Mythic Patterns and Satiric Effect in Eudora Welty's 'Petrified Man.'" *Studies in Contemporary Satire* 4 (1977): 21–27.
Berlant, Lauren. "Re-writing the Medusa: Welty's 'Petrified Man.'" *Studies in Short Fiction* 26 (Winter 1989): 59–70.
Capers, Charlotte. "The Narrow Escape of 'The [sic] Petrified Man': Early Eudora Welty Stories." *Journal of Mississippi History* 41 (Feb. 1979): 25–32.
Cochran, Robert W. "Welty's 'Petrified Man.'" *Explicator* 27 (Dec. 1968): item 25.
Helterman, Jeffrey. "Gorgons in Mississippi: Eudora Welty's 'Petrified Man.'" *Notes on Mississippi Writers* 7 (Spring 1974): 12–20.
Jones, Libby F. "The Stories of Welty's 'Petrified Man.'" *Notes on Mississippi Writers* 18.1 (1986): 65–72.
Jones, William M. "Welty's 'Petrified Man.'" *Explicator* 15 (Jan. 1957): item 21.
Kraus, W. Keith. "Welty's 'Petrified Man.'" *Explicator* 29 (Apr. 1971): item 63.
Richmond, Lee J. "Symbol and Theme In Eudora Welty's 'Petrified Man.'" *English Journal* 60 (Dec. 1971): 1201–03.
Ringe, Donald A. "Welty's 'Petrified Man.'" *Explicator* 18 (Feb. 1960): item 32.
Walker, Robert G. "Another Medusa Allusion in Welty's 'Petrified Man.'" *Notes on Contemporary Literature* 9 (Mar. 1979): 10.

"THE KEY"

Harris, Wendell V. "Welty's 'The Key.'" *Explicator* 17 (June 1959): item 61.

"KEELA, THE OUTCAST INDIAN MAIDEN"

Cochran, Robert. "Lost and Found Identities in Welty's 'Keela, the Outcast Indian Maiden.'" *Notes on Modern American Literature* 2 (Spring 1978): item 14.

Coulthard, A. R. "'Keela, the Outcast Indian Maiden': A Dissenting View." *Studies in Short Fiction* 23 (Winter 1986): 35–41.

Fischer, John Irwin. "'Keela, the Outcast Indian Maiden': Studying It Out." *Studies in Short Fiction* 15 (Spring 1978): 165–71.

Hussein, Ayman. "A Freudian Reading of Eudora Welty's 'Keela, the Outcast Indian Maiden.'" *Midwest Quarterly* 31 (Summer 1990): 523–36.

May, Charles E. "*Le Roi Mehaigne* in Welty's 'Keela, the Outcast Indian Maiden.'" *Modern Fiction Studies* 18 (Winter 1972–73): 559–66.

McDonald, W. U., Jr. "Welty's 'Keela': Irony, Ambiguity, and the Ancient Mariner." *Studies in Short Fiction* 1 (Fall 1963): 59–61.

McFarland, Ronald E. "Vision and Perception in the Works of Eudora Welty." *Markham Review* 2 (Feb. 1971): 94–99.

"WHY I LIVE AT THE P.O."

Du Priest, Travis. "'Why I Live at the P.O.': Eudora Welty's Epic Question." *Christianity and Literature* 31.4 (1982): 45–54.

Graves, Nora Calhoun. "Shirtly-T. in Eudora Welty's 'Why I Live at the P.O.'" *Notes on Contemporary Literature* 7 (Mar. 1977): 6–7.

Herrscher, Walter. "Is Sister Really Insane? Another Look at 'Why I Live at the P.O.'" *Notes on Contemporary Literature* 5 (Jan. 1975): 5–7.

May, Charles E. "Why Sister Lives at the P.O." *Southern Humanities Review* 12 (Summer 1978): 243–49. Rpt. in Champion 43–49.

Nissen, Axel. "Occasional Travelers in China Grove: Welty's 'Why I Live at the P.O.' Reconsidered." *Southern Quarterly* 32 (Fall 1993): 72–79.

Whitaker, Elaine E. "Welty's 'Why I Live at the P.O.'" *Explicator* 50.2 (Winter 1992): 115–17.

"THE WHISTLE"

McDonald, W. U., Jr. "Welty's Social Consciousness: Revisions of 'The Whistle.'" *Modern Fiction Studies* 16 (Summer 1970): 193–98.

Yaeger, Patricia. "Edible Labor." *Southern Quarterly* 30 (Winter–Spring 1992): 150–79.

"THE HITCH-HIKERS"

Hardy, John Edward. "The Achievement of Eudora Welty." *Southern Humanities Review* 2 (Summer 1968): 269–78.

Tamir-Ghez, Nomi. "Binary Oppositions and Thematic Decoding in e.e. cummings and Eudora Welty." *PTL: A Journal for Descriptive Poetics and Theory of Literature* 3 (Apr. 1978): 235–48.

Walter, James. "The Fate of the Story Teller in Eudora Welty's 'The Hitch-Hikers.'" *South Central Review* 2 (Spring 1985): 57–70.

"A Memory"

Ginsberg, Elaine. "The Female Initiation Theme in American Fiction." *Studies in American Fiction* 3 (Spring 1975): 27–37.

Gray, Richard J. "Eudora Welty: A Dance to the Music or Order." *Canadian Review of American Studies* 7 (Spring 1976): 57–65. Rpt. in *The Literature of Memory*. Baltimore: Johns Hopkins UP, 1977. 150–52, 174–85, 261.

Lief, Ruth Ann. "A Progression of Answers." *Studies in Short Fiction* 2 (Summer 1965): 343–50.

Prenshaw, Peggy Whitman. "Two Jackson Excursions." *Eudora Welty Newsletter* 2.1 (Winter 1978): 3–4.

"Clytie"

Griffith, Albert J. "The Numinous Vision: Eudora Welty's 'Clytie'" *Studies in Short Fiction* 4 (Fall 1966): 80–82.

Jones, William. "Growth of a Symbol: The Sun in Lawrence and Eudora Welty." *University of Kansas Review* 26 (Oct. 1959): 68–73.

"Old Mr. Marblehall"

Brooks, Cleanth, and Robert Penn Warren. "Interpretation." *Understanding Fiction*. Ed. Brooks and Warren. New York: Appleton, 1943. 479–81.

Coulthard. A. R. "Point of View in Eudora Welty's 'Old Mr. Marblehall.'" *Notes on Mississippi Writers* 8 (Spring 1975): 22–27.

Davis, Charles E. "Welty's 'Old Mr. Marblehall.'" *Explicator* 30 (Jan. 1972): item 40.

Detweiler, Robert. "Eudora Welty's Blazing Butterfly: The Dynamics of Response." *Language and Style* 6 (Winter 1973): 58–71.

Travis, Mildred K. "A Note on 'Wakefield' and 'Old Mr. Marblehall.'" *Notes on Contemporary Literature* 4 (May 1974): 9–10.

"Flowers for Marjorie"

Gretlund, Jan Nordby. "Welty's Photos of New York in the Depression and 'Flowers for Marjorie.'" *Eudora Welty Newsletter* 5.2 (Summer 1981): 4–5.

McDonald, W. U., Jr. "Eudora Welty, Reviser: Some Notes on 'Flowers for Marjorie.'" *Delta* 5 (Nov. 1977): 35–48.

"A Curtain of Green"

Arnold, St. George Tucker, Jr. "The Raincloud and the Garden: Psychic Regression as Tragedy in Welty's 'A Curtain of Green.'" *South Atlantic Bulletin* 44 (Jan. 1979): 53–60.
Brown, Alan. "Welty's 'A Curtain of Green.'" *Explicator* 51 (Summer 1993): 242–43.
Carson, Gary. "The Romantic Tradition in Eudora Welty's 'A Curtain of Green.'" *Notes on Mississippi Writers* 9 (Fall 1976): 97–100.
Tabakowska, Elzbieta. "The Function of Referent-Establishing Relative Clauses in Eudora Welty's 'A Curtain of Green.'" *Litterae et Lingua: In Honorem Premislavi Mroczkowski.* Wroclaw, Pol.: Akad. Nauk, 1984. 193–98.

"A Visit of Charity"

Bradham, Jo Allen. "'A Visit of Charity': Menippean Satire." *Studies in Short Fiction* 1 (Summer 1964): 258–63.
Hartley, Lodwick. "Proserpina and the Old Ladies." *Modern Fiction Studies* 3 (Spring 1957): 350–54.
Kelly, Edward E. "Eudora Welty's Hollow Women." *Notes on Modern American Literature* 6 (Autumn 1982): item 15.
May, Charles E. "The Difficulty of Loving in 'A Visit of Charity.'" *Studies in Short Fiction* 6 (Spring 1969): 338–41.
Palmer, Melvin Delmar. "Welty's 'A Visit of Charity.'" *Explicator* 22 (May 1964): item 69.
Prenshaw, Peggy Whitman. "Two Jackson Excursions." *Eudora Welty Newsletter* 2.1. (Winter 1978): 3–4.
Toole, William B., III. "The Texture of 'A Visit of Charity.'" *Mississippi Quarterly* 20 (Winter 1966–67): 43–46.

"Death of a Traveling Salesman"

Clark, Eleanor. "Old Glamour, New Gloom." *Partisan Review* 16 (June 1949): 631–36.
Dessner, Lawrence Jay. "Vision and Revision in Eudora Welty's 'Death of a Traveling Salesman.'" *Studies in American Fiction* 15.2 (Autumn 1987): 145–59.
Griffith, Albert J. "Welty's 'Death of a Traveling Salesman.'" *Explicator* 20 (Jan. 1962): item 38.

Heilman, Robert B. "Salesmen's Deaths: Documentary and Myth." *Shenandoah* 20 (Spring 1969): 20–28.

Hoberman, Michael. "Demythologizing Myth Criticism: Folklore and Modernity in Eudora Welty's 'Death of a Traveling Salesman.'" *Southern Quarterly* 30.1 (Fall 1991): 23–34.

Jones, William M. "Eudora Welty's Use of Myth in 'Death of a Traveling Salesman.'" *Journal of American Folklore* 73 (Jan.–Mar. 1960): 18–23.

Manning, Carol S. "Welty, Tyler, and Traveling Salesmen: The Wandering Hero Unhorsed." *The Fiction of Anne Tyler*. Ed. C. Ralph Stephens. Jackson: UP of Mississippi, 1990. 110–18.

McFarland, Ronald E. "Vision and Perception in the Works of Eudora Welty." *Markham Review* 2 (Feb. 1971): 94–99.

McGinnis, Wayne D. "Welty's 'Death of a Traveling Salesman' and William Blake Once Again." *Notes on Mississippi Writers* 11 (Winter 1979): 52–54.

Mortimer, Gail L. "'The Way to Get There': Journeys and Destinations in the Stories of Eudora Welty." *Southern Literary Journal* 19.2 (Spring 1987): 61–69.

Piwinski, David J. "The Mule in the Window: The Theme of Sterility in Eudora Welty's 'Death of a Traveling Salesman.'" *Notes on Mississippi Writers* 22.2 (1990): 65–67.

Romines, Ann. "The Powers of the Lamp: Domestic Ritual in Two Stories by Eudora Welty." *Notes on Mississippi Writers* 12 (Summer 1979): 1–16.

Schorer, Mark. "Comment." *The Story: A Critical Anthology*. Englewood Cliffs: Prentice, 1950. 354–57.

Sederberg, Nancy B. "Welty's 'Death of a Traveling Salesman.'" *Explicator* 42.1 (Fall 1983): 52–54.

Vickery, John B. "William Blake and Eudora Welty's 'Death of a Salesman [sic].'" *Modern Language Notes* 76 (Nov. 1961): 625–32.

"POWERHOUSE"

Adams, Timothy Dow. "A Curtain of Black: White and Black Jazz Styles in 'Powerhouse.'" *Notes on Mississippi Writers* 10 (Winter 1977): 57–61.

Albert, Richard N. "Eudora Welty's Fats Waller: 'Powerhouse.'" *Notes on Mississippi Writers* 19.2 (1987): 63–71.

Appel, Alfred, Jr. "Powerhouse's Blues." *Studies in Short Fiction* 2 (Spring 1965): 221–34.

Balliett, Whitney. "Jazz Fats." *New Yorker* 10 Apr. 1978: 110–12, 114–17.

Bates, Jonathan. "Welty's Improvisation of Powerhouse: Is This the Portrayal Fats Would Have Wanted?" *Notes on Mississippi Writers* 22.2 (1990): 81–94.

Cohn, Alan M. "Welty, Waller, and 'Hold Tight': A Footnote." *Notes on Mississippi Writers* 20.2 (1988): 75–77.

Getz, Thomas H. "Eudora Welty: Listening to 'Powerhouse.'" *Kentucky Review* 4 (Winter 1983): 40–48.

Gretlund, Jan Nordby. "Eudora Welty: Early Acrobatics." *Notes on Mississippi Writers* 24 (Jan. 1992): 35–49.

Griffith Benjamin W. "'Powerhouse' As a Showcase of Eudora Welty's Methods and Themes." *Mississippi Quarterly* 19 (Spring 1966): 79–84.

Kirkpatrick, Smith. "The Anointed Powerhouse." *Sewanee Review* 77 (Jan.–Mar. 1969): 94–108.

Lampkin, Loretta M. "Musical Movement and Harmony in Eudora Welty's 'Powerhouse.'" *CEA Critic* 45 (Nov. 1982): 24–28.

Stone, William B. "Eudora Welty's Hydrodynamic 'Powerhouse.'" *Studies in Short Fiction* 11 (Winter 1974): 93–96.

Thomas, Leroy. "Welty's 'Powerhouse.'" *Explicator* 36 (Summer 1978): 15–17.

West, Ray B., Jr. "Three Methods of Modern Fiction: Ernest Hemingway, Thomas Mann, Eudora Welty." *College English* 12 (Jan. 1951): 193–203.

———, and Robert Wooster Stallman. "Analysis: Form Through Theme." *The Art of Modern Fiction*. Ed. Ray B. West, Jr., and Robert Wooster Stallman. New York: Rinehart, 1949. 403–08.

"A Worn Path"

Ardolino, Frank R. "Life Out of Death: Ancient Myth and Ritual in Welty's 'A Worn Path.'" *Notes on Mississippi Writers* 9 (1976): 1–9.

Bartel, Roland. "Life and Death in Eudora Welty's 'A Worn Path.'" *Studies in Short Fiction* 14 (1977): 288–90. Rpt. in Sarcone 45–48.

Brans, Jo. "Struggling Against the Plaid: An Interview with Eudora Welty." Prenshaw, *Conversations* 296–307.

Butters, Ronald R. "Dialect at Work: Eudora Welty's Artistic Purposes." *Mississippi Folklore* 16 (Fall 1982): 33–39.

Butterworth, Nancy K. "From Civil War to Civil Rights: Race Relations in Welty's 'A Worn Path.'" Trouard, *Eye* 165–72. Rpt. in Johnston 225–34 and Sarcone 60–70.

Byrne, Mary Ellen. "Welty's 'A Worn Path' and Walker's 'Everyday Use': Companion Pieces." *Teaching English in Two Year Colleges* 16.2 (May 1989): 129–33.

Cooley, John R. "Blacks and Primitives in Eudora Welty's Fiction." *Ball State University* 14 (Summer 1973): 20–28.

———. *Savages and Naturals: Black Portraits by White Writers in Modern American Literature*. Newark: U of Delaware P, 1982.

Daly, Saralyn R. "'A Worn Path' Retrod." *Studies in Short Fiction* 1 (Winter 1964): 133–39.

Davis, Charles E. "Eudora Welty's Blacks: Name and Cultural Identity." *Notes on Mississippi Writers* 17.1 (1985): 1–8.
Dazey, Mary A. "Phoenix Jackson and the Nice Lady: A Note on Eudora Welty's 'A Worn Path.'" *American Notes and Queries* 17 (1979): 92–93.
Donlan, Dan. "'A Worn Path': Immortality of Stereotype." *English Journal* 62 (1973): 549–50.
Gardner, Joseph H. "Errands of Love: A Study in Black and White." *Kentucky Review* 12 (Autumn 1993): 69–78. Rpt. in Sarcone 97–106.
Hardy, John Edward. "Eudora Welty's Negroes." *Images of the Negro in American Literature*. Ed. Seymour L. Gross and John Hardy. Chicago: U of Chicago P, 1966. 221–32.
Howard, Maureen. "A Collection of Discoveries." A Review of *The Collected Stories of Eudora Welty*. *New York Times Book Review* 2 Nov. 1980: 1, 31–32.
Howell, Elmo. "Eudora Welty's Negroes: A Note on 'A Worn Path.'" *Xavier University Studies* 9 (Spring 1970): 28–32. Rpt. in Sarcone 37–41.
Isaacs, Neil D. "Life for Phoenix." *Sewanee Review* 71.1 (Jan.–Mar. 1963): 75–81. Rpt. in Champion 37–42.
Jones, William M. "Welty's 'A Worn Path.'" *Explicator* 15 (1957): item 57.
———. "Name and Symbol in the Prose of Eudora Welty." *Southern Folklore Quarterly* 22 (Dec. 1958): 173–85.
Keys, Marilynn. "'A Worn Path': The Way of Dispossession." *Studies in Short Fiction* 16 (Fall 1979): 354–56.
Maclay, Joanna. "A Conversation with Eudora Welty." Prenshaw, *Conversations* 268–77.
Mortimer, Gail L. "'The Way to Get There': Journeys and Destinations in the Stories of Eudora Welty." *Southern Literary Journal* 19.2 (Spring 1987): 61–69.
Moss, Grant, Jr. "'A Worn Path' Retrod." *College Language Assn. Journal* 15 (Dec. 1971): 144–52.
Nostrandt, Jeanne R. "Welty's 'A Worn Path.'" *Explicator* 34 (1976): item 33. Rpt. in Sarcone 44–45.
Orr, Elaine. "'Unsettling Every Definition of Otherness': Another Reading of Eudora Welty's 'A Worn Path.'" *South Atlantic Review* 57.2 (1992): 57–72. Rpt. in Sarcone 70–84.
Pingatore, Diana R. "The Worn Path." *A Reader's Guide to the Short Stories of Eudora Welty*. New York: Hall, 1996. 169–82.
Pollack, Harriet. "Photographic Convention and Story Composition: Eudora Welty's Uses of Detail, Plot, Genre, and Expectation from 'A Worn Path' through *The Bride of the Innisfallen*." *South Central Review* 14.2 (Summer 1997): 15–34.
Robinson, David. "A Nickel and Dime Matter: Teaching Eudora Welty's 'A Worn Path.'" *Notes on Mississippi Writers* 19.1 (1987): 23–27. Rpt. in Sarcone 56–60.

Sarcone, Elizabeth, ed. *The Harcourt Brace Casebook Series in Literature: "A Worn Path."* Fort Worth: Harcourt, 1998.

Saunders, James Robert. "'A Worn Path': The Eternal Quest of Welty's Phoenix Jackson." *Southern Literary Journal* 25 (Fall 1992): 62–73. Rpt. in Sarcone 86–97.

Seidl, Frances. "Eudora Welty's Phoenix." *Notes on Mississippi Writers* 6 (Fall 1973): 53–55.

Smith, Evans Lansing. "Eudora Welty." *The Hero Journey in Literature: Parables of Poesis.* Ed. Evans Lansing Smith. Lanham, MD: UP of America, 1997. 446–52.

Trefman, Sara. "Welty's 'A Worn Path.'" *Explicator* 24 (Feb. 1966): item 56.

Walter, James. "Love's Habit of Vision in Eudora Welty's Phoenix Jackson." *Journal of the Short Story in English* 7 (Autumn 1986): 77–85. Rpt. in Sarcone 48–56.

Welty, Eudora. "Artists on Criticism of Their Art: 'Is Phoenix Jackson's Grandson Really Dead?'" *Critical Inquiry* 1 (1974): 219–28. Rpt. in *The Eye of the Story* 157–62 and Sarcone 41–43.

———. ["Comment"] *This Is My Best.* Ed. Whit Burnett. Garden City: Doubleday, 1970. 532.

———. "Must the Novelist Crusade?" *Atlantic* Oct. 1965: 265–74. Rpt. in *The Eye of the Story* 141–58. Rpt. in Sarcone 28–37.

THE ROBBER BRIDEGROOM, 1942

Akin, Warren, IV. "*The Robber Bridegroom:* An Oedipal Tale of the Natchez Trace." *Literature and Psychology* 30.3–4 (1980): 112–18.

Arnold, Marilyn. "Eudora Welty's Parody." *Notes on Mississippi Writers* 11 (Spring 1978): 15–22. Rpt. in Turner and Harding 32–38.

Bishop, John Peale. "The Violent Country." *New Republic* 16 Nov. 1942: 646–47. Rpt. in *The Collected Essays of John Peale Bishop.* Ed. Edmund Wilson. New York: Scribners, 1948. 257–59. Also rpt. in Champion 53–54.

Brown, Ashley. "Eudora Welty and the Mythos of Summer." *Shenandoah* 20 (Spring 1969): 29–35.

Carson, Barbara Harrell. "Eudora Welty's Dance with Darkness: *The Robber Bridegroom.*" *Southern Literary Journal* 20.2 (Spring 1988): 51–68. Rpt. in Champion 64–81. Rev. and rpt. in *Two Pictures* 51–71.

Clark, Charles C. "*The Robber Bridegroom:* Realism and Fantasy on the Natchez Trace." *Mississippi Quarterly* 26 (Fall 1973): 625–38.

Cook, Bernard. "Ritual Abduction in Early Mississippi." *Mississippi Quarterly* 36 (Winter 1982–83): 72–73.

Davis, Charles E. "Eudora Welty's *The Robber Bridegroom* and Old Southwest Humor: A Doubleness of Vision." Desmond 71–81.

Ellis, Nancy S. "Kickin' Up Dust on the Natchez Trace." *POMPA.* 1993: 13–21.

French, Warren. "'All Things Are Double': Eudora Welty as a Civilized Writer." Prenshaw, *Critical Essays* 179–88.
Graulich, Melody. "Pioneering the Imagination: Eudora Welty's *The Robber Bridegroom.*" *Women and Western American Literature.* Ed. Helen Winter Stauffer and Susan J. Rosowski. Troy, NY: Whitson, 1982. 283–96.
Hattenhauer, Darryl. "Absurdism and Dark Humor in Welty's *The Robber Bridegroom.*" *University of Mississippi Studies in English* 10 ns (1992): 167–69.
———. "Welty's *The Robber Bridegroom.*" *South Dakota Review* 30.4 (Winter 1992): 98–111.
Kreyling, Michael. "Clement and the Indians: Pastoral and History in *The Robber Bridegroom.*" Dollarhide and Abadie 25–45. Rev. and rpt. in *Achievement* 32–51.
Miller, Lisa K. "The Dark Side of Our Frontier Heritage: Eudora Welty's Use of the Turner Thesis in *The Robber Bridegroom.*" *Notes in Mississippi Writers* 14 (1981): 18–26.
Randisi, Jennifer. "Eudora Welty's *The Robber Bridegroom* as American Romance." *Mid-Hudson Language Studies* 3 (1980): 101–15.
Skaggs, Merrill Maguire. "The Uses of Enchantment in Frontier Humor and *The Robber Bridegroom.*" *Studies in American Humor* 3 (Oct. 1976): 96–102. Rpt. in Champion 57–63.
Slethaug, Gordon E. "Initiation in Eudora Welty's *The Robber Bridegroom.*" *Southern Humanities Review* 7 (Winter 1973): 77–87.
Smith, Carol. "The Journey Motif in Eudora Welty's *The Robber Bridegroom.*" *Shippensburg State College Review,* Shippensburg [PA] State College, 1973: 18–32.
Theodosiadou, Youli. "Welty Meets Bakhtin: Some Elements of the Carnivalesque in *The Robber Bridegroom.*" *Year Book of the English Department* [Thessaloniki Aristotle University] 3 (1993): 311–17.
Trilling, Lionel. "American Fairy Tale." *Nation* 19 Dec. 1942: 686–87. Rpt. in Turner and Harding 31–32 and in Champion 55–56.
Walker, Ellen L., and Gerda Seaman. "*The Robber Bridegroom* as a Capitalistic Fable." *Southern Quarterly* 26.4 (1988): 57–68.
Wilson, Deborah. "The Altering/Alterity of History in Eudora Welty's *The Robber Bridegroom.*" *Southern Quarterly* 32 (Fall 1993): 62–71.

THE WIDE NET AND OTHER STORIES, 1943

Davenport, F. Gavin, Jr. "Renewal and Historical Consciousness in *The Wide Net.*" Prenshaw, *Critical Essays* 189–200.
Donaldson, Susan V. "Meditations on Nonpresence: Re-Visioning the Short Story in Eudora Welty's *The Wide Net.*" *Journal of the Short Story in English* 11 (Autumn 1988): 75–91. Rpt. in *Modern American Short Story Sequences: Composite Fictions and Fictive Communities.* Ed. J. Gerald Kennedy. Cambridge: Cambridge UP, 1995. 98–113.

Rosenfield, Isaac. "Consolations of Poetry." *New Republic* 18 Oct. 1943: 525–26. Rpt. in Champion 89–90.

Trilling, Diana. "Fiction in Review." *Nation* 2 Oct. 1943: 386–87. Rpt. in Turner and Harding 39–42 and in Champion 85–88.

"First Love"

Arnold, Marilyn. "Somnambulism in San Francisco: Eudora Welty's Western Story." *Southern Quarterly* 27 (Summer 1989): 16–24.

Arnold, St. George Tucker, Jr. "Eudora Welty's 'First Love' and the Personalizing of Southern Regional History." *Journal of Regional Cultures* 1 (Fall–Winter 1981): 97–105.

Devlin, Albert J. "Eudora Welty's Historicism: Method and Vision." *Mississippi Quarterly* 30 (Spring 1977): 213–24.

Marrs, Suzanne. "The Conclusion of Eudora Welty's 'First Love': Historical Backgrounds." *Notes on Mississippi Writers* 13 (1981): 73–78.

McFarland, Ronald E. "Vision and Perception in the Works of Eudora Welty." *Markham Review* 2 (Feb. 1971): 94–99.

Thompson, Victor H. "Aaron Burr in Eudora Welty's 'First Love.'" *Notes on Mississippi Writers* 8 (Winter 1976): 75–83.

Warner, John M. "Eudora Welty: The Artist in 'First Love.'" *Notes on Mississippi Writers* 9 (Fall 1976): 77–87.

"The Wide Net"

Arnold, St. George Tucker, Jr. "The Dragon in the Delta: The Hero Archetype in Eudora Welty's 'The Wide Net.'" *Journal of Evolutionary Psychology* 4 (Aug. 1983): 133–44.

Bolsterli, Margaret. "A Fertility Rite in Mississippi." *Notes on Mississippi Writers* 8 (Fall 1975): 69–71.

Cluck, Nancy Anne. "*The Aeneid* of the Natchez Trace: Epic Structure in Eudora Welty's 'The Wide Net.'" *Southern Review* 19 (Summer 1983): 510–18.

Orr, Linda. "The Duplicity of the Southern Story: Reflections on Reynolds Price's *The Surface of Earth* and Eudora Welty's 'The Wide Net.'" *South Atlantic Quarterly* 91 (Winter 1992): 111–37. Rpt. in *Eloquent Obsession: Writing Cultural Criticism*. Ed. Marianna Torgovnick. Durham: Duke UP, 1994. 50–75.

"A Still Moment"

Cluck, Nancy Anne. "Audubon: Images of the Artist in Eudora Welty and Robert Penn Warren." *Southern Literary Journal* 17 (Spring 1985): 41–53.

Corrigan, Lesa Carnes. "Snapshots of Audubon: Photographic Perspectives from

Eudora Welty and Robert Penn Warren." *Mississippi Quarterly* 48.1 (Winter 1994–95): 83–91.

Curley, Daniel. "Eudora Welty and the Quondam Obstruction." *Studies in Short Fiction* 5 (Spring 1968): 209–24.

Davenport, F. Garvin. "Renewal and Historical Consciousness in *The Wide Net*. Prenshaw, *Critical Essays* 189–200.

Devlin, Albert J. "Eudora Welty's Historicism: Method and Vision." *Mississippi Quarterly* 30 (Spring 1977): 213–34. Rpt. in *Chronicle* 41–79.

———. "From Horse to Heron: A Source for Eudora Welty" *Notes on Mississippi Writers* 10 (Winter 1977): 62–68.

Gibley, Kevin Charles. "'Half-Concealed and Half-Sought For': Eudora Welty's 'A Still Moment' as Aesthetic Allegory." *Journal of the Short Story in English* 18 (1992): 43–51.

Jolly, John. "The Schillerian Dialectic and Eudora Welty's 'A Still Moment.'" *Notes on Mississippi Writers* 15 (1983): 65–71.

Marrs, Suzanne. "Eudora Welty's Snowy Heron." *American Literature* 53 (Jan. 1982): 723–25.

———. "John James Audubon in Fiction and Poetry: Literary Portraits by Eudora Welty and Robert Penn Warren." *Southern Studies* 20 (Winter 1981): 378–83.

McHaney, Pearl Amelia. "Eudora Welty's Snowy Heron." *American Literature* 53 (Jan. 1982): 723–25.

———. "Historical Perspectives in 'A Still Moment.'" In Turner and Harding 52–69.

Prenshaw, Peggy Whitman. "Coates' *The Outlaw Years* and Welty's 'A Still Moment.'" *Notes on Modern American Literature* 2 (Spring 1978): item 17.

Rosenblum, Joseph. "A New England Heron on the Natchez Trace: Sarah Orne Jewett's 'A White Heron' as Possible Source for Eudora Welty's 'A Still Moment'" *Notes on Mississippi Writers* 22.2 (1990): 69–74.

Thompson, Victor H. "The Natchez Trace in Eudora Welty's 'A Still Moment.'" *Southern Literary Journal* 6 (Fall 1973): 59–69.

"ASPHODEL"

Cole, Hunter M. "Windsor in Spencer and Welty: A Real and an Imaginary Landscape." *Notes on Mississippi Writers* 7 (Spring 1974): 2–11.

Hodgins, Audrey. "The Narrator as Ironic Device in a Short Story of Eudora Welty." *Twentieth Century Literature* 1 (Jan. 1956): 215–19.

Phillips, K. J. "Maligning the God: The Case Against Hades." *Dying Gods in Twentieth-Century Fiction*. Lewisburg, PA: Bucknell UP. 179–202.

"THE WINDS"

Manning, Carol S. "Little Girls and Sidewalks: Glasgow and Welty on Childhood's Promise." *Southern Quarterly* 21 (Spring 1983): 67–76.

"Livvie"

Henley, Elton F. "Confinement-Escape Symbolism in Eudora Welty's 'Livvie.'" *Iowa English Yearbook* 10 (Fall 1965): 60–63.
Kloss, Robert J. "The Symbolic Structure of Eudora Welty's 'Livvie.'" *Notes on Mississippi Writers* 7 (Winter 1975): 70–82.
Prenshaw, Peggy Whitman. "Persephone in Eudora Welty's 'Livvie.'" *Studies in Short Fiction* 17.2 (Spring 1980): 149–55. Rpt. in Champion 91–97.
Smith, Julian. "'Livvie'—Eudora Welty's Song of Solomon." *Studies in Short Fiction* 5 (Fall 1967): 73–74.

"At the Landing"

Arnold, St. George Tucker, Jr. "Woman's Psyche and the Archetypal Odyssey: First Voyaging in Eudora Welty's 'At the Landing.'" *Journal of Evolutionary Psychology* 8.3–4 (Aug. 1987): 330–40.
Brookhart, Mary Hughes, and Suzanne Marrs. "More Notes on River Country." *Mississippi Quarterly* 39 (Fall 1986): 507–19. Rpt. in Devlin, *A Life* 82–95.
Ferguson, Mary Anne. "The Female Novel of Development and the Myth of Psyche." *Denver Quarterly* 17.4 (Winter 1983): 58–74.
Ginsberg, Elaine. "The Female Initiation Theme in American Fiction." *Studies in American Fiction* 3 (Spring 1975): 27–37.

Delta Wedding, 1946

Basso, Hamilton. "Look Away, Look Away, Look Away." *New Yorker* 11 May 1946: 89. Rpt. in Champion 106–07.
Bookhart, Mary Alice. "Eudora Welty." *The Clarion-Ledger* 28 Apr. 1946: 8. Rpt. in Champion 101–02.
Bradford, M. E. "Fairchild as Composite Protagonist in *Delta Wedding*." Prenshaw, *Critical Essays* 201–07.
Cannon, Kelly D. "The Power of Silence in *Delta Wedding*." *University of Mississippi Studies in English* 8 (1990): 127–36.
Childers, Joseph W. "Character and Context: The Paradox of the Family Myth in Eudora Welty's *Delta Wedding*." *Essays in Literature* 14.2 (Fall 1987): 241–50.
Devlin, Albert J. "The Making of *Delta Wedding*: Or, Doing 'Something Diarmuid Thought I Could Do.'" *Biographies of Books: The Compositional Histories of Notable American Writers*. Ed. James Barber and Tom Quirk. Columbia: U of Missouri P, 1996. 226–61.
Devlin, Albert J. "Meeting the World in *Delta Wedding*." In Turner and Harding 90–109.
———. "Modernity and the Literary Plantation: Eudora Welty's *Delta Wedding*." *Mississippi Quarterly* 43 (Spring 1990): 163–72.

Donaldson, Susan. "Gender and History in Eudora Welty's *Delta Wedding*." *South Central Review* 14.2 (Summer 1997): 3–14.
Fabricant, Dan. "Onions and Hyacinths: Unwrapping the Fairchilds in *Delta Wedding*." *Southern Literary Journal* 18.1 (Fall 1985): 50–60.
Glenn, Sharlee Mullins. "In and Out of the Circle: The Individual and the Clan in Eudora Welty's *Delta Wedding*." *Southern Literary Journal* 22.1 (Fall 1989): 50–60.
Goeller, Allison Deming. "*Delta Wedding* as Pastoral." *Interpretations: A Journal of Ideas, Analyses and Criticism* 13 (Fall 1981): 59–72.
Gray, Richard J. "Eudora Welty: A Dance to the Music of Order." *Canadian Review of American Studies* 7 (Spring 1976): 57–65. Rpt. in *The Literature of Memory*. Baltimore: Johns Hopkins UP, 1977. 174–84.
Griffin, Dorothy. "The House as Container: Architecture and Myth in Eudora Welty's *Delta Wedding*." *Mississippi Quarterly* 39 (Fall 1986): 521–35. Rpt. in Devlin, *A Life* 96–112.
Harder, Louise M. "How Eudora Welty Speaks to Us Through Her Use of Names in *Delta Wedding*." *Literary Onomastics Studies* 10 (1983): 133–46.
Hardy, John Edward. "*Delta Wedding* as Region and Symbol." *Sewanee Review* 60 (Summer 1952): 397–417. Rpt. in *Man in the Modern Novel*. Seattle: U of Washington P, 1964. Also rpt. in Turner and Harding 75–89.
Howell, Elmo. Eudora Welty's "Comedy of Manners." *South Atlantic Quarterly* 69 (Autumn 1970): 469–79.
———. "Eudora Welty and the Poetry of Names: A Note on *Delta Wedding*." *Love and Wrestling, Butch and O.K.* Ed. Fred Tarpley. Publication 2. South Central Names Institute. Commerce, TX: Names Institute Press, 1973. 73–78.
Krause, Florence Phyfer. "Emasculating Women in *Delta Wedding*." *Publications of the Missouri Philological Association* 1 (1976): 48–57.
Ladd, Barbara. "'Coming Through': The Black Initiate in *Delta Wedding*." *Mississippi Quarterly* 41 (Fall 1988): 541–51.
Leonard, J. S. "*Delta Wedding*: Eudora Welty's Plunge into Freudian Symbolism." *West Virginia University Philological Papers* 34 (1988): 110–17.
Marrs, Suzanne. "'The Treasure Most Dearly Regarded': Memory and Imagination in *Delta Wedding*." *Southern Literary Journal* 25.2 (1993): 79–91.
Messerli, Douglas. "The Problem of Time in Welty's *Delta Wedding*." *Studies in American Fiction* 5 (Autumn 1977): 227–40. Rpt. in Champion 108–21.
Moore, Carol A. "Aunt Studney's Sack." *Southern Review* 16 (Summer 1980): 591–96.
Ransom, John Crowe. "Delta Fiction." *Kenyon Review* 8 (Summer 1946): 503–07. Rpt. in Turner and Harding 71–75.
Rosenfeld, Isaac. "Double Standard." *New Republic* 29 Apr. 1946: 633–34.
Sprengnether, Madelon. "*Delta Wedding* and the Kore Complex." *Southern Quarterly* 25 (Winter 1987): 120–30.
Trilling, Diana. "Fiction in Review." *Nation* 11 May 1946: 578. Rpt. in Champion 103–05.

Wall, Carey. "Eudora Welty's *Delta Wedding* and Victor Turner's 'Liminality.'" *Southern Studies* 25 (Fall 1986): 220–34.
Westling, Louise. "Demeter and Kore, Southern Style." *Pacific Coast Philology* 19 (Nov. 1984): 101–07.
———. "Food, Landscape and the Feminine in *Delta Wedding*." *Southern Quarterly* 30.2–3 (1992): 29–40.
Yakimenko, Natalia. "Idyllic Chronotope in *Delta Wedding*." *Southern Quarterly* 32 (Fall 1993): 21–26.

THE GOLDEN APPLES, 1949

Blackwell, Louise. "Eudora Welty: Proverbs and Proverbial Phrases in *The Golden Apples*." *Southern Folklore Quarterly* 30 (Dec. 1966): 332–41.
Bowen, Elizabeth. "*The Golden Apples*." *Seven Winters: Memories of a Dublin Childhood and Afterthoughts: Pieces on Writing*. New York: Knopf, 1962. 215–18.
Bryant, J. A., Jr. "Seeing Double in *The Golden Apples*." *Sewanee Review* 82 (Spring 1974): 300–15. Rpt. in Turner and Harding 142–53.
Cannon, Lee E. "Main Street in Dixie." *The Christian Century* 7 Sept. 1949: 1039–40. Rpt. in Champion 125–26.
Carson, Franklin D. *Eudora Welty's* The Golden Apples *and the Problem of the Collection–Novel*. Chicago. 1971.
———. "Recurring Metaphors: An Aspect of Unity in *The Golden Apples*." *Notes on Contemporary Literature* 5 (Sept. 1975): 4–7.
———. "'The Song of Wandering Aengus': Allusions in Eudora Welty's *The Golden Apples*." *Notes on Mississippi Writers* 6 (Spring 1973): 14–17.
Demmin, Julia L., and Daniel Curley. "Golden Apples and Silver Apples." Prenshaw, *Critical Essays* 242–57. Rpt. in Prenshaw, *Thirteen* 130–45.
Devoize, Jeanne. "Some Narrative Variations in Eudora Welty's *The Golden Apples*." *Journal of the Short Story in English* 18 (Spring 1992): 53–62.
Donaldson, Susan V. "Recovering Otherness in *The Golden Apples*." *American Literature* 63.3 (Sept. 1991): 489–506.
Fritz-Piggot, Jill. "'The Sword and the Song:' Moments of Intensity in *The Golden Apples*." *Southern Literary Journal* 18.2 (Spring 1986): 27–39.
Gerlach, John. "Faulkner's *Unvanquished* and Welty's *Golden Apples:* The Boundaries of Story, Cycle, and Novel." *Short Story* 2.2 (Winter–Spring 1992): 51–62.
Hankins, Leslie Kathleen. "Alas, Alack! or A Lass, a Lack? Quarrels of Gender and Genre in the Revisionist *Kunstlerroman:* Eudora Welty's *The Golden Apples*." *Mississippi Quarterly* 44 (Fall 1991): 391–409.
Harris, Wendell V. "'The Thematic Unity of Welty's *The Golden Apples*." *Texas Studies in Literature and Language* 6 (Spring 1964): 92–95. Rpt. in Champion 131–34.

Hurst, Mary Jane. "Fire Imagery." *PMLA* 100 (Mar. 1985): 236–37.
Jones, William M. "The Plot as Search." *Studies in Short Fiction* 5 (Fall 1967): 37–43.
Kreyling, Michael. "The Reginald Burch Illustration in *The Golden Apples*." *Eudora Welty Newsletter* 1 (Winter 1977): 3–5.
Ladd, Barbara. "'Too Positive a Shape Not to Be Hurt': *Go Down, Moses*, History and the Woman Artist in Eudora Welty's *The Golden Apples*." *Bucknell Review* 39.1 (1995): 79–103.
McHaney, Thomas L. "Eudora Welty and the Multitudinous Golden Apples." *Mississippi Quarterly* 26 (Fall 1973): 589–624. Rpt. in Turner and Harding 113–41.
———. "Falling into Cycles: *The Golden Apples*." Trouard, *Eye* 173–89.
Mark, Rebecca. *The Dragon's Blood: Feminist Intertextuality in Eudora Welty's* The Golden Apples." Jackson: UP of Mississippi, 1994.
Marshall, Margaret. "Notes by the Way." *Nation* 10 Sept. 1949: 256. Rpt. in Champion 127–28 and in Turner and Harding 111–12.
Messerli, Douglas. "Metronome and Music: The Encounter Between History and Myth in *The Golden Apples*." Desmond 82–102.
Morris, H. C. "Zeus and the Golden Apples: Eudora Welty." *Perspective* 5 (Autumn 1952): 190–99.
Mortimer, Gail L. "Memory, Despair, and Welty's MacLain Twins." *South Central Review* 14.2 (Summer 1997): 35–44.
Pawlowski, Robert S. "The Process of Observation: *Winesburg, Ohio* and *The Golden Apples*." *University Review* 37 (June 1971): 292–98.
Pei, Lowry. "Dreaming the Other in *The Golden Apples*." *Modern Fiction Studies* 28 (Autumn 1982): 415–33.
Phillips, Robert L., Jr. *An Introduction to Eudora Welty's* The Golden Apples. Jackson: Mississippi Library Commission, 1977.
Pingree, Allison. "The Circles of Ran and Eugene MacLain: Welty's Twin Plots in *The Golden Apples*." *The Significance of Sibling Relationships in Literature*. Ed. JoAnna Stephens Mink and Janet Doubler Ward. Bowling Green: Popular, 1992. 83–97.
Pitavy-Souques, Daniele. "Technique as Myth: The Structure of *The Golden Apples*." Prenshaw, *Critical Essays* 258–68. Rpt. in Prenshaw, *Thirteen* 146–56.
Pugh, Elaine Upton. "The Duality of Morgana: The Making of Virgie's Vision, The Vision of *The Golden Apples*." *Modern Fiction Studies* 28 (Autumn 1982): 435–51.
Rubin, Louis D., Jr. "Art and Artistry in Morgana, Mississippi." *Missouri Review* 4 (Summer 1981): 101–16. Rpt. in *A Gallery of Southerners*. Baton Rouge: Louisiana State UP, 1982. 49–66.
———. "The Golden Apples of the Sun." *The Faraway Country*. Seattle: U of Washington P, 1963. 131–54.

Skaggs, Merrill Maguire. "Eudora Welty's 'I' of Memory." In Turner and Harding 153–65.

———. "Morgana's Apples and Pears." Prenshaw, *Critical Essays* 220–41.

Yaeger, Patricia S. "'Because a Fire Was in My Head': Eudora Welty and the Dialogic Imagination." *PMLA* 99 (Oct. 1984): 955–73. Rev. and rpt. in *Mississippi Quarterly* 39 (Fall 1986): 561–86; in Devlin, *A Life* 139–67; and in Johnston 201–24.

"JUNE RECITAL"

Arnold, Marilyn. "When Gratitude Is No More: Eudora Welty's 'June Recital.'" *South Carolina Review* 13 (Spring 1981): 62–72.

Caminero-Santangelo, Marta. "The Madwoman Can't Speak: Postwar Culture, Feminist Criticism, and Welty's 'June Recital.'" *Tulsa Studies in Women's Literature* 15 (Spring 1996): 123–46.

Corcoran, Neil. "The Face That Was in the Poem: Art and 'Human Truth' in 'June Recital.'" *Delta* 5 (Nov. 1977): 27–34.

Evans, Elizabeth. "Eudora Welty and the Dutiful Daughter." Trouard, *Eye* 57–68.

Lindsay, Creighton. "Music as Metaphor in Welty's 'June Recital.'" *Southern Studies* 4.1 (Spring 1993): 1–17.

Pitavy-Souques, Daniele. "Watchers and Watching: Point of View in Eudora Welty's 'June Recital.'" Trans. Margaret Tomarchio. *Southern Review* ns 19 (Summer 1983): 483–509.

Wall, Carey. "'June Recital': Virgie Rainey Saved." Trouard, *Eye* 14–31.

"SIR RABBIT"

Carson, Franklin D. "The Passage of Time in Eudora Welty's 'Sir Rabbit.'" *Studies in Short Fiction* 12 (Summer 1975): 284–86.

Kendig, Daun. "Realities in 'Sir Rabbit': A Frame Analysis." Trouard, *Eye* 119–32.

Rubin, Louis D., Jr. "Five Southerners." *Hopkins Review* 3 (Spring 1950): 44–45. Rpt. in Champion 129–30.

"MOON LAKE"

Arnold, Marilyn. "The Edge of Adolescence in Eudora Welty's 'Moon Lake.'" *Southern Quarterly* 32 (Fall 1993): 49–61.

Garbarini, Arline. "'Moon Lake' and the Recreation of Brian Kent." *Eudora Welty Newsletter* 2 (Winter 1978): 1–3.

Lepaludier, Laurent. "Womanhood in Eudora Welty's 'Moon Lake.'" *Journal of the Short Story in English* 21 (Autumn 1993): 63–77.

Manning, Carol S. "Male Initiation, Welty Style." *Regionalism and the Female Imagination* 4.2 (1978): 53–60.

Mortimer, Gail L. "A Source for a Name and a Question of Naming in Eudora Welty's 'Moon Lake.'" *Southern Quarterly* 32.4 (Summer 1994): 81–83.
Scott, Michael. "Easter as Sexual Pathfinder in Eudora Welty's 'Moon Lake.'" *Crossroads* 1.1 (Fall 1992): 35–38.
Yaeger, Patricia S. "The Case of the Dangling Signifier: Phallic Imagery in Eudora Welty's 'Moon Lake.'" *Twentieth Century Literature* 28 (Winter 1982): 431–52. Rpt. in *Faith of a (Woman) Writer*. Ed. Alice Harris Kessler and William McBrien. Westport: Greenwood, 1988. 253–71.

"MUSIC FROM SPAIN"

Arnold, Marilyn. "Somnambulism in San Francisco: Eudora Welty's Western Story." *Southern Quarterly* 27 (Summer 1989): 16–24.

THE PONDER HEART, 1954

Arnold, Marilyn. "The Strategy of Edna Earle Ponder." Trouard, *Eye* 69–77.
Barber, Bette E. "Eudora Welty's *The Ponder Heart* Gets Rave Notices at Broadway." *Clarion-Ledger* 19 Feb. 1956, sec. 1: 6. Rpt. in Champion 151–53.
Carson, Barbara Harrell. "In the Heart of Clay: Eudora Welty's *The Ponder Heart*." *American Literature* 59.4 (1987): 609–25. Rpt. in *Two Pictures* 100–16.
Chapman, John. "Witless on the Delta." *Dallas Morning News* 10 Jan. 1954, sec. 6: 15.
Cornell, Brenda G. "Ambiguous Necessity: A Study of *The Ponder Heart*." Prenshaw, *Critical Essays* 208–19.
Drake, Robert Y., Jr. "The Reasons of the Heart." *Georgia Review* 11 (Winter 1957): 420–26.
Hains, Frank. "*Ponder Heart* Now out in Dramatic Version." *Clarion-Ledger* 27 May 1956, sec. 4: 6. Rpt. in Champion 149–50.
Holland, Robert B. "Dialogue as a Reflection of Place in *The Ponder Heart*." *American Literature* 35 (Nov. 1963): 352–58. Rpt. in Turner and Harding 168–74.
Idol, John L., Jr. "Edna Earle Ponder's Good Country People." *Southern Quarterly* 20.3 (Spring 1982): 66–75. Rpt. in Champion 141–48.
Kornfeld, Eve. "Out of Order: The Challenge of Outsider Jurisprudence and Eudora Welty's (Extra) Legal Vision to the American Rule of Law." Spec. issue of *Canadian Review of American Studies*. Part I (1992): 117–40.
Peden, William. "A Trial with No Verdict." *Saturday Review* 16 Jan. 1954: 14. Rpt. in Turner and Harding 167–68.
Pritchett, V. S. "Bossy Edna Earle Had a Word for Everything." *New York Times Book Review* 10 Jan. 1954: 5. Rpt. in Champion 137–38.
Seaman, Gerda, and Ellen L. Walker. "'It's All in a Way of Speaking': A Discussion of *The Ponder Heart*." *Southern Literary Journal* 23.2 (1991): 65–76.

Synder, Lynn. "Rhetoric in *The Ponder Heart.*" *Southern Literary Journal* 21.2 (1989): 17–26.
Varis, Sharon Deykin. "Welty's Philosophy of Friendship: Meanings Treasured in *The Ponder Heart.*" *Southern Literary Journal* 27.2 (Spring 1995): 43–61.
Weiner, Rachel V. "Eudora Welty's *The Ponder Heart:* The Judgment of Art." *Southern Studies* 19 (Fall 1980): 261–73.

THE BRIDE OF THE INNISFALLEN AND OTHER STORIES, 1955

Bornhauser, Fred. "*The Bride of the Innisfallen.*" *Shenandoah* 7 (Autumn 1955): 71, 77–78. Rpt. in Champion 157–60.
Harris, Frank. "Miss Welty Magnificent in Newest Short Pieces." *Clarion-Ledger* 10 Apr. 1955, sec. 4: 6. Rpt. in Champion 161–62.
Peden, William. "The Incomparable Welty." *Saturday Review of Literature* 38 (1955): 18.
Polk, Noel. "A Possible Source in 'Little Gidding' for *The Bride of Innisfallen.*" *Eudora Welty Newsletter* 4.1 (1980): 11.
Rubin, Louis D., Jr. "Two Ladies of the South." *Sewanee Review* 63 (1955): 671–81. Excerpted in Turner and Harding 175–81.

"NO PLACE FOR YOU, MY LOVE"

Devlin, Albert J. "'The Sharp Edge of Experiment': The Poetics of 'No Place for You, My Love.'" In Champion 163–70.
Gretlund Jan Nordby. "Out of Life into Fiction: Eudora Welty and the City." *Notes on Mississippi Writers* 14 (1982): 45–62.

"THE BURNING"

Gallafent, Edward. "The Landscape of 'The Burning.'" *Delta* 5 (Nov. 1977): 19–26.
Howell, Elmo. "Eudora Welty's Civil War Story." *Notes on Mississippi Writers* 2 (1969): 3–12.
McBurney, William H. "Welty's 'The Burning.'" *Explicator* 16 (1957): item 9.

"THE BRIDE OF THE INNISFALLEN"

Harrell, Don. "Death in Eudora Welty's 'The Bride of the Innisfallen.'" *Notes on Contemporary Literature* 3 (Sept. 1973): 2–7.
Liscio, Lorraine. "The Female Voice of Poetry in 'The Bride of the Innisfallen.'" *Studies in Short Fiction* 21.4 (Fall 1984): 357–62.

Toman, Marshall. "Welty's 'The Bride of the Innisfallen.'" *Explicator* 43.2 (Winter 1985): 42–44.

"LADIES IN SPRING"

Boisterli, Margaret. "Mythic Elements in 'Ladies in Spring.'" *Notes on Mississippi Writers* 6 (Winter 1974): 69–72.

"CIRCE"

Goudie, Andrea. "Eudora Welty's Circe: A Goddess Who Strove with Men." *Studies in Short Fiction* 13 (Fall 1976): 481–89.

"GOING TO NAPLES"

Polk, Noel. "Going to Naples and Other Places in Eudora Welty's Fiction." Trouard, *Eye* 153–64.

LOSING BATTLES, 1970

Aldridge, John W. "Eudora Welty: Metamorphosis of a Southern Lady Writer." *Saturday Review* 11 Apr. 1970: 21–23, 35–36. Rpt. as "The Emergence of Eudora Welty" in *The Devil in the Fire*. New York: Harper, 1972. 249–56.
Bass, Eben F. "The Languages of *Losing Battles*." *Studies in American Fiction* 21 (Spring 1993): 67–82.
Boatwright, James. "I Call This a Reunion to Remember, All!" *New York Times Book Review* 12 Apr. 1970: 1, 32–34.
———. "Speech and Silence in *Losing Battles*." *Shenandoah* 25.3 (Spring 1974): 3–14. Rpt. in Champion 208–17.
Bradford, M. E. "'Looking Down from a High Place': The Serenity of Miss Welty's *Losing Battles*." *Recherches Anglaises et Americaines* 4 (1971): 92–97. Rpt. in Desmond 103–09.
Dollarhide, Louis. "Eudora Welty's *Losing Battles* Is Magnificent Feast." *Mississippi Library News* June 1970: 96–98. Rpt. in Champion 193–95.
Donaldson, Susan V. "'Contradictors, Interferers, and Prevaricators': Opposing Modes of Discourse in Eudora Welty's *Losing Battles*." Trouard, *Eye* 32–43.
Drake, Robert. "Miss Welty's Wide World." *Christian Century* 17 June 1970: 766–67. Rpt. in Champion 205–07.
Ferguson, Mary Anne. "*Losing Battles* as a Comic Epic in Prose." Prenshaw, *Critical Essays* 305–24.
Goodin, Gayle. *An Introduction to Eudora Welty's* Losing Battles. Jackson, Mississippi Library Commission. 1976.
Gossett, Louise Y. "Eudora Welty's New Novel: The Comedy of Loss." *South-*

ern Literary Journal 3 (Fall 1970): 122–37. Rpt. in Turner and Harding 193–205.

———. "*Losing Battles:* Festival and Celebration." Prenshaw, *Critical Essays* 341–50.

Gross, Seymour. "A Long Day's Living: The Angelic Ingenuities of *Losing Battles.*" Prenshaw, *Critical Essays* 325–40. Rpt. in Prenshaw, *Thirteen* 193–208.

Gretlund, Jan Nordby. "Welty's *Losing Battles.*" *Explicator* 51 (Fall 1992): 49–50.

Hains, Frank. "Eudora Welty Talks about Her New Book, *Losing Battles.*" *Clarion-Ledger* 5 Apr. 1970: 6F. Rpt. in Champion 189–192.

Heilman, Robert B. "*Losing Battles* and Winning the War." Prenshaw, *Critical Essays* 269–304. Rpt. in Prenshaw, *Thirteen* 157–92.

Kornfeld, Eva. "Reconstructing American Law: The Politics of Narrative and Eudora Welty's Empathic Vision." *Journal of American Studies* 26 (Apr. 1992): 23–39.

Kreyling, Michael. "Myth and History: The Foes of *Losing Battles.*" *Mississippi Quarterly* 26 (Fall 1973): 639–49. Rev. and rpt. in *Achievement* 140–52.

Landess, Thomas. "More Trouble in Mississippi: Family vs. Antifamily in Miss Welty's *Losing Battles.*" *Sewanee Review* 79 (Autumn 1971): 626–34.

Magee, Rosemary M. "Eudora Welty's *Losing Battles:* A Patchwork Quilt of Stories." *South Atlantic Review* 49 (May 1984): 67–79.

Marrs, Suzanne. "The Making of *Losing Battles:* Jack Renfro's Evolution." *Mississippi Quarterly* 37 (Fall 1984): 469–74.

———. "The Making of *Losing Battles:* Judge Moody Transformed." *Notes on Mississippi Writers* 17 (1985): 47–53.

———. "The Making of *Losing Battles:* Plot Revision." *Southern Literary Journal* 18 (Fall 1985): 40–49.

McMillan, William E. "Conflict and Resolution in Welty's *Losing Battles.*" *Critique* 15.1 (1973): 110–24. Rpt. in Turner and Harding 205–17.

Messerli, Douglas. "'A Battle with Both Sides Using the Same Tactics': The Language of Time in *Losing Battles.*" Prenshaw, *Critical Essays* 351–66.

Moore, Carol A. "The Insulation of Illusion and *Losing Battles.*" *Mississippi Quarterly* 26 (Fall 1973): 651–58.

Murrey, Loretta Martin. "From Religious Ritual to Family Ritual: The 'Holiness of Life' in Eudora Welty's *Losing Battles.*" *Southern Folklore* 47.3 (1990): 239–47.

Oates, Joyce Carol. "Eudora's Web." *Atlantic* Apr. 1970: 118–120, 122.

Prenshaw, Peggy Whitman. "The Harmonies of *Losing Battles.*" *Modern American Fiction: Form and Function.* Ed. Thomas Daniel Young. Baton Rouge: Louisiana State UP, 1989. 184–97.

Price, Reynolds. "Frightening Gift." In *Things in Themselves: Essays and Scenes.* By Price. New York: Atheneum, 1972. 139–42.

Reynolds, Larry J. "Enlightening Darkness: Theme and Structure in Eudora Welty's *Losing Battles.*" *Journal of Narrative Technique* 8 (Spring 1978): 133–40. Rpt. in Turner and Harding 217–24.

Rubin, Louis D., Jr. "Everything Brought Out in the Open: Eudora Welty's *Losing Battles. Hollins Critic* 7.3 (June 1970): 1–12. Rpt. in Champion 196–204.
Stroup, Sheila. "'We're All Part of It Together': Eudora Welty's Hopeful Vision in *Losing Battles*," *Southern Literary Journal* 15 (Spring 1983): 42–58.
Walter, James. "Place Dissolved in Grace: Welty's *Losing Battles*." *Southern Literary Journal* 21.1 (Fall 1988): 39–53.
Zverev, Aleksei "*Losing Battles* Against the Background of the Sixties." *Southern Quarterly* 32 (Fall 1993): 27–30.

ONE TIME, ONE PLACE, 1971

Armitage, Shelley. "The Eye and the Story: The Photographs of Eudora Welty." *Women's Work: Essays in Cultural Studies.* Ed. Shelley Armitage. West Cornwall, CT: Locust Hill Press, 1995. 41–48.
Bradford, M. E. "Miss Eudora's Picture Book." *Mississippi Quarterly* 26 (Fall 1973): 659–62.
East, Charles. "The Welty Photographs." *Southern Review* 26 (Spring 1990): 449–55.
Mann, Charles. "Eudora Welty, Photographer." *History of Photography: An International Quarterly.* 6 (Apr. 1982): 145–49.
McKenzie, Barbara. "The Eye of Time: The Photographs of Eudora Welty." Prenshaw, *Critical Essays* 386–400. Rpt. in Prenshaw, *Thirteen* 209–23.
Westling, Louise. "The Loving Observer of *One Time, One Place*." *Mississippi Quarterly* 39 (Fall 1986): 587–604. Rpt. in Devlin, *A Life* 168–87.

THE OPTIMIST'S DAUGHTER, 1972

Arnold, Marilyn. "Images of Memory in Eudora Welty's *The Optimist's Daughter.*" *Southern Literary Journal* 14.2 (Spring 1982): 28–38. Rpt. in Turner and Harding 238–48.
Blair, John. "Nicholas and the Judge: The 'Wrong Book' In Eudora Welty's *The Optimist's Daughter.*" *Notes on Mississippi Writers* 24 (Jan. 1992): 25–33.
Boatwright, James. "The Continuity of Love." *New Republic* 10 June 1972: 24–25. Rpt. in Champion 221–25.
Brinkmeyer, Robert H., Jr. "New Orleans, Mardi Gras, and Eudora Welty's *The Optimist's Daughter.*" *Mississippi Quarterly* 44 (Fall 1991): 429–41.
Brooks, Cleanth. "The Past Reexamined: *The Optimist's Daughter.*" *Mississippi Quarterly* 26 (Fall 1973): 577–87. Rpt. in Champion 226–34.
Carson, Barbara Harrell. "Eudora Welty's Heart of Darkness, Heart of Light." *South Central Review* 4.1 (Spring 1987): 106–22.
Chaudhary, Jasbir. "Patterns of Love and Isolation: Eudora Welty's *The Optimist's Daughter.*" *Panjab University Research Bulletin (Arts)* 13 Oct. 1982: 65–72.

Desmond, John F. "Patterns and Vision in *The Optimist's Daughter.*" Desmond 118–38.
Harris, A. Leslie. "The Mystic Vision in *The Optimist's Daughter.*" *Studies in the Humanities* 13.1 (June 1986): 31–41.
Kreyling, Michael. "Life with People: Virginia Woolf, Eudora Welty and *The Optimist's Daughter.*" *Southern Review* ns 13 (Apr. 1977): 250–71.
Landry, Donna E. "Genre and Revision: The Example of Welty's *The Optimist's Daughter.*" *Postscript* 1 (1983): 90–98.
Long, Kim Martin. "'The Freed Hands': The Power of Images in Eudora Welty's *The Optimist's Daughter.*" In Champion 235–44.
Mortimer, Gail L. "Image and Myth in Eudora Welty's *The Optimist's Daughter.*" *American Literature* 62 (1990): 617–33.
Pepperdene, Margaret W. "'When Our Separate Journeys Converge': Notes on *The Optimist's Daughter.*" *Mississippi Quarterly* 42 (Spring 1989): 147–60.
Phillips, Robert L. "Patterns of Vision in Welty's *The Optimist's Daughter.*" *Southern Literary Journal* 14.1 (1981): 10–23.
Prenshaw, Peggy Whitman. *An Introduction to Eudora Welty's* The Optimist's Daughter. Jackson: Mississippi Library Commission, 1977.
Price, Reynolds. "The Onlooker, Smiling: An Early Reading of *The Optimist's Daughter.*" *Shenandoah* 20 (Spring 1969): 58–73. Rpt. in Turner and Harding 225–38. Rpt. with "Postscript" in *Things Themselves: Essays and Scenes.* By Price. New York Atheneum, 1972. 114–38. Also rpt. in *Eudora Welty.* Ed. Harold Bloom. New York: Chelsea House, 1986. 75–88.
Shepherd, Allen. "Delayed Exposition in Eudora Welty's *The Optimist's Daughter.*" *Notes on Contemporary Literature.* 4.4 (1974): 10–13.
Spacks, Patricia Meyer. *The Female Imagination.* New York: Knopf, 1975. 261, 264–75.
Stanford, Donald E. "Eudora Welty and the Pulitzer Prize." *Southern Review* ns 9 (Autumn 1973): xx–xxiii.
Stuckey, William J. "The Use of Marriage in Welty's *The Optimist's Daughter.*" *Critique* 17.2 (1975): 36–46.
Thornton, Naoka Fuwa. "Medusa-Perseus Symbolism in Eudora Welty's *The Optimist's Daughter.*" *Southern Quarterly* 23 (Summer 1985): 64–76.
Tiegreen, Helen H. "Mothers, Daughters, and One Writer's Revisions." *Mississippi Quarterly* 39 (Fall 1986): 605–26. Rpt. in Devlin, *A Life* 188–211.
Watkins, Floyd C. "Death and the Mountains in *The Optimist's Daughter.*" *Essays in Literature* 15.1 (Spring 1988): 77–85.
———. "The Journey to Baltimore in *The Optimist's Daughter.*" *Mississippi Quarterly* 38 (Fall 1985): 435–39.
Weston, Ruth D. "The Feminine and Feminist Texts of Eudora Welty's *The Optimist's Daughter.*" *South Central Review* 4 (Winter 1987): 74–91.
Wolff, Sally. "'Among Those Missing': Phil Hand's Disappearance from *The Optimist's Daughter.*" *Southern Literary Journal* 25.1 (1992): 74–78.

Young, Thomas Daniel. "Social Form and Social Order: An Examination of *The Optimist's Daughter*." Prenshaw, *Critical Essays* 367–85. Rpt. in *The Past in the Present: A Thematic Study of Modern Southern Literature*. Ed. Young. Baton Rouge: Louisiana State UP, 1981. 87–115.

THE COLLECTED STORIES OF EUDORA WELTY, 1980

Clemons, Walter. "Songs of the South." *Newsweek* 3 Nov. 1980: 85–86. Rpt. in Champion 280–82.
Drake, Robert. "The Loving Vision." *Modern Age* 27.1 (Winter 1983): 96–97. Rpt. in Champion 293–95.
Gray, Paul. "Life, with a Touch of the Comic." *Time* 3 Nov. 1980: 110.
Howard, Maureen. "A Collection of Discoveries." *New York Times Book Review* 2 Nov. 1980: 1, 31–32.
Price, Reynolds. "The Collected Stories of Eudora Welty." *New Republic* 1 Nov. 1980: 31–34. Rpt. in Johnston 173–78.
Tyler, Anne. "The Fine, Full World of Welty." *Washington Evening Star* 26 Oct. 1980, sec. D: 1, 7. Rpt. in Champion 275–79.
Uglow, Jennifer. "Journeys out of Separateness." *Times Literary Supplement* 8 Jan. 1982: 26. Rpt. in Champion. 283–87.

UNCOLLECTED STORIES

Polk, Noel E. "Continuity and Change in Eudora Welty's 'Where Is the Voice Coming From?' and 'The Demonstrators.'" *Turning Points, Mississippi Mindscape*. Jackson: Mississippi Committee for the Humanities, 1986. 7–12.

"WHERE IS THE VOICE COMING FROM"

Clerc, Charles. "Anatomy of Welty's 'Where Is the Voice Coming From?'" *Studies in Short Fiction* 23 (Fall 1986): 389–400.
Hargrove, Nancy D. "Portrait of an Assassin: Eudora Welty's 'Where Is the Voice Coming From?'" *Southern Literary Journal* 20 (Fall 1987): 74–88.
Vande Keifi, Ruth M. "'Where Is the Voice Coming From': Teaching Eudora Welty." Trouard, *Eye* 190–204.

"THE DEMONSTRATORS"

Ferguson, Suzanne. "'The Assault of Hope': Style's Substance in Welty's 'The Demonstrators.'" Trouard, *Eye* 44–54.

Prenshaw, Peggy Whitman. "Elegies for Gentlemen: Walter Percy's *The Last Gentleman* and Eudora Welty's 'The Demonstrators.'" *Walker Percy: Novelist and Philosopher.* Ed. Jan Nordby and Karl-Heinz Westarp Gretlund. Jackson: UP of Mississippi, 84–95.

Vande Kieft, Ruth M. "Demonstrators in a Stricken Land." *The Process of Fiction.* Ed. Barbara McKenzie. New York: Harcourt. 342–49.

ELECTRONIC AND OTHER MEDIA

Film, TV Broadcasts, and Video

"Eye of Memory." *American Playhouse.* Prod. Calvin Skaggs. PBS. Lumiere Productions and KERA-TV, Dallas. 1987. ("Transcript of Eudora Welty's Comments on Katherine Anne Porter." Included in Merrill Maguire Skaggs. "Eudora Welty's 'I' of Memory." In Turner and Harding 161–64.)

Haines, Frank. *Interview with Eudora Welty.* Mississippi Authority for Educational Television. 26 Oct. 1971.

Henley, Beth. *Interview with Eudora Welty.* Dir. John Reid and Claudia Velasco. Videocassette. Harcourt, 1994.

"The Key." By Eudora Welty. Videocassette. Filmed for deaf community. New Orleans: Key Films, 1996.

Moore, Richard R. *Eudora Welty.* Writer in America Series. Sausalito, 1971.

———. *Four Women Artists: Interviews with Eudora Welty, Ethel Mohammed, Theora Hamblett, and Pecolia Warner.* Videocassette. Memphis: Center for Southern Folklore, 1977.

Mudd, Roger. "Interview with Eudora Welty." *MacNeil/Lehrer Newshour.* PBS. WNET, New York. Show no. 3613. 19 Nov. 1989.

"The Southern Imagination." *Firing Line.* Prod. Warren Steibel. Hosted by William F. Buckley, Jr. PBS. WMAA, Jackson. Taped 12 Dec. 1972. Broadcast 24 Dec. 1972.

"The Wide Net." By Eudora Welty. Adapted by Anthony Herrera. *American Playhouse.* PBS. 2 Feb. 1987.

"A Worn Path." By Eudora Welty. Dir. John Reid and Claudia Velasco. Perf. Cora Lee Day and Conchita Ferrell. Videocassette. Harcourt, 1994.

Sound Recordings

Welty, Eudora. *Eudora Welty Reading from Her Works: "Why I Live at the P.O.," "A Memory," and "A Worn Path."* Caedmon Records TC-100-A, 1952. Reissued as Caedmon Cassette CDL5 1010, 1986.

———. *Eudora Welty Reads Her Stories "Powerhouse" and "Petrified Man."* Caedmon Records TC-1626, 1979. Reissued as Caedmon Cassette CDL5 1626.
———. *On Story Telling.* Columbia, MO: Audio Forum, 1961.
———. *The Optimist's Daughter.* Audiocassette. New York: Random, 1986.

CD-ROM

Welty, Eudora. *Selected Stories of Eudora Welty.* Modern Library Edition. NY: Harcourt, 1954. Macintosh version. CD-ROM. Expanded Books. Santa Monica: Voyager, 1993.

WWW Sites

"Eudora Welty." Online posting. 31 May 1997. *Mississippi Writers Page.* <http://www.olemiss.edu/depts/english/ms-writers/dir/welty_eudora/>.
Eudora Welty Newsletter. Ed. Pearl A. McHaney. Atlanta: Georgia State U. Available <http://www.gsu.edu/~wwweng/ewn>.

Adaptations for the Stage

Lily Daw and the Three Ladies. By Eudora Welty. Adapted by Gloria Baxter. Memphis State University. Feb. 1981. Pamphlet.
Lily Daw and the Three Ladies. By Eudora Welty. Adapted by Ruth Perry. Chicago: Dramatic Publishing, 1972.
The Ponder Heart. By Eudora Welty. Adapted by Joseph Fields and Jerome Chodorov. Broadway. 16 Feb. 1956. Pub. New York: Random [1956?] and New York: Samuel French, 1956.
The Ponder Heart. By Eudora Welty. Opera. Adapted by Alice Parker. New State Theatre, Jackson, MS. 10 Sept.1982.
A Season of Dreams. Adaptation of several Welty works. New Stage Theatre, Jackson, MS. 22 May 1968. Broadcast version. Mississippi ETV. 19 Nov. 1970.
The Shoe Bird. By Eudora Welty. Ballet. Jackson, MS. 20 Apr. 1968.
Sister and Miss Lexie. By David Kaplan and Brenda Currin. Adaptations of "June Recital," *Losing Battles,* and "Why I Live at the P.O." By Eudora Welty. Chelsea Theatre, NY. 1981.
The Robber Bridegroom. By Eudora Welty. Musical. Adapted by Alfred Uhry and Robert Waldman. Broadway. 9 Oct. 1976. Pub. Drama Book Specialists [1978].
Why I Live at the P.O. By Eudora Welty. Adapted by Gloria Baxter. Memphis State U. Feb. 1981.

REFERENCE GUIDES AND BIBLIOGRAPHIES

"Checklist of Welty Scholarship." *Eudora Welty Newsletter.* Ed. W.U. McDonald, Jr. University of Toledo. Winter 1977–Spring 1997. Ed. Pearl A. McHaney. Georgia State University. Winter 1997.

Marrs, Suzanne. *The Welty Collection: A Guide to the Eudora Welty Manuscripts and Documents at the Mississippi Department of Archives and History.* Jackson: UP of Mississippi, 1988.

McHaney, Pearl A. "A Eudora Welty Checklist, 1973–1986." *Mississippi Quarterly* 39 (1986): 651–97. Rpt. in Devlin, *A Life* 266–302.

Pingatore, Diana R. *A Reader's Guide to the Short Stories of Eudora Welty.* New York: Hall, 1996.

Polk, Noel. *Eudora Welty: A Bibliography of Her Work.* Jackson: UP of Mississippi, 1994.

"A Eudora Welty Checklist, 1936–1972." *Mississippi Quarterly* 39 (Fall 1973): 663–93. Rev. and rpt. in Devlin, *A Life* 238–65.

Prenshaw, Peggy Whitman. "Eudora Welty." *American Women Writers: Bibliographical Essays.* Ed. Maurice Duke, Jackson R. Bryer, and M. Thomas Inge. Westport: Greenwood, 1983. 233–67.

Swearington, Bethany C. *Eudora Welty: A Critical Bibliography, 1936–1958.* Jackson: UP of Mississippi, 1984.

Thompson, Victor H. *Eudora Welty: A Reference Guide.* Boston: Hall, 1976.

Appendix: Documenting Sources

A Guide to MLA Documentation Style

Documentation is the acknowledgment of information from an outside source that you use in a paper. In general, you should give credit to your sources whenever you quote, paraphrase, summarize, or in any other way incorporate borrowed information or ideas into your work. Not to do so—on purpose or by accident—is to commit **plagiarism,** to appropriate the intellectual property of others. By following accepted conventions of documentation, you not only help avoid plagiarism, but also show your readers that you write with care and precision. In addition, you enable them to distinguish your ideas from those of your sources and, if they wish, to locate and consult the sources you cite.

Not all ideas from your sources need to be documented. You can assume that certain information—facts from encyclopedias, textbooks, newspapers, magazines, and dictionaries, or even from television and radio—is common knowledge. Even if the information is new to you, it need not be documented as long as it is found in several reference sources and as long as you do not use the exact wording of your source. Information that is in dispute or that is the original contribution of a particular person, however, *must* be documented. You need not, for example, document the fact that Arthur Miller's *Death of a Salesman* was first performed in 1949 or that it won a Pulitzer Prize for drama. (You could find this information in any current encyclopedia.) You would, however, have to document a critic's interpretation of a performance or a scholar's analysis of an early draft of the play, even if you do not use your source's exact words.

Students of literature use the documentation style recommended by the Modern Language Association of America (MLA), a professional organization of more than twenty-five thousand teachers and students of English and other languages. This method of documentation, the one that you should use any time you write a literature paper, has three components: *parenthetical references in the text, a list of works cited,* and *explanatory notes.*

Parenthetical References in the Text

MLA documentation uses references inserted in parentheses within the text that refer to an alphabetical list of works cited at the end of the paper. A typical **parenthetical reference** consists of the author's last name and a page number.

> Gwendolyn Brooks uses the sonnet form to create poems that have a wide social and aesthetic range (Williams 972).

If you use more than one source by the same author, include a shortened title in the parenthetical reference. In the following entry, "Brooks's Way" is a shortened form of the complete title of the article "Gwendolyn Brooks's Way with the Sonnet."

> Brooks not only knows Shakespeare, Spenser, and Milton, but she also knows the full range of African-American poetry (Williams, "Brooks's Way" 972).

If you mention the author's name or the title of the work in your paper, only a page reference is necessary.

> According to Gladys Margaret Williams in "Gwendolyn Brooks's Way with the Sonnet," Brooks combines a sensitivity to poetic forms with a depth of emotion appropriate for her subject matter (972-73).

Keep in mind that you use different punctuation for parenthetical references used with *paraphrases and summaries*, with *direct quotations run in with the text*, and with *quotations of more than four lines*.

Paraphrases and Summaries

Place the parenthetical reference after the last word of the sentence and before the final punctuation:

> In her works Brooks combines the pessimism of Modernist poetry with the optimism of the Harlem Renaissance (Smith 978).

Direct quotations run in with the text

Place the parenthetical reference after the quotation marks and before the final punctuation:

> According to Gary Smith, Brooks's <u>A Street in Bronzeville</u> "conveys the primacy of suffering in the lives of poor Black women" (980).
>
> According to Gary Smith, the poems in <u>A Street in Bronzeville</u>, "served notice that Brooks had learned her craft . . ." (978).
>
> Along with Thompson we must ask, "Why did it take so long for critics to acknowledge that Gwendolyn Brooks is an important voice in twentieth-century American poetry?" (123)

Quotations set off from the text

Omit the quotation marks and place the parenthetical reference one space after the final punctuation.

> For Gary Smith, the identity of Brooks's African-American women is inextricably linked with their sense of race and poverty:
>> For Brooks, unlike the Renaissance poets, the victimization of poor Black women becomes not simply a minor chord but a predominant theme of <u>A Street in Bronzeville</u>. Few, if any, of her female characters are able to free themselves from a web of poverty that threatens to strangle their lives. (980)

[Quotations of more than four lines are indented ten spaces (or one inch) from the margin and are not enclosed within quotation marks. The first line of a single paragraph of quoted material is not indented further. If you quote two or more paragraphs, indent the first line of each paragraph three additional spaces (one-quarter inch).]

SAMPLE REFERENCES

The following formats are used for parenthetical references to various kinds of sources used in papers about literature. (Keep in mind that the parenthetical reference contains just enough information to enable readers to find the source in the list of works cited at the end of the paper.)

An entire work

> August Wilson's play <u>Fences</u> treats many themes frequently expressed in modern drama.

[When citing an entire work, state the name of the author in your paper instead of in a parenthetical reference.]

A work by two or three authors

> Myths cut across boundaries and cultural spheres and reappear in strikingly similar forms from country to country (Feldman and Richardson 124).

> The effect of a work of literature depends on the audience's predispositions that derive from membership in various social groups (Hovland, Janis, and Kelley 87).

A work by more than three authors

> Hawthorne's short stories frequently use a combination of allegorical and symbolic methods (Guerin et al. 91).

[The abbreviation *et al.* is Latin for "and others."]

A work in an anthology

> In his essay "Flat and Round Characters" E. M. Forster distinguishes between one-dimensional characters and those that are well developed (Stevick 223-31).

[The parenthetical reference cites the anthology (edited by Stevick) that contains Forster's essay; full information about the anthology appears in the list of works cited.]

A work with volume and page numbers

> In 1961 one of Albee's plays, <u>The Zoo Story</u>, was finally performed in America (Eagleton 2:17).

An indirect source

> Wagner observed that myth and history stood before him "with opposing claims" (qtd. in Winkler 10).

[The abbreviation *qtd. in* (quoted in) indicates that the quoted material was not taken from the original source.]

A play or poem with numbered lines

> "Give thy thoughts no tongue," says Polonius, "Nor any unproportioned thought his act" (<u>Ham</u>. 1.3.59-60).

[The parentheses contain the act, scene, and line numbers, separated by periods. When included in parenthetical references, titles of the books of the Bible and well-known literary works are often abbreviated—*Gen.* for *Genesis* and *Ado* for *Much Ado about Nothing*, for example.]

> "I muse my life-long hate, and without flinch / I bear it nobly as I live my part," says Claude McKay in his bitterly ironic poem "The White City" (3-4).

[Notice that a slash [/] is used to separate lines of poetry run in with the text. The parenthetical reference cites the lines quoted.]

The List of Works Cited

Parenthetical references refer to a **list of works cited** that includes all the sources you refer to in your paper. (If your list includes all the works consulted, whether you cite them or not, use the title *Works Consulted.*) Begin the works cited list on a new page, continuing the page numbers of the paper. For example, if the text of the paper ends on page six, the works cited section will begin on page seven.

Center the title *Works Cited* one inch from the top of the page. Arrange entries alphabetically, according to the last name of each author (or the first word of the title if the author is unknown). Articles—*a, an,* and *the*—at the beginning of a title are not considered first words. Thus, *A Handbook of Critical Approaches to Literature* would be alphabetized under *H.* In order to conserve space, publishers' names are abbreviated—for example, *Harcourt* for Harcourt Brace College Publishers. Double-space the entire works cited list between and within entries. Begin typing each entry at the left margin, and indent subsequent lines five spaces or one-half inch. The entry itself generally has three divisions—author, title, and publishing information—separated by periods.*

A book by a single author

Kingston, Maxine Hong. <u>The Woman Warrior: Memoirs of a Girlhood among Ghosts</u>. New York: Knopf, 1976.

A book by two or three authors

Feldman, Burton, and Robert D. Richardson. <u>The Rise of Modern Mythology</u>. Bloomington: Indiana UP, 1972.

[Notice that only the *first* author's name is in reverse order.]

A book by more than three authors

Guerin, Wilfred, et al., eds. <u>A Handbook of Critical Approaches to Literature</u>. 3rd. ed. New York: Harper, 1992.

[Instead of using *et al.,* you may list all the authors' names in the order in which they appear on the title page.]

Two or more works by the same author

Novoa, Juan-Bruce. <u>Chicano Authors: Inquiry by Interview</u>, Austin: U of Texas P, 1980.

---

* The fourth edition of the *MLA Handbook for Writers of Research Papers* (1995) shows a single space after all end punctuation.

162 APPENDIX: DOCUMENTING SOURCES

> ---. "Themes in Rudolfo Anaya's Work." Address given at New Mexico State University, Las Cruces. 11 Apr. 1987.

[List two or more works by the same author in alphabetical order by title. Include the author's full name in the first entry; use three unspaced hyphens followed by a period to take the place of the author's name in second and subsequent entries.]

An edited book

> Oosthuizen, Ann, ed. <u>Sometimes When It Rains: Writings by South African Women</u>. New York: Pandora, 1987.

[Note that the abbreviation *ed.* stands for *editor.*]

A book with a volume number

> Eagleton, T. Allston. <u>A History of the New York Stage</u>. Vol. 2. Englewood Cliffs: Prentice. 1987.

[All three volumes have the same title.]

> Durant, Will, and Ariel Durant. <u>The Age of Napoleon: A History of European Civilization from 1789 to 1815</u>. New York: Simon, 1975.

[Each volume has a different title, so you may cite an individual book without referring to the other volumes.]

A short story, poem, or play in a collection of the author's work

> Gordimer, Nadine. "Once upon a Time." <u>"Jump" and Other Stories</u>. New York: Farrar, 1991. 23-30.

A short story in an anthology

> Salinas, Marta. "The Scholarship Jacket." <u>Nosotros: Latina Literature Today</u>. Ed. Maria del Carmen

Boza, Beverly Silva, and Carmen Valle. Binghamton: Bilingual, 1986. 68-70.

[The inclusive page numbers follow the year of publication. Note that here the abbreviation *Ed.* stands for *Edited by.*]

A poem in an anthology

Simmerman, Jim. "Child's Grave, Hale County, Alabama." <u>The Pushcart Prize, X: Best of the Small Presses</u>. Ed. Bill Henderson. New York: Penguin, 1986. 198-99.

A play in an anthology

Hughes, Langston. <u>Mother and Child</u>. <u>Black Drama Anthology</u>. Ed. Woodie King and Ron Miller. New York: NAL, 1986. 399-406.

An article in an anthology

Forster, E. M. "Flat and Round Characters." <u>The Theory of the Novel</u>. Ed. Philip Stevick. New York: Free, 1980. 223-31.

More than one selection from the same anthology

If you are using more than one selection from an anthology, cite the anthology in one entry. In addition, list each individual selection separately, including the author and title of the selection, the anthology editor's last name, and the inclusive page numbers.

Kirszner, Laurie G., and Stephen R. Mandell, eds. <u>Literature: Reading, Reacting, Writing</u>. 3rd ed. Fort Worth: Harcourt, 1997.
Rich, Adrienne. "Diving into the Wreck." Kirszner and Mandell 874-76.

A translation

Carpentier, Alejo. <u>Reasons of State</u>. Trans. Francis Partridge. New York: Norton, 1976.

An article in a journal with continuous pagination in each issue

> LeGuin, Ursula K. "American Science Fiction and the Other." <u>Science Fiction Studies</u> 2 (1975): 208-10.

An article with separate pagination in each issue

> Grossman, Robert. "The Grotesque in Faulkner's 'A Rose for Emily.'" <u>Mosaic</u> 20.3 (1987): 40-55.

[20.3 signifies volume 20, issue 3.]

An article in a magazine

> Milosz, Czeslaw. "A Lecture." <u>New Yorker</u> 22 June 1992: 32.
> "Solzhenitsyn: An Artist Becomes an Exile." <u>Time</u> 25 Feb. 1974: 34+.

[34+ indicates that the article appears on pages that are not consecutive; in this case the article begins on page 34 and then continues on page 37. An article with no listed author is entered by title on the works cited list.]

An article in a daily newspaper

> Oates, Joyce Carol. "When Characters from the Page Are Made Flesh on the Screen." <u>New York Times</u> 23 Mar. 1986, late ed.: C1+.

[C1+ indicates that the article begins on page 1 of Section C and continues on a subsequent page.]

An article in a reference book

> "Dance Theatre of Harlem." <u>The New Encyclopaedia Britannica: Micropaedia</u>. 15th ed. 1987.

[You do not need to include publication information for well-known reference books.]

> Grimstead, David. "Fuller, Margaret Sarah." <u>Encyclopedia of American Biography</u>. Ed. John A. Garraty. New York: Harper, 1974.

[You must include publication information when citing reference books that are not well known.]

A CD-ROM: Entry with a print version

> Zurbach, Kate. "The Linguistic Roots of Three Terms." <u>Linguistic Quarterly</u> 37 (1994): 12-47. <u>Infotrac: Magazine Index Plus</u>. CD-ROM. Information Access. Jan. 1996.

[When you cite information with a print version from a CD-ROM, include the publication information, the underlined title of the database (<u>Infotrac: Magazine Index Plus</u>), the publication medium (CD-ROM), the name of the company that produced the CD-ROM (Information Access), and the electronic publication date.]

A CD-ROM: Entry with no print version

> "Surrealism." <u>Encarta 1996</u>. CD-ROM. Redmond: Microsoft, 1996.

[If you are citing a part of a work, include the title in quotation marks.]

> <u>A Music Lover's Multimedia Guide to Beethoven's 5th</u>. CD-ROM. Spring Valley: Interactive, 1993.

[If you are citing an entire work, include the underlined title.]

An online source: Entry with a print version

> Dekoven, Marianne. "Utopias Limited: Post-sixties and Postmodern American Fiction." <u>Modern Fiction Studies</u> 41.1 (Spring 1995): 121-34. 17 Mar. 1996 <http://muse.jhu.edu/journals/MFS/v041/41.1 dekoven.html>.

[When you cite information with a print version from an online source, include the publication information for the printed source, the number of pages (*n. pag.* if no pages are given), and the date of access. Include the electronic address, or URL, in angle brackets. Information from a commercial computer service—America Online, Prodigy, and CompuServ, for example—will not have an electronic address.]

O'Hara, Sandra. "Reexamining the Canon." Time 13 May
    1994: 27. America Online. 22 Aug. 1994.

An online source: Entry with no print version

"Romanticism." Academic American Encyclopedia. Sept.
    1996. Prodigy. 6 Nov. 1995.

[This entry shows that the material was accessed on November 6, 1996.]

An online source: Public Posting

Peters, Olaf. "Studying English through German."
    Online posting. 29 Feb. 1996. Foreign Language
    Forum, Multi Language Section. CompuServe.
    15 Mar. 1996.
Gilford, Mary. "Dog Heroes in Children's Litera-
    ture." 4 Oct. 1996. Newsgroup alt.animals.dogs.
    America Online. 23 Mar. 1996.

[**WARNING:** Using information from online forums and newsgroups is risky. Contributors are not necessarily experts, and frequently they are incorrect and misinformed. Unless you can be certain that the information you are receiving from these sources is reliable, do not use it in your papers.]

An online source: Electronic Text

Twain, Mark. The Adventures of Huckleberry Finn.
    From The Writing of Mark Twain. Vol. 13.
    New York: Harper, 1970. Wiretap.spies.
    13 Jan. 1996
    <http.//www.sci.dixie.edu/DixieCollege/Ebooks/
    huckfin.html>.

[This electronic text was originally published by Harper. The name of the repository for the electronic edition is Wiretap.spies.]

An online source: E-Mail

Adkins, Camille. E-Mail to the author. 8 June 1995.

An interview

>Brooks, Gwendolyn. "Interviews." <u>Triquarterly</u> 60 (1984): 405-10.

A lecture or address

>Novoa, Juan-Bruce. "Themes in Rudolfo Anaya's Work." New Mexico State University, Las Cruces, 11 Apr. 1987.

A film or videocassette

>"<u>A Worn Path</u>." By Eudora Welty. Dir. John Reid and Claudia Velasco. Perf. Cora Lee Day and Conchita Ferrell. Videocassette. Harcourt, 1994.

[In addition to the title, the director, and the year, include other pertinent information such as the principal performers.]

Explanatory Notes

Explanatory notes, indicated by a superscript (a raised number) in the text, may be used to cite several sources at once or to provide commentary or explanations that do not fit smoothly into your paper. The full text of these notes appears on the first numbered page following the last page of the paper. (If your paper has no explanatory notes, the works cited page follows the last page of the paper.) Like works cited entries, explanatory notes are double-spaced within and between entries. However, the first line of each explanatory note is indented five spaces (or one-half inch), with subsequent lines flush with the left-hand margin.

TO CITE SEVERAL SOURCES

In the paper

>Surprising as it may seem, there have been many attempts to define literature.[1]

In the note

[1] For an overview of critical opinion, see Arnold 72; Eagleton 1-2; Howe 43-44; and Abrams 232-34.

To Provide Explanations

In the paper

In recent years gothic novels have achieved great popularity.[3]

In the note

[3] Gothic novels, works written in imitation of medieval romances, originally relied on supernatural occurrences. They flourished in the late eighteenth and early nineteenth centuries.

Credits

Roland Bartel, "Life and Death in Eudora Welty's 'A Worn Path'" by Roland Bartel from STUDIES IN SHORT FICTION 14 (1977): 288–90. Copyright 1977 by Newberry College. Reprinted by permission.

Nancy K. Butterworth, "From Civil War to Civil Rights: Race Relations in Welty's 'A Worn Path'" by Nancy K. Butterworth from THE EYE OF THE STORYTELLER edited by Dawn Trouard. Copyright © 1989. Reprinted by permission of The Kent State University Press.

Joseph Gardner, "Errand of Love: A Study in Black and White" by Joseph Gardner as appeared in KENTUCKY REVIEW 12 (Autumn 1993), pp. 69–78. Reprinted by permission of the author.

Elmo Howell, "Eudora Welty's Negroes: A Note on 'A Worn Path'" by Elmo Howell as appeared in XAVIER UNIVERSITY STUDIES 9.1 (Spring 1970): 28–32. Reprinted by permission.

Jeanne R. Nostrandt, "Welty's 'A Worn Path'" by Jeanne R. Nostrandt from EXPLICATOR, January 1976. Reprinted with permission of the Helen Dwight Reid Educational Foundation. Published by Heldref Publications, 1319 Eighteenth St., N.W., Washington, D.C. 20036-1802. Copyright © 1976.

Elaine Orr, "Unsettling Every Definition of 'Otherness': Another Reading of Welty's 'A Worn Path'" by Elaine Orr. This essay originally appeared in the SOUTH ATLANTIC REVIEW 57 (May 1992): 57–72.

David Robinson, "A Nickel and Dime Matter: Teaching Eudora Welty's 'A Worn Path'" by David Robinson as appeared in NOTES ON MISSISSIPPI WRITERS 19.1 (1987). Used with permission.

James Robert Saunders, "'A Worn Path': The Eternal Quest of Welty's Phoenix Jackson" by James Robert Saunders from SOUTHERN LITERARY JOURNAL, 25, Fall 1992. Copyright © by the Department of English-University of North Carolina at Chapel Hill. Used by permission of the publisher.

James Walter, "Love's Habit of Vision in Eudora Welty's Phoenix Jackson" by James Walter from JOURNAL OF THE SHORT STORY IN ENGLISH 7 (Autumn 1986): 77–85. Reprinted by permission.

Eudora Welty, "Must the Novelist Crusade?" from THE EYE OF THE STORYTELLER: SELECTED ESSAYS AND REVIEWS by Eudora Welty. Copyright © 1978 by Eudora Welty. Reprinted by permission of Random House, Inc.

"Is Phoenix Jackson's Grandson Really Dead?" from THE EYE OF THE STORY: SELECTED ESSAYS AND REVIEWS by Eudora Welty. Copyright © 1978 by Eudora Welty. Reprinted by permission of Random House, Inc.

"A Worn Path" from A CURTAIN OF GREEN AND OTHER STORIES, copyright 1941 and renewed 1969 by Eudora Welty, reprinted by permission of Harcourt Brace & Company.

Eudora Welty photo p. 12 from AP/Wide Photos.